THE FIRST SEASON

2011 — 2012

A YEAR IN REVIEW

Celebrating the first year
of the return of NHL hockey
to Winnipeg

THE FIRST SEASON

ISBN ISBN 978-0-9682575-7-9

Printed in Canada

LIBRARY AND ARCHIVES CANADA CATALOGUING IN PUBLICATION

Turner, Randy, 1961-
THE FIRST SEASON / by Randy Turner

ISBN 978-0-9682575-7-9

1. Winnipeg Jets (hockey team) 2. National Hockey League 3. Hockey-Manitoba-Winnipeg-History

First printing

Written by: Randy Turner, with contributions from Adam Wazny, Gary Lawless, Ed Tait and Tim Campbell
Project editor: Margo Goodhand
Art director / production: Gordon Preece
Photo editor: Mike Aporius
Photo processing: Mike Deal
Research: Adam Wazny
Copy editor: Andrew Maxwell, Ron Campbell and Jason Bell

On the front: Jets captain Andrew Ladd — Jonathan Kozub / Winnipeg Jets Hockey Club
Background shot by Boris Minkevich / Winnipeg Free Press

WINNIPEG

Jets

Trevor Hagan / Winnipeg Free Press

Evander Kane, Alex Burmistrov

Foreword

Feature reporter

Randy Turner

SOMETIMES, when Mark Chipman sees me coming, he sighs.

That's because for the last two summers of documenting the return of the Jets — both for *Back in the Bigs* and *The First Season* — I have subjected him to hours of interviews and countless questions. He's never said "No."

It's always amazed me, frankly, that people with so much on their collective plates not only take the time to provide their insight on one of the most historically significant events in Winnipeg history, but do so with the utmost patience and generosity.

My thanks to the aforementioned Mr. Chipman, along with his tireless True North team of Jim Ludlow, Norva Riddell, Dorian Morphy, Scott Brown, Dwayne Green, Kevin Cheveldayoff and Craig Heisinger for their assistance in this project.

Also, thanks to players Blake Wheeler and former goaltender Chris Mason for their insight. As Mason said of *The First Season*: "This is the year they (the Jets) came back. I'll never forget it."

Editor / Winnipeg Free Press

Margo Goodhand

I'VE always liked the Jets' slogan, Fuelled by Passion.

It describes the players, of course, and their pumped-up fans across Manitoba. But even more so, it describes the folks who brought this team back to life in Winnipeg.

This book is dedicated to the Winnipeg Jets True North Foundation, the charitable arm of the team and its home rink, which raises funds for a variety of registered children's charities in Manitoba.

Thanks to Randy Turner, for bringing it to life. To sportswriters Adam Wazny, Ed Tait, Gary Lawless and Tim Campbell. To *Free Press* photographers and photo editor Mike Aporius. To art director Gordon Preece, who giftwrapped the whole project, and copy editors Andrew Maxwell, Ron Campbell and Jason Bell.

Fuelled by Passion also describes the *Winnipeg Free Press* newsroom. Here's to many seasons more.

REGULAR-SEASON GAME **SUMMARIES**

HOME› AWAY›

FEATURES

Phil Hossack / Winnipeg Free Press

Ondrej Pavelec

THE TEAM

BACK ROW (L-R) — Michael Flaman, Kyle Wellwood, Aaron Gagnon, Johnny Oduya, Alexander Burmistrov, Tanner Glass, Mark Stuart, Ben Maxwell, Jim Slater, Bryan Little, Derek Meech, Kenndal McArdle, Tim Stapleton, Al Pritchard, Michaël Roy

Lance Thomson / Winnipeg Jets Hockey Club

MIDDLE ROW (L-R) — Joseph Enright, Brad Shaw, Jason McMaster, Ryan Bowness, Randy Jones, Brett MacLean, Chris Thorburn, Eric Fehr, Nik Antropov, Blake Wheeler, Ron Hainsey, Zach Bogosian, Mark Scheifele, Evander Kane, Tony Borgford, Rob Milette, Mark Grehan, Lee Stubbs

FRONT ROW (L-R) — Ondrej Pavelec, Dustin Byfuglien, Wade Flaherty, Charlie Huddy, Craig Heisinger, Kevin Cheveldayoff, Mark Chipman, Andrew Ladd, David Thomson, Claude Noel, Jim Ludlow, Pascal Vincent, Larry Simmons, Tobias Enstrom, Chris Mason

THE ANNOUNCEMENT

'Today, on behalf of my family, our partner David Thomson and our entire organization, I'm excited beyond words to announce our purchase of the Atlanta Thrashers. In a sense, I guess you could say that True North, our city and our province have received the call we've long since been waiting for'

— Winnipeg Jets co-owner and chairman Mark Chipman.

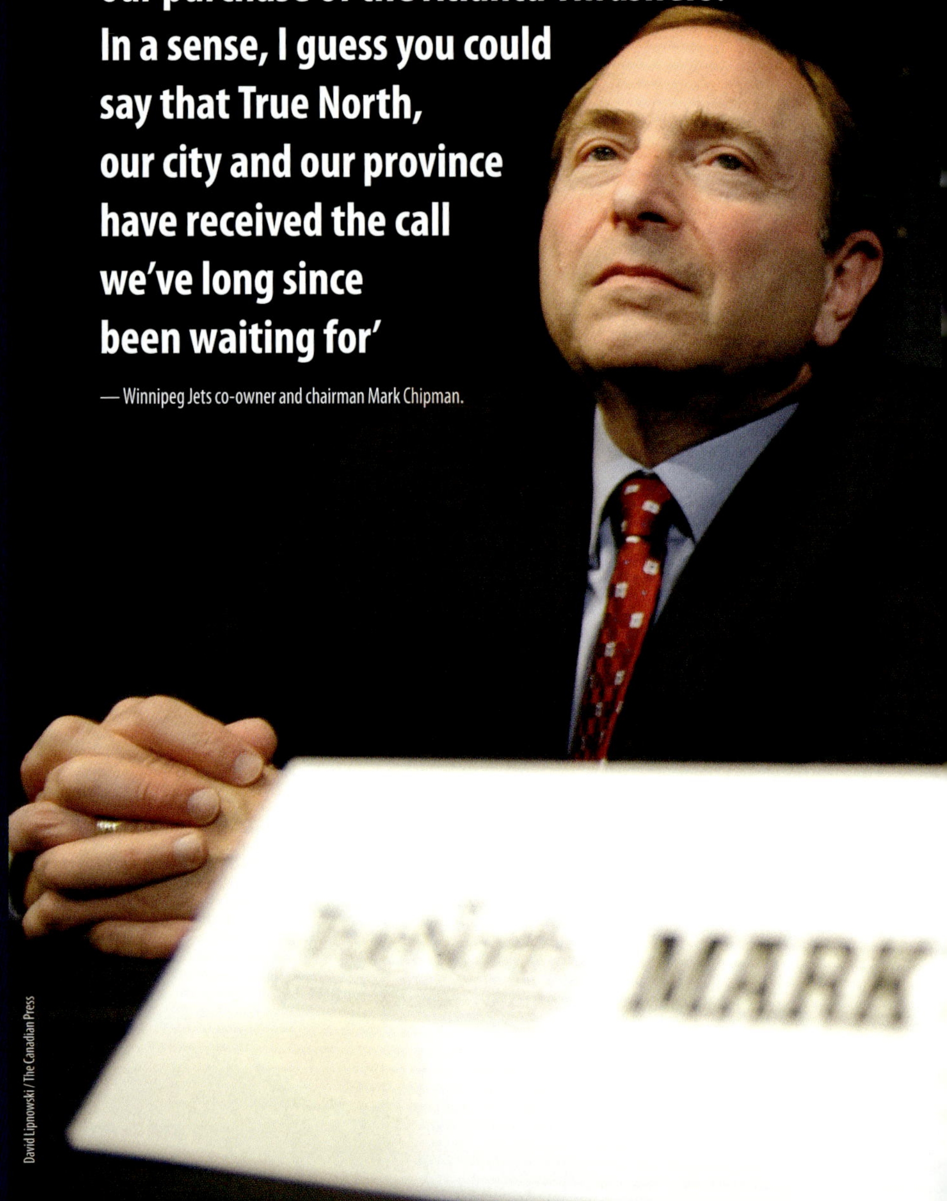

David Lipnowski / The Canadian Press

Mark Chipman, NHL commissioner Gary Bettman at purchase announcement.

TrueNorth
MTS
NHL
MTS centre
HIPMAN

Everybody loves a comeback story

THE words came just after 11 a.m. on May 31, 2011, during a hastily called press conference that included NHL commissioner Gary Bettman, who hadn't set foot in Manitoba since the Jets' bitter departure 15 years ago.

Sure, the announcement was highly anticipated: The Thrashers organization was failing, and the Phoenix Coyotes — the team Winnipeg hockey fans and media had long expected to return to Manitoba — had just been bailed out again, by a $25-million subsidy from the City of Glendale.

Yet that simmering expectation didn't dampen the spontaneous, city-wide celebration that saw thousands of fans flood to Portage and Main even before Mark Chipman strode to the podium in a conference room in the bowels of the MTS Centre.

Police shut down Portage Avenue, where ball-hockey games broke out, the most expansive being at the corner of Portage and Main, the iconic intersection where Bobby Hull was first introduced as a Winnipeg Jet in 1972 and where, some years later, the Jets introduced future star Dale Hawerchuk in 1981.

"It's nice to be back in Winnipeg after all these years," said Bettman. "Mark (Chipman) has been pursuing the NHL for a number of years, quietly and obviously quite effectively.

"This venue, the MTS Centre, will be a fine, fine home for an NHL club, and there is the strength of the prospective ownership group," Bettman said. "We get to be back in a place we wish we had never left in 1996."

Bettman, however, wasn't nearly as delirious as the fans who migrated to The Forks, chanting "Go Jets Go!" and "We Want Teemu!"

Ruth Bonneville / Winnipeg Free Press

"We didn't think they were going to come back," said Dale Wolgemuth, standing amid the celebration at The Forks with his grandson, Judah, and son, Matt. "We thought we were done. We tried to cheer for the Coyotes, but that didn't work. We went to Toronto for a game, but it wasn't the same. It was very hard. Very hard. I mean, it was our team. I followed them since 1972. I used to listen to them on a little transistor radio.

"We lost them once. But they're coming back. And I'd say that's a feel-good story if there ever was one."

It was a story that spread far beyond Manitoba boundaries. CBC-TV's *The National* led with the Jets' return that night, with Peter Mansbridge intoning, "Hockey is coming home to Winnipeg."

And though that historic press conference was finalized at the last minute, few Winnipeggers knew how much effort True North officials had expended behind the scenes — and late into the evening of May 30 — to ensure the return of the NHL's seventh Canadian franchise went off without a glitch.

After all, this was arguably one of the most-watched press conferences relating to the NHL and Canada since the tearful Wayne Gretzky was dealt to Bruce McNall's Los Angeles Kings on Aug. 9, 1988 — another seismic geographical shift that a few years later would become a factor in the demise of the Jets.

True North knew the hockey world would be paying attention, once again, to a small-market Canadian Prairie city, and there was no room for error.

"We were working on the fact that all of this city, all of the province, would watch... and a lot of people across North America," noted True North director of communications Scott Brown. "This was a monumental event, and it was a team coming back to a market no one thought it would come back to. I said out loud, 'This is going to be the first impression of True North Sports & Entertainment. We were going to be judged on that first impression.' "

Jets fans at The Forks (left) and Portage and Main (right) watch and roar their approval on the big day.

Ken Gigliotti / Winnipeg Free Press

In fact, though this was admittedly a fast-track sale and relocation, the announcement also showcased an organization that had been preparing to adopt an NHL team for more than a year. In late May of 2010, True North had made preparations to hold a press conference announcing the acquisition of the Phoenix Coyotes — only to be scuttled by another cash infusion into the money-losing franchise by Glendale councillors.

They had spent the subsequent year constantly tweaking their presentation, price points and refining their website design.

"We couldn't have been more ready," True North president Jim Ludlow said. "In fact, if we had carried it on any further into the year (a delay in acquiring the Thrashers), we might have lost our edge."

Crucial to the announcement was Ludlow's presentation of the new team's season-ticket drive. He practised it several times May 30, well into the night. A camera crew even filmed it, having been required to sign non-disclosure documents.

"I'll never forget," Ludlow recalled. "We were going all night long."

There was only one problem: Even as early as 4 a.m., the agreement to purchase the Thrashers had yet to be finalized, with documents still requiring signatures from the banks.

Chipman and Ludlow agonized over whether to announce a major press conference at 11 a.m. or (if the deal hit a snag) simply update the status of negotiations. Around 6 a.m., Ludlow told Chipman, "Go with it. We'll get those signatures."

Thomson and the NHL's top officials, including Bettman, got on a plane to Winnipeg.

The deal was inked at around 9:30 a.m. And minutes later, Bettman and his entourage arrived at the MTS Centre.

"Nice building," he said. "This will do."

That brief statement is one of the few moments of that hectic day Chipman remembers. "You try to tell yourself to slow down and take things in, and it's hard. (But) I will always remember that."

Joe Bryksa / Winnipeg Free Press

Thomson, Selinger, Bettman, Chipman at announcement.

Ludlow, meanwhile, was working on about two hours' sleep. He kept thinking, "Is this really happening?"

Then came a moment that, for Ludlow, made the happening very real. Unbeknownst to all those involved in the bunker bubble of negotiations, hockey fans were spilling off Portage Avenue and into the MTS lobby, transfixed on the in-house television sets, waiting for the press conference to begin.

"You're way downstairs," he said. "There's no light. Nothing. And we begin to hear all this cheering above us, coming down the stairwell. It sent a chill up my spine. Those experiences don't come along every day. All of a sudden we realized there's this community all around us that had been waiting for decades for what this group was about to announce.

"It's funny how quickly those kind of moments go by," Ludlow added. "But nobody's going to forget that day."

Joe Bryksa / Winnipeg Free Press

Mark Chipman (from left), Gary Bettman, Premier Greg Selinger and David Thomson arrive.

The owners

One man's father started with a dirt parking lot on Portage Avenue; the other man's father, the 2nd Baron Thomson of Fleet, inherited a media empire worth $17 billion.

Yet, Winnipeg businessman Mark Chipman and Toronto's David Thomson, co-owners of the Winnipeg Jets, share three things — a passion for hockey, an unassuming demeanour and a belief in this small-market Canadian city.

"There's a heartfelt sense of community in Winnipeg, in Manitoba," said Thomson. "I've always felt inspired by the leadership and ambitions."

Thomson and Chipman first got together to form True North Sports & Entertainment, which opened the MTS Centre, in 2004. It is the city's leading concert and entertainment venue, as well as the home of the Winnipeg Jets.

Trevor Hagan / Winnipeg Free Press

David Thomson

Mark Chipman

THE ANNOUNCEMENT

Gary Bettman addresses the media on the big day.

Joe Bryksa / Winnipeg Free Press

Ken Gigliotti / Winnipeg Free Press

Fans take in the announcement at Portage and Main.

Jets
HOCKEY

'Sold out every night'

IN the euphoria unleashed as the return of the National Hockey League to Winnipeg was made official May 31, it took but a few minutes before reality came front and centre... in the form of NHL commissioner Gary Bettman.

From rejoice to revenue. From mania to money.

"To be candid," Bettman intoned, with Chipman's historic announcement still hanging in the air at the MTS Centre, "it isn't going to work very well unless this building is sold out every night."

Indeed, the NHL's board of governors still had to approve the deal to purchase the Atlanta Thrashers when they met on June 21. And raw enthusiasm doesn't buy tickets.

But behind the scenes, True North had spent months studying ticket sponsorship pricing in similarly sized Canadian-based markets such as Edmonton and Ottawa. The organization was ready to unveil its season-ticket vision, called the Drive to 13,000, on national television.

Wayne Glowacki / Winnipeg Free Press

True North's Jim Ludlow outlines the season-ticket plan.

True North president and CEO Jim Ludlow stepped to the stage and spent the next few minutes showing Winnipeg hockey fans not only the price of season-ticket packages, but the organization's bold ask of three- to five-year commitments from fans. It was a strategy no other NHL team had ever attempted.

It was a gamble that had top True North officials holding their breath. After all, there was no Plan B. If Manitobans didn't respond at the box office, all the hysteria and hype would be for naught.

"If sales were soft... if we sold 8,000 tickets, I don't know what we would have done," recalled Norva Riddell, True North's senior vice-president of sales and marketing.

Package prices, per game, ranged from $39 to $129 — a total of $1,755 to $5,805 per 45-game season.

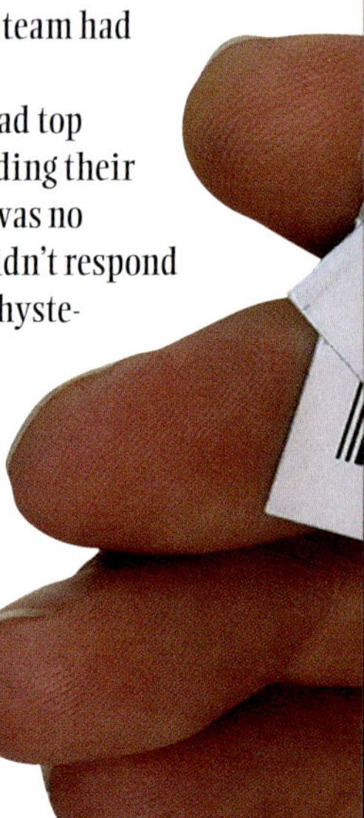

SEC: 121
ROW: 10
SEAT: 10
PRICE: $117.50
FUELLED BY PASSION
PRESEASON
GAME 01
JETS
SEC: 121
ROW: 10
SEAT: 11
PRICE: $117.50
FUELLED BY PASSION
PRESEASON
GAME 01
JETS
VS
COLUMBUS BLUE JACKETS
SEPTEMBER 20, 2011
PUCK DROP 7:30PM
TrueNorth
PAYMENT PLANS
PRE-SALE
GENERAL ON SALE
Top 10 Things You Need to Know
DRIVE TO 13,000
4,000*
DRIVE TO 13,000

Season tickets were first sold to existing Manitoba Moose season-ticket holders and corporate advertising partners. Within minutes of Ludlow's announcement, they were notified by email of their options. The website was up and running, which provided walk-through information on ticket purchasing to the general public.

More than 7,100 were sold.

When the remaining tickets were made available to the general public four days later, on June 4, they were snapped up in 90 seconds. It took about 17 minutes before the final transaction was completed. In addition, a waiting list for season tickets was established — True North cut it off at 8,000; it could have been five figures — a development that stunned even the most optimistic in the organization.

To review: The announcement was made on Tuesday. Moose season-ticket holders snapped up over half the available tickets by Friday. The Drive to 13,000 was history by Saturday at 12:17 p.m.

In addition, the club's 55 suites (the number was expanded by seven during the

'We couldn't afford to fail... It was the most critical element to say to the NHL and the other 29 teams that Winnipeg is a market and a force to be reckoned with'

— Jim Ludlow (below), president and CEO of True North Sports & Entertainment, smiles after announcing all 13,000 Jets season tickets sold in minutes.

Jonathan Hayward / The Canadian Press

Mike Deal / Winnipeg Free Press

off-season) were sold immediately.

For the first time, True North officials let out a collective breath.

"That was such a significant project," Riddell said. "That it worked and the community sent such a strong message."

"We couldn't afford to fail," Ludlow added. "It was the most critical element to say to the NHL and the other 29 teams that Winnipeg is a market and a force to be reckoned with."

Again, what might have appeared like an overnight success, almost literally, was the result of months of calculated strategizing behind closed doors.

"Those time sales were scripted to the minute," Ludlow noted. "It was bang, bang, bang."

At their headquarters in New York, the NHL heard: ka-ching, ka-ching, ka-ching.

On June 21, 2011, the NHL board of governors unanimously approved the sale of the Atlanta Thrashers to True North Sports & Entertainment.

Cheveldayoff in charge

IT took just eight days after landing the franchise for 41-year-old Kevin Cheveldayoff to be introduced as general manager on June 8, and the true lineage of what would become the Winnipeg Jets began to materialize.

From the outside, at least, Cheveldayoff's appointment might have been considered — as they like to say at the annual teenage draft — off the board.

After all, Cheveldayoff wasn't just a rookie GM in the National Hockey League; he was chosen ahead of far more high-profile and experienced candidates, the least of whom would have been former Thrashers GM Rick Dudley or Toronto Maple Leafs assistant GM Dave Nonis.

Yet in retrospect, Cheveldayoff's ascension to the Jets GM post was practically preordained, dating back to one of those random hockey crossings of paths with an acerbic-tongued trainer at the age of 16.

Cheveldayoff was a highly touted Brandon Wheat Kings defenceman from Blaine Lake, Sask. The trainer was a bundle of tough love named Craig Heisinger, then in in his early 20s.

In a league of 18- to 21-year-old opponents, the rookie Cheveldayoff backed down from no one, racking up a team-high 259 penalty minutes. Yet Heisinger would good-naturedly needle the rookie about his puck-handling skills, or lack thereof.

"It's not as though we tried to become friends. We just did," Cheveldayoff recalled. "He (Heisinger) was able to control the room and make it lighthearted. Quick-witted. Certainly I was very easy for him to pick fun at on a lot of occasions."

(To this day, when the Jets management staff hunker down to discuss draft prospects and the subject of a player's puck-handling ability is raised, Heisinger will ask his scouts: "Better than Chevy's or worse than Chevy's?" The room will crack up.)

Heisinger eventually became general manager of the Manitoba Moose in 2002. And Chevaldayoff, who was drafted 16th overall by the New York Islanders in 1998, but derailed by a severe leg injury in his final year of junior — began to work his way up in management through the IHL, AHL and finally the NHL Chicago Blackhawks.

His front-office career includes three Turner Cups (one as the assistant GM of the Utah Grizzles in 1996, two as GM of the Wolves) in the IHL; two Calder Cups (also with the AHL's Wolves) and a Stanley Cup in 2010 as assistant GM with the Blackhawks. Given the shared history between the Moose and Wolves — an often intense rivalry and respect — and his long-standing friendship with Heisinger, who had already assumed the title of director of hockey operations and assistant Jets GM, Cheveldayoff didn't hesitate when the Jets came calling.

"There was no background checking needed," Cheveldayoff noted. "There were no third- or fourth-party phone calls to ask about Mark (Chipman) or Craig or David Thomson. The evidence was proven itself about how the Moose operated."

And vice versa.

Joe Bryksa / Winnipeg Free Press

Joe Bryksa / Winnipeg

"We were always competitive against (the Wolves)," Chipman said, when Cheveldayoff was introduced at a jam-packed press conference at the MTS Centre. "But, honestly, an admiration grew, not just from (Heisinger), because he has known him for a long time, but from myself as well. He always conducted himself with the utmost professionalism; win, lose or draw. To bring that (championship) quality into our organization is huge."

Of note, no other GM candidate was interviewed.

In Cheveldayoff and Heisinger, the franchise's hockey operations were now being steered by two old friends and fierce competitors with western roots, who had both risen up the AHL ladder by unconventional routes — one a former trainer, the other who took his first executive positions at the age of 24.

"They've always had to work harder," the team co-owner said. "They've always felt like they have to prove themselves, whether they did or didn't. There is just an extraordinary work ethic in both of them that propels them."

From the outset, Cheveldayoff's philosophy in building the Jets organization was to preach patience and instil the franchise with character players. One of Cheveldayoff's first acts of business was to lock up Jets captain Andrew Ladd to a five-year, $22-million extension, along with power forward Blake Wheeler (two years, $5.1 million), the latter responding with a career season (17 G, 47 A) in 2011-2012.

"I want a team that emulates the region that we're in," Cheveldayoff said. "I want a team that comes to play very hard, that has a passion for the game that the people cheering for them have. I want them to enjoy playing and be willing to pay the price to ultimately win the championship. That's the ultimate goal."

It didn't take Cheveldayoff long to immerse himself in the fledgling Jets culture. His knee brace has a team logo and colours. His new Manitoba licence plates are "WJ 2011" and "WJ 0608," the former for the year the team was reborn, the latter for the day Cheveldayoff was hired.

"It's your life," he said. "It becomes part of you. It's like my wife says, 'There's two things in this family: there's winning, then there's hell.' When you don't win, you feel it. They feel it. You take that very, very seriously. It's no different than when I was with the Wolves or the Grizzlies or the Blackhawks. You live it. It becomes tattooed."

Cole Breiland / Winnipeg Free Press

John Woods / Winnipeg Free Press

Kevin Cheveldayoff's swift appointment as Jets GM was a no-brainer, given his hockey pedigree. No other candidate was interviewed.

Cheveldayoff's approach is to pursue 'a team that emulates the region that we're in.'

k / Winnipeg Free Press

Vaulted into the big leagues

HE was 55 years old and had never held a full-time position as head coach in the National Hockey League.

Never thought he would, either.

That was the realistic, star-crossed attitude of Claude Noel, a career minor-league bench boss who was convinced Murphy's Law was his fate in hockey: If something could go wrong, it would.

Not this time. After one season at the helm of the Manitoba Moose, during the AHL club's swan song, Noel landed his first full-time gig as an NHL head coach on June 24, at a press conference held just prior to the 2011 Entry Draft in St. Paul, Minn.

Newly appointed general manager Kevin Cheveldayoff made the decision a few days before and reached Noel by phone with the good news.

"I was shopping at Superstore with my wife and sons," Noel said. "I leaned over a can of tomatoes and it took about a minute before they decided to tell me I had it or not... I would have just rather him say 'You got the job' but he didn't and I went through a living hell for a minute."

Then there was joy, a word the head coach spouted at almost every press conference thereafter.

Indeed, if there was one developing storyline of the Jets' 2011-12 season, it was the emergence of the affable Noel as must-see TV during televised post-game press conferences.

In one YouTube moment, in fact, the head coach — in response to a question about one of the first music albums he ever bought — started to sing the first few bars of Iron Butterfly's rock opus *In-A-Gadda-Da-Vida*.

Recalled True North communications director Scott Brown: "I could feel my knees buckle. An NHL coach singing at the podium."

Classic Noel. And the hits kept coming all season long (courtesy of Jets beat writers Tim Campbell and Ed Tait):

OCT. 11: On cracking the whip at practice with a few curse words... and his sister in the stands watching:

"She had no influence on my behaviour at all. She knows I swore because it's just the way it happens in the season — you start to swear a lot. I'm trying not to get influenced by Charlie Huddy, because he REALLY swears a lot. It's not my fault."

OCT. 27: Trying to explain the unexplainable — a wild 9-8 victory over the Philadelphia Flyers.

"I thought to myself, 'Self, you're a sick man trying to make logic of this.' "

FEB. 18: On winning and losing.

"I know one thing today: I like winning more than I like losing. That's good, eh? Write that down... winning is better than losing. That's going to be the quote of the day. 'Winning is better than losing.' Should I attach my name to that one? That's C. Noel."

Noel is a product of a hardscrabble mining town in northern Ontario called Kirkland Lake and began his pro career as a grinding forward with the Buffalo Norsemen of the North American Hockey League. Eventually, he rose through the minor-league ranks to suit up for seven games with the dreadful Washington Capitals during the 1979-80 season.

As a coach, Noel started at the bottom again, with the East Coast Hockey League's Roanoke Valley Rebels. Again, he persevered and in 2003 won a Calder Cup with the Milwaukee Admirals and was named the AHL coach of the year.

In February of 2010, Noel was named interim head coach of the Columbus Blue Jackets, replacing his mentor Ken Hitchcock. The Blue Jackets finished 10-8-6 under Noel, who was nonetheless passed over for the head-coaching job the next season — by none other than former Moose head coach Scott Arniel.

In a stroke of irony, Noel then replaced Arniel behind the Moose bench in 2011, setting in motion the events that would lead to his emotional hiring by the Jets.

"My heart was jumping," Noel said the day of the announcement. "There were a lot of emotions. I was really appreciative. Almost tears of appreciation for me. I've gone through this process a few times and I'm a little older (55) and I thought, 'I hope my day is coming.' I thought my day would come."

Trevor Hagan / Winnipeg Free Press

A usually restrained Noel questions a referee's call from behind the bench.

Joe Bryksa / Winnipeg Free Press

LEFT: Winnipeg Jets head coach Claude Noel briefs goalies Chris Mason (centre) and Ondrej Pavelec.

BELOW: Noel outlines a drill at practice.

Trevor Hagan / Winnipeg Free Press

Pick for future has links to past

KEVIN Cheveldayoff winked, and Mark Scheifele smiled.

In one moment, the Winnipeg Jets were reborn. In the next, the franchise had its first draft pick, which evoked both a glorious ghost of the old Jets and a fresh, baby face of the future.

The Jets selected Mark Scheifele seventh overall in the 2011 NHL Entry Draft June 24 in St. Paul's Xcel Energy Center, but not before the GM, on the way to the podium, looked up into the stands and winked at the 18-year-old Barrie Colts centreman.

"I wasn't sure if he caught it or not," Cheveldayoff said later.

Didn't matter. Following his selection, the 6-3 teenager from Kitchener — whose head coach with the Colts was none other than former Winnipeg Jet Hall of Fame centre Dale Hawerchuk — couldn't contain his unbridled joy.

"I'm just so excited right now," a beaming Scheifele told a horde of reporters. "This is a moment I've always dreamed about, and to go to the Jets and a team that has such a great organization, and be the first pick since they've been back... there's no other feeling like walking up the stage."

Andy King / The Canadian Press

Kevin Cheveldayoff (from left), Mark Scheifele and Claude Noel on draft day.

Talk about a new adventure unfolding. Scheifele was the only player taken in the first round who didn't pull his team's NHL jersey over his head because, well, the Jets didn't have a jersey yet. Or a logo, for that matter.

So Scheifele came into his post-draft press conference wearing a generic black NHL sweater and a 1,000-watt smile.

"All the guys were saying 'You're going to be on all these trivia questions,'" he said. "I'm kind of starting to soak it in. To be able to go to Winnipeg and a franchise that's just starting, it's unbelievable."

Hawerchuk, a former Jets icon whom Winnipeg selected first overall in the 1981 draft, had already told Scheifele about the old portrait of Queen Elizabeth that hung in the rafters at the old Winnipeg Arena. He told his protege Winnipeg fans would love him. Oh, and one last piece of advice: "Bring a parka," Hawerchuk said.

Dozens of Jets fans who made the trek to the Minneapolis draft roared when Cheveldayoff announced the pick — even if they didn't know yet exactly how Scheifele's name was prounounced (Shy-flea). That's OK, neither did the Jets management during pre-draft player interviews.

Dave Sandford / NHLI via Getty Images

The Jets crew at their table at the draft in St. Paul, Minn. The newly minted franchise didn't have a logo yet.

NHL
WINNIPEG
2011-12
EJ

Meanwhile, around 4,000 fans who had gathered back home in the MTS Centre also celebrated the unofficial welcome of the first pure Winnipeg Jet into the franchise.

"It was definitely really cool to have that many fans here and hear them screaming," Scheifele said. "They told me back in the arena in Winnipeg they were going bonkers. It's great to have a great fan base."

Interestingly, Scheifele was ranked 16th by Central Scouting and the Jets passed on the opportunity to grab another highly ranked centre, Sean Couturier, who was selected ninth overall by the Philadelphia Flyers. The *Hockey News* had Scheifele ranked 41st overall.

The Jets brain trust acknowledged from the outset they had selected Scheifele based on a projected arch that would someday make him a No. 1 centre in the NHL. Said Jets assistant GM Craig Heisinger: "Character and hockey sense are first and foremost for us and we don't want to lose sight of that. In three years we'll know."

"When I sat there with my scouts and they talked about this player, they talked with passion and they said if we get a chance to draft him, we'd like to draft him," added Cheveldayoff. "They watch the players night in and night out. They were passionate about him. When I talked about the values I wanted to bring to this organization, they just shook their heads and said this guy's got all of those."

Scheifele at first tantalized Jets fans by scoring twice and adding two assists in the club's first exhibition game against the Columbus Blue Jackets. He was signed to an entry-level contract Oct. 3, 2011, and — after making the big club to open the season — scored his first career NHL goal Oct. 19 against the Toronto Maple Leafs at the Air Canada Centre.

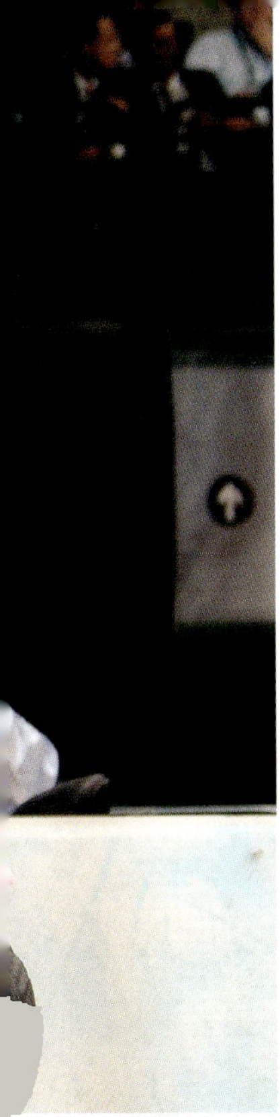

Dave Sandford / NHLI via Getty Images

John Woods / Winnipeg Free Press

Dave Sandford / NHLI via Getty Images

FAR LEFT: NHL commissioner Gary Bettman greets Jets pick Mark Scheifele onstage at the draft.

ABOVE: Jets fans at the MTS Centre await Winnipeg's NHL draft pick.

LEFT: The draft pick meets the Jets brass.

Ultimately, however, Jets management determined the teenager, who only had one junior A season with the Colts, needed to continue developing his game in Barrie. On Oct. 23, Scheifele was sent back to Hawerchuk and his OHL teammates, where he scored 63 points in 47 games during the 2011-12 season, adding 12 points in 13 playoff games. Scheifele also played for Team Canada at the world junior championship in Calgary/Edmonton, winning a bronze medal.

"(Colts coach Dale Hawerchuk) was working very hard at teaching him the pro game," Cheveldayoff said of Scheifele's progress last season. "It wasn't just all about goals and assists and racking up minutes. In Mark's case, Dale wanted to make sure he spent time teaching him the two-way pro game. The assessment from that aspect went well.

"His understanding of the game continued to grow. Those are things that are going to have to continue in order for him to keep on maturing."

Of course, Scheifele was just the first of eight Jets selections at the 2011 draft.

The club made two deals to move up — one with the Montreal Canadiens, the other with the San Jose Sharks — and chose left-winger Adam Lowry (third round, 67th overall, Swift Current Broncos, OHL), followed by defenceman Brennan Serville (78th overall, Stouffville Spirit, OJHL), defenceman Zach Yuen (fourth round, 119th, Tri-City Americans, WHL), right-winger Austen Brassard (fifth round, 149th overall, Bellville), Portage Terriers goaltender Jason Kasdorf (sixth round, 157th overall, MJHL) and defenceman Aaron Harstad (seventh round, 187th overall, Green Bay Gamblers, USHL).

The internal moniker debate

TRUE story: Just before taking the podium at the 2011 NHL Entry Draft in St. Paul, Mark Chipman turned to his newly minted general manager, Kevin Cheveldayoff, with a request.

It was the evening of June 24, and they were about to claim Winnipeg's first pick, seventh overall.

"And Mark goes, 'Chevy, you're going to go up there and name the team,' " said Chevaldayoff. "And I said, 'Well, I don't know, that depends.' "

Chipman seemed taken aback. "What do you mean, that depends?'" the owner asked.

Replied the GM: "What's the name of the team?"

For such a highly anticipated moment in the return of the NHL to Winnipeg, the moment couldn't have been more understated. Without any fanfare or preamble, Chipman rose to stand at the podium and asked Cheveldayoff to make the pick "on behalf of the Winnipeg Jets."

Cue the bedlam. Back at the MTS Centre, where some 4,000 faithful had gathered for a draft party, the building erupted. Until that moment, although the NHL had returned to Winnipeg, the Jets had not.

Mike Debrowski, a 23-year-old fan wearing a 16-year-old Keith Tkachuk jersey, proclaimed: "It's like I've woken up on Christmas morning and gotten everything I ever wanted."

Kevin Cheveldayoff didn't know the franchise was going with the Jets identity until the last minute.

Trevor Hagan / Winnipeg Free Press

The Jets moniker perhaps sparked more internal debate at True North's senior management table than any other aspect of the NHL's return.

From the outset, there was a resistance to the past and a yearning for a fresh start — and what better place to start than the name?

"To us, this was about the return of the NHL, not the return of the Jets," True North CEO Jim Ludlow said of those initial discussions. "We were moving forward."

Added Chipman: "If it was Phoenix (that relocated to Winnipeg), probably a no-brainer (to keep the Jets name). But if it wasn't Phoenix, maybe we should start fresh."

There were plenty of other viable candidates:

THE VICTORIAS — An amateur senior club that won the Stanley Cup three times at the turn of the last century.

The Winnipeg Victorias, turn-of-the-century Stanley Cup champions.

The Canadian Press / HO-Farpoint Films

Fans at the MTS Centre rejoice when they hear the Jets name recited at the draft.

John Woods / Winnipeg Free Press

THE FALCONS — A Winnipeg-based group of underdog Icelandic amateurs who won Canada's first-ever Olympic gold medal in hockey in 1920.

THE MOOSE — Of course.

THE MANITOBA BEARS — Most intriguing to True North brass, a polar bear concept (logo).

The bear idea had been floating as far back as 2007, when the NHL first asked True North to "kick the tires" of a failing Nashville franchise. Chipman was partial to "Predators," and his logical follow was that, hey, isn't a polar bear the ultimate predator in Manitoba?

Trevor Hagan / Winnipeg Free Press

In fact, at the time of the NHL's announced return, in the following few weeks, there was about a 50-50 chance Winnipeg's franchise would be Moose or Bears.

"I remember specifically him (Chipman) coming into my office the day before (the June 24 draft) and there were still two options," noted Dorian Morphy, True North's senior director of marketing and brand management. "That's how close it was."

But, ultimately, an organization built on independence and distancing itself from a doomed NHL past came to realize the fans had spoken. And yelled. And chanted.

Just hours before first uttering "Winnipeg Jets" at that St. Paul podium, Chipman was sitting in a hotel restaurant, chewing on his lunch and reality.

"It isn't all about True North and our desires" he said. "I'm not trying to sound altruistic here, but when they say you own the team... well, you do and you don't. It's not right just to impose our will on this. It (the Jets name) has almost taken on mythical proportions.

"Besides, that's how I got in... to save the Winnipeg Jets. I thought long and hard about how much it meant back then and how much it means to the community. It was the right thing to do."

Interestingly, Chipman said no one from NHL headquarters ever pressured True North on the naming of the franchise, one way or another. And given the unconditional love displayed by hockey fans in the wake of the Thrashers purchase, it's almost certain that Moose or Bears would have eventually been embraced. But...

"I think we all acknowledge in retrospect it was the right choice," Morphy concluded."

In the end, the passion of Jets fans won the day.

Ken Gigliotti / Winnipeg Free Press

The brand's the thing

A franchise logo can be at least as critical as the name itself.

In the beginning, True North had neither.

The seeds of what would become the brand of the Winnipeg Jets — a fighter jet layered over a red Maple Leaf, centred inside an RCAF trademark roundel, with Polar Midnight blue as the predominant colour and Air Force wings as shoulder patches — began in January of 2010, when longtime True North employee Dorian Morphy was approached with a top-secret mission: Become the senior member of a team with the task of designing the new Jets NHL logo.

Morphy, True North senior director of marketing and brand management, was understandably giddy — not just at the prospect of the NHL's return to his hometown, but at being on the ground floor of a brand manager's dream.

"I had to pinch myself," Morphy said. "To be able to be involved in creating a logo that could last 50 years, it's a true honour."

Morphy started with the basics, first identifying the most popular colour schemes of professional teams (red and blue, 80 per cent), dissecting the number of teams that incorporated the city name into their logo, how many nicknames included animals. The options were endless.

How many names/logos involved industry (Edmonton Oilers, Milwaukee Brewers, Pittsburgh Steelers), how many were geographical in nature (Colorado Avalanche, Miami Heat), how many were cultural (St. Louis Blues, San Francisco 49ers, Dallas Cowboys), how many were nationalistic (Ottawa Senators, Washington Capitals, New England Patriots)?

The design team was asked to design at least two logos — focusing on (polar) bears and Jets. And even as they honed in on the Jets concept, it was agreed the logo would be a complete departure from the original Jets design or its later incarnations.

"We were fully aware what the Jets meant to the community," Morphy explained. "But we wanted to be thorough. Jets 2.0 is what we called it."

Despite Morphy's head start, at the time of the announced return of the NHL, True North was still wrestling over both the name and logo. Enter Reebok, the global athletic apparel company that is the NHL's official outfitter. So crunched was True North for time — the NHL usually requires 18 months to develop a jersey and logo scheme — that Reebok's entire NHL design team was thrown onto the project. Said Chipman: "Every square inch (of Reebok's Boston studio) was covered in some sort of Air Force imagery."

Indeed, the ultimate design didn't evolve so much from concrete designs as images and ideas. True North had long been associated with Winnipeg's 17 Wing through the Manitoba Moose.

In 2008, Moose military tribute jerseys were based on the 1948 RCAF Flyers uniforms, which were baby blue with a bright red roundel as a logo. That was the bestseller of all Moose tribute jerseys.

The Reebok team pitched six versions of a new RCAF-ish logo, but nothing stuck. "It was like shooting in the dark," Chipman noted. "It didn't connect."

38:45
Jets

Winnipeg Jets

The Reebok team brainstormed and ended up submittting six new versions of an Air Force-style logo, but nothing clicked.

'Every square inch (of Reebok's Boston studio) was covered in some sort of Air Force imagery'

— Mark Chipman

Mike Deal / Winnipeg Free Press

But once the designers at Reebok — under the guidance of True North — married the RCAF concept with silhouettes of CF-18 and F-35 fighter jets, a new logo was born.

There were some trademark issues. First, the Toronto Maple Leafs had to sign off on the red Maple Leaf, for obvious reasons. Next, True North undertook a month of friendly negotiations to secure approval from the Department of National Defence on behalf of the Canadian Forces for use of the RCAF's patented roundel symbol. "Once we got permission from the DND," Chipman said, "we were off to the races."

True North president CEO Jim Ludlow called the fusion of the old and new "a flash of brilliance. That's absolutely historic. That drew instant pedigree to our logo."

The final leg of the process took three weeks, before a set of home and away jerseys was sent to the True North offices, where they remained locked in Morphy's desk drawer.

All that stealth, however, couldn't stop a major security leak.

In the late afternoon of Friday, July 22, photos of what appeared to be the new Jets logo on T-shirts began to surface on the Internet.

Turns out, some of the boxes of original merchandise — T-shirts and hats, not jerseys — had been opened.

The logo was out of the bag. Within an hour, True North scrambled together perhaps the first-ever press conference held at 5 p.m. on a Friday in July at the MTS Iceplex.

"That," Chipman remembered, "was the antithesis of May 31 in terms of preparation. We did it very quickly... and it probably came off that way."

Regardless, the Winnipeg Jets had a name and a bouncing new baby image. And so little Jets 2.0 was born.

Lance Thomson / Winnipeg Jets Hockey Club

WINNIPEG Jets

WINNIPEG JETS

The silhouettes of fighter jets added to the RCAF visual concept proved to be the winning combination.

John Woods / The Canadian Press

Winnipeg Jets players (from left) Mark Stuart, Andrew Ladd, Eric Fehr and Nik Antropov emerge from a Hercules plane, officially unveiling the home and away jerseys.

John Woods / The Canadian Press

Jets captain Andrew Ladd

The jerseys

ON Sept. 6, 2011, on a brilliant fall afternoon, four Winnipeg Jets strode out of the back hatch of a Canadian Forces Hercules aircraft on the grounds of Air Force base 17 Wing.

They were dressed in their brand-new team uniforms, unveiled for fans and players alike for the first time.

Home darks sported trim of Aviator Blue and white, with a double, thick white strip over the elbows and a white and Aviator Blue trim around the bottom. Away whites had the Polar Night Blue band down the outside of both sleeves with a silver-bordered Aviator Blue double stripe over the elbows.

"I think they're great," said team captain Andrew Ladd, who got to model the new look, along with Mark Stuart, Eric Fehr and Nik Antropov.

The Canadian Press / John Woods

“They’re clean, they’re simple and hopefully something that’ll last a long, long time and that we’ll be proud to wear. I think it’ll look good on the ice. It’s finally exciting to throw them on.”

Jets GM Kevin Cheveldayoff described the unveiling as “one of the final pieces of the puzzle in what has been one of the most exciting summers in the history of sports in this province.”

But it was the stylized fighter-jet logo, centred in the Air Force roundel, which carried the day on the Canadian Air Force base.

“Our men and women in uniform are delighted by the gracious manner in which the Winnipeg Jets... have sought to pay tribute to our time-honoured relationship with this city,” said Col. Blaise Frawley, commander of 17 Wing. “Today’s announcement at our home in Winnipeg certainly lends a boost to our morale.”

Frawley also acknowledged that the military personnel on hand for the unveiling were grateful for the Jets’ plans to donate $1 million over a 10-year period to the Soldier On, Military Family and Military Heritage funds.

Members of the Air Force were thrilled with the tip of the hat in the new Jets logo.

The Jets Gear store at the MTS Centre was swamped from the beginning, and the logo was soon to be found everywhere.

Everyone wants a piece of Jets 2.0

SURE, it wasn't an ideal launch, as Jet takeoffs go. But as soon as Jets merchandise hit the streets, it soared off the shelves.

Within minutes of Mark Chipman's rushed confirmation of the logo July 22, fans were lined up around the block at the Jets Gear store at the MTS Centre. By the next afternoon, all 1,900 hats in stock were sold out. By mid-Saturday, the team had processed more than 1,200 on-site transactions. By the end of Saturday, only men's T-shirts were left of $200,000 in stock.

Of course, it was only the beginning.

Before long, the Jets logo was everywhere. Flying from car flags. Every conceivable type of clothing, including bikinis (for both babies and adults). The options were seemingly endless: shot glasses, blankets, pet accessories. Even a "Jets toaster," which will burn the team logo into your daily bread.

As the initial season progressed and the Jets logo became omnipresent in the city and province, even Chipman was taken aback.

"You can buy a Winnipeg Jets air freshener while you get your gas," the co-owner and chairman said. "It's bananas. You can get a Jets toaster — and a waffle maker, too!"

Ken Gigliotti / Winnipeg Free Press

Chipman has a thick file of photos of entire extended families wearing Jets gear.

After opening the original Jets Gear store in September of 2011, located at the northwest corner of the MTS Centre, the club opened a second store at the St. Vital Centre mall in the fall. A smaller, third outlet is located at the MTS Iceplex.

Although the NHL keeps their sales figures confidential, the Jets did confirm the team was the No. 1-selling brand in the league during the 2011-12 season— not too surprising for a Canadian franchise making such a dramatic return to the NHL.

In addition, an initial run of 20,000 individualized Jets licence plates Manitoba Public Insurance issued sold out in just eight days at a cost of $70 each. Another 5,000 were printed in December 2011.

The sale of merchandise was a phenomenon this city had never experienced. During home games, the MTS Centre was awash in fans wearing team jerseys. It was the embodiment of the Jets 2.0 slogan, Fuelled by Passion.

"There wasn't a better way to describe what was going on in the community," said Norva Riddell, True North's senior VP of sales and marketing.

Signed, sealed, delivered

What's the best way to buy a Winnipeg Jets commemorative stamp?

With a Winnipeg Jets commemorative coin, of course.

On the eve of the Jets' opening regular-season game with the Montreal Canadiens, Prime Minister Stephen Harper unveiled one of two commemorative coins Winnipeg's Royal Canadian Mint produced, marking the team's return to the NHL.

The mint issued a 50-cent piece and a pure-silver $20 coin; the former sold for $14.95, while the latter cost $94.95.

In November, Canada Post introduced three Jets Picture Postage stamps. The first featured the fighter jet poised on a red Maple Leaf. The second featured crossed hockey sticks resting on military-style wings. The third commemorated the first goal scored at the MTS Centre by a Jets player, Nik Antropov, on opening night, Oct. 9.

The logo stamps sold in sheets of 21 for $24.95. The limited-edition first-goal stamp sold for $34.95 per sheet.

Ken Gigliotti / Winnipeg Free Press

A Canada Post stamp commemorated Nik Antropov's historic goal on opening night.

Phil Hossack / Winnipeg Free Press

Coach Claude Noel shows drills on the board as the Jets hit the ice at the MTS Iceplex as a crowd looks on.

Business on ice draws throng

FANS began arriving at the site at dawn. By 9 a.m., as the team's first practice began, upwards of 1,500 fans were crammed into the MTS Iceplex, chanting "Go Jets Go!"

Among the crowd, Kevin Storimans held up his young son, Trevor, to get a better look at the likes of Andrew Ladd, Zach Bogosian and Tobias Enstrom.

"Probably not going to be able to see a game, the way they sell out and everything," said Storimans, who had missed the boat on season tickets for the upcoming season. "This might be as close as we get this year."

John Woods / The Canadian Press

"It's very historic," added John Palson, standing rinkside with his six-year-old daughter, Jessica. "My daughter wasn't even alive when they left. I used to be a very dedicated fan and it's exciting to be here for the very first practice."

The Jets newcomers, in turn, were getting their first impression of their fans.

"I'm not used to practising in front of a crowd like that, but it's great. The fans are excited, we're excited," said defenceman Zach Bogosian. "We had some good turnouts (in Atlanta) the first day of training camp, but I didn't think it would be anything like this... There's a lot of people here and when they're screaming 'Go Jets Go' it kind of gives you goosebumps."

Added captain Andrew Ladd: "It felt going out there like we were about to play a game."

Even before camp opened, recalled backup Jets goaltender Chris Mason — a good old Prairie boy from Red Deer — the buzz in town was palpable.

"I think I was the first one (Jets player) there," Mason said. "I just remember driving down Portage (Avenue in mid-August) and seeing all the Jets stuff they had downtown. It was unbelievable." Wherever Jets casually got together just to scrimmage, he noted, reporters started hanging out as well.

And by the time camp opened, said Mason, "It was awesome. It was wall-to-wall people."

Mason was part of the third group of Jets players to leave the dressing room at the MTS Iceplex. "Other players were coming back and telling us, 'Wait until you see this.

"The lobby (leading to the ice) was packed," the netminder said. "They had a path for the players roped off. When we stepped on the ice, everybody started cheering. It was absolutely unbelievable. It just gave you shivers."

There were just three workouts at the Iceplex, and then the team moved to the MTS Centre for workouts that were closed to the public.

Sixty-five players started camp, either under NHL contract, AHL contract to St. John's or by invitation.

The list included the majority of players who had participated in the Vancouver Canucks Young Stars tournament in Penticton, B.C., earlier in the week. The Jets rookies went 2-1 in their three games, scoring shutout wins over San Jose and Vancouver. One of the headliners at the rookie tournament was Winnipeg's first-round draft pick from June, 18-year-old centre Mark Scheifele.

Fans greet Zach Bogosian and other Jets as they head to the ice for practice.

John Woods / The Canadian Press

Goalie Ondrej Pavelec confers with goaltending coach Wade Flaherty.

John Woods / The Canadian Press

2011 PLAYERS AT CAMP

FORWARDS

PLAYER	HT	WT	SHOT	BIRTHPLACE	BORN	2010-11 CLUB	GP	G	A	PTS	PIM	GP	G	A	PTS	PIM
Aliu, Akim	6-3	205	R	Okene, Nigeria	4/24/1989	Chicago (AHL)	43	4	5	9	53	-	-	-	-	-
						Gwinnett (ECHL)	16	12	8	20	22	-	-	-	-	-
						Peoria (AHL)	16	5	4	9	20	2	1	0	1	6
Antropov, Nik	6-6	245	L	Ust-Kamenogorsk, KZ	2/18/1980	Atlanta (NHL)	76	16	25	41	42	-	-	-	-	-
Brassard, Austen	6-2	191	R	Windsor, ON	1/14/1993	Belleville (OHL)	67	19	15	34	78	4	1	0	1	4
Burmistrov, Alex	6-1	180	L	Kazan, Russia	10/21/1991	Atlanta (NHL)	74	6	14	20	27	-	-	-	-	-
Clark, Kevin	5-8	155	R	Winnipeg, MB	12/29/1987	Manitoba (AHL)	43	6	8	14	22	11	3	3	6	10
Cormier, Patrice	6-2	215	L	Moncton, NB	6/14/1990	Atlanta (NHL)	21	1	1	2	4	-	-	-	-	-
						Chicago (AHL)	11	2	3	5	14	-	-	-	-	-
Forney, Mike	6-2	185	R	Thief River Falls, MN	5/14/1988	Chicago (AHL)	9	0	2	2	0	-	-	-	-	-
						Gwinnett (ECHL)	66	21	45	66	79	-	-	-	-	-
Glass, Tanner	6-1	210	L	Regina, SASK	11/29/1983	Vancouver (NHL)	73	3	7	10	72	20	0	0	0	18
Gregoire, Jason	6-0	196	L	Winnipeg, MB	2/24/1989	U. of ND (WCHA)	35	25	18	43	8	-	-	-	-	-
Holzapfel, Riley	6-0	185	L	Regina, SASK	8/18/1988	Chicago (AHL)	68	12	15	27	20	-	-	-	-	-
Jaffray, Jason	6-1	205	L	Olds, AB	6/30/1981	Manitoba (AHL)	6	1	1	2	2	14	3	6	9	6
Kane, Evander	6-2	195	L	Vancouver, BC	8/2/1991	Atlanta (NHL)	73	19	24	43	68	-	-	-	-	-
Klingberg, Carl	6-3	205	R	Gotenburg, Sweden	1/28/1991	Atlanta (NHL)	1	0	0	0	0	-	-	-	-	-
						Vastra Frolunda (SEL)	38	2	1	3	12	-	-	-	-	-
						Timra IK (SEL)	11	3	2	5	2	-	-	-	-	-
						Chicago (AHL)	8	1	0	1	6	-	-	-	-	-
Ladd, Andrew	6-3	205	L	Maple Ridge, BC	12/12/1985	Atlanta (NHL)	81	29	30	59	39	-	-	-	-	-
Little, Bryan	5-11	185	R	Edmonton, AB	11/12/1987	Atlanta (NHL)	76	18	30	48	33	-	-	-	-	-
Lowry, Adam	6-4	184	L	Calgary, AB	3/29/1993	Swift Current (WHL)	66	18	27	45	84	-	-	-	-	-
Machacek, Spencer	6-1	195	R	Lethbridge, AB	10/14/1988	Chicago (AHL)	67	21	32	53	45	-	-	-	-	-
						Atlanta (NHL)	10	0	0	0	0	-	-	-	-	-
Maxwell, Ben	6-1	195	L	North Vancouver, BC	3/30/1988	Hamilton (AHL)	47	11	29	40	32	-	-	-	-	-
						Chicago (AHL)	2	0	1	1	0	-	-	-	-	-
						Atlanta (NHL)	12	1	1	2	9	-	-	-	-	-
McArdle, Kenndal	5-11	190	L	Toronto, ON	1/4/1987	Florida (NHL)	11	0	0	0	16	-	-	-	-	-
						Rochester (AHL)	54	14	12	26	106	-	-	-	-	-
O'Dell, Eric	6-1	181	R	Ottawa, ON	6/21/1990	Sudbury (OHL)	39	20	24	44	34	8	7	5	12	15
Rosa, Marco	6-0	180	L	Scarborough, ON	1/15/1982	Manitoba (AHL)	51	13	21	34	20	14	6	11	17	4
Scheifele, Mark	6-2	181	R	Kitchener, ON	3/15/1993	Barrie (OHL)	66	22	53	75	35	-	-	-	-	-
Slater, Jim	6-0	200	L	Petosky, MI	12/9/1982	Atlanta (NHL)	36	5	7	12	19	-	-	-	-	-
Stapleton, Tim	5-9	180	R	Forest Park, IL	7/19/1982	San Antonio (AHL)	20	8	7	15	2	-	-	-	-	-
						Atlanta (NHL)	45	5	2	7	12	-	-	-	-	-
						Chicago (AHL)	4	1	3	4	2	-	-	-	-	-
Telegin, Ivan	6-3	199	L	Novokuznetsk, Russia	2/28/1992	Saginaw (OHL)	59	20	41	61	35	12	2	8	10	8
Thorburn, Chris	6-3	230	R	Sault Ste. Marie, ON	6/3/1983	Atlanta (NHL)	82	9	10	19	77	-	-	-	-	-
Weller, Shawn	6-2	199	L	Glen Falls, NY	7/8/1986	Manitoba (AHL)	67	12	11	23	50	10	0	0	0	4
Wellwood, Kyle	5-10	180	R	Windsor, ON	5/16/1983	Mytishchi (KHL)	25	5	3	8	2	-	-	-	-	-
						San Jose (NHL)	35	5	8	13	0	18	1	6	7	0
Wheeler, Blake	6-5	205	R	Robbinsdale, MN	8/31/1986	Boston (NHL)	58	11	16	27	32	-	-	-	-	-
						Atlanta (NHL)	23	7	10	17	14	-	-	-	-	-

DEFENCE

PLAYER	HT	WT	SHOT	BIRTHPLACE	BORN	2010-11 CLUB	GP	G	A	PTS	PIM	GP	G	A	PTS	PIM
Bogosian, Zach	6-3	215	R	Massena, NY	7/15/1990	Atlanta (NHL)	71	5	12	17	29	-	-	-	-	-
Byfuglien, Dustin	6-5	265	R	Minneapolis, MN	3/27/1985	Atlanta (NHL)	81	20	33	53	93	-	-	-	-	-
Chiarot, Ben	6-3	224	L	Hamilton, ON	5/9/1991	Sudbury (OHL)	25	5	8	13	62	-	-	-	-	-
						Saginaw (OHL)	39	5	19	24	51	12	1	4	5	21
Enstrom, Tobias	5-10	180	L	Nordingra, Sweden	11/5/1984	Atlanta (NHL)	72	10	41	51	54	-	-	-	-	-
Festerling, Brett	6-1	208	L	Prince George, BC	3/3/1986	Syracuse (AHL)	32	3	9	12	41	-	-	-	-	-
						Anaheim (NHL)	1	0	0	0	0	-	-	-	-	-
						Hamilton (AHL)	16	0	4	4	15	-	-	-	-	-
						Chicago (AHL)	5	0	0	0	0	-	-	-	-	-
Flood, Mark	6-1	195	R	Charlottetown, PEI	9/29/1984	Manitoba (AHL)	63	11	29	40	29	14	0	6	6	2
Hainsey, Ron	6-3	210	L	Bolton, CT	3/24/1981	Atlanta (NHL)	82	3	16	19	24	-	-	-	-	-
Jones, Randy	6-2	210	L	Quispamisis, NB	7/23/1981	Tampa Bay (NHL)	61	1	12	13	15	5	0	1	1	2
Kulda, Arturs	6-2	195	L	Riga, Latvia	7/25/1988	Chicago (AHL)	69	5	12	17	73	-	-	-	-	-
						Atlanta (NHL)	2	0	0	0	2	-	-	-	-	-
McFaull, Kendall	6-2	185	L	Rosetown, SASK	4/10/1992	Moose Jaw (WHL)	69	1	6	7	78	6	0	1	1	12
Meech, Derek	5-11	205	L	Winnipeg, MB	4/21/1984	Grand Rapids (AHL)	74	10	27	37	81	-	-	-	-	-
Melchiori, Julian	6-4	209	L	Richmond Hill, ON	12/6/1991	Kitchener (OHL)	63	1	18	19	55	3	0	0	0	0
Oduya, Johnny	6-0	190	L	Stockholm, Sweden	10/1/1981	Atlanta (NHL)	82	2	15	17	22	-	-	-	-	-
Owuya, Sebastian	6-4	207	L	Hagersten, Sweden	10/8/1991	Medicine Hat (WHL)	66	0	10	10	69	14	1	5	6	18
Postma, Paul	6-3	195	R	Red Deer, AB	2/22/1989	Chicago (AHL)	69	12	33	45	20	-	-	-	-	-
						Atlanta (NHL)	1	0	0	0	0	-	-	-	-	-
Ramsey, Travis	6-5	225	R	Lakewood, CA	5/16/1983	Manitoba (AHL)	57	0	12	12	63	14	0	3	3	6
Redmond, Zach	6-2	205	R	Traverse City, MI	7/26/1988	Ferris State (CCHA)	26	7	13	20	20	-	-	-	-	-
						Chicago (AHL)	3	0	0	0	4	-	-	-	-	-
Sol, Cody	6-5	242	L	Woodstock, ON	2/11/1991	Kitchener (OHL)	60	4	13	17	114	7	0	3	3	10
Stuart, Mark	6-2	213	R	Rochester, MN	4/27/1984	Boston (NHL)	31	1	4	5	23	-	-	-	-	-
						Atlanta (NHL)	23	1	0	1	24	-	-	-	-	-
Yuen, Zachary	6-0	205	R	Vancouver, BC	3/3/1993	Tri-City (WHL)	72	8	24	32	65	10	0	3	3	12

GOALTENDERS

PLAYER	HT	WT	CATCH	BIRTHPLACE	BORN	2010-11 CLUB	GP	W-L-OT	AVG	SO	GP	W-L	AVG
Carrozzi, Chris	6-2	185	L	Nepean, ON	3/2/1990	Gwinnett (ECHL)	47	16-20-6	3.23	2	-	-	-
						Chicago (AHL)	1	0-1-0	5.55	0	-	-	-
Mannino, Peter	6-1	195	L	Farmington Hills, MI	2/17/1984	Atlanta (NHL)	2	0-0-0	4.11	0	-	-	-
						Chicago (AHL)	42	16-17-4	3.12	0	-	-	-
Mason, Chris	6-0	195	L	Red Deer, AB	4/20/1976	Atlanta (NHL)	33	13-13-3	3.39	1	-	-	-
Pasquale, Edward	6-3	210	L	Toronto, ON	11/20/1990	Chicago (AHL)	24	11-11-1	2.93	1	-	-	-
						Gwinnett (ECHL)	12	7-4-0	3.69	0	-	-	-
Pavelec, Ondrej	6-3	220	L	Kladno, Czech Rep.	8/31/1987	Atlanta (NHL)	58	21-23-9	2.73	4	-	-	-
						Chicago (AHL)	1	0-1-0	3.10	0	-	-	-

EXHIBITION SEASON

uesday,
eptember 29, 2011
@ Winnipeg
Vinnipeg 6
olumbus 1

uesday,
eptember 29, 2011
@ Columbus
olumbus 5
Vinnipeg 1

riday,
eptember 24, 2011
@ Nashville
ville 4
Vinnipeg 0

Monday,
eptember 26, 2011
@ St. John's
Vinnipeg 3
Ottawa 1

Vednesday,
eptember 28, 2011
@ Winnipeg
Vinnipeg 3
Carolina 1

Vednesday,
eptember 30, 2011
@ Winnipeg
Nashville 3
Vinnipeg 2 (SO)

John Woods / The Canadian Press

Scheifele grabs early spotlight

FROM the opening pre-season game — a split-squad exhibition between the Columbus Blue Jackets on Sept. 20 — one story dominated the Jets camp: Mark Scheifele.

At the outset, the highly touted centreman was widely expected to eventually return to the OHL's Barrie Colts, where he would resume his junior hockey tutelage under the guidance of former Winnipeg Jets great Dale Hawerchuk.

That notion, however, began to change the moment the 18-year-old notched two goals and two assists in the Jets' 6-1 rout of the Blue Jackets at the MTS Centre. Suddenly, Scheifele became the darling of the capacity crowd at the MTS Centre (15,004) for what would become an emotional precursor to the team's season opener a few weeks later.

The outpouring of passion that literally spilled into the streets when it was first announced the Jets would return to the NHL was at last concentrated in full view of a team that had officially returned — right before their collective eyes.

"It's almost like 15 years of vented emotion... " Jets head coach Claude Noel told reporters. "As soon as the anthem started, everybody sang. It just gave you goose-bumps, like everybody was singing. It almost brought tears to your eyes. It was beautiful."

Scheifele wasn't the only Jet player to endear himself to the adoring crowd. Brawny blue-liner Dustin Byfuglien dropped his gloves against Blue Jackets forward Cody Bass less than a minute after the opening faceoff. Quipped Noel: "Between Byfuglien and the fans, it was like the Stanley Cup final."

Scheifele was just as impressed with the fans' performance. "To hear how loud they were I couldn't even hear myself think. It was just unbelievable and I wanted to feed off that energy and give it back to them," he said.

Just a few nights later, on Sept. 26, Scheifele scored in the 3-1 Jets victory over the Ottawa Senators in St. John's, N.L. — home of the club's newly minted American Hockey League farm team, the St. John's IceCaps.

Scheifele finished with eight points (4 G, 4 A) in just five pre-season games. On Oct. 3, the Jets signed the 6-3 forward to an entry-level contract, paving the way for the rookie to start the NHL season in Winnipeg.

"He's showing great potential," Jets GM Kevin Cheveldayoff said. "Certainly we're very excited about his training camp and very happy to have him signed to a contract. There really are no expectations. He'll be in the lineup opening night and we'll take it day by day in those regards. There are no guarantees of anything."

No guarantees, to be sure, but Scheifele's pre-season fling was definitely one of the fairy-tale storylines as the first regular season loomed.

The opening exhibition game against the Columbus Blue Jackets was as emotional an affair as one can see in pre-season hockey.

Fans at the 4Play Sports Bar downtown watch on TV as the anthem is sung across the street at the MTS Centre.

Wayne Glowacki / Winnipeg Free Press

THE OPENING NIGHT

Trevor Hagan / Winnipeg Free Press

OCTOBER 9, 2011

Jets' Bryan Little faces off against the Montreal Canadiens' Tomas Plekanec to start the historic home opener

Eager fans stream into the MTS Centre on opening night.

Trevor Hagan / Winnipeg Free Press

We'll remember
JETS

'The city is waking up again'

IT was a day celebrating a lost love refound, the renewal of vows and the promise to stay wedded through good times and bad — till death or skyrocketing salaries do us part.

And that was just for a hockey team.

Then there was Rachel Wu, standing in the foyer of the MTS Centre on Oct. 9, 2011, resplendent in her white wedding dress.

On the ice, the reborn Winnipeg Jets were doing battle with the legendary Montreal Canadiens to officially herald the NHL's return.

"It's such a great game," gushed Wu — a hockey player, obviously — surrounded by her wedding party during the first intermission. "And nothing is more exciting to watch live."

So exciting, in fact, that Rachel and Gabriel Wu exchanged vows at the Messiah Lutheran Church in Westwood at 2 p.m. Then headed to the arena, where they had Jets season tickets — and weren't about to miss the 2011-12 season opener.

"We went to the first period," Rachel said. "Now we're heading to our reception."

How fresh were the wedding vows? When a reporter asked them to spell their names, the bride said, "I'm Rachel Wu." Said the groom: "That's the first time I've heard her say that (last) name."

So it was that fans 15 years divorced from the NHL welcomed back the Jets, coming by the thousands to settle in the pews of their Portage Avenue shrine of hockey worship. Some came carrying their childhood memories. Some carried a belief that the return of the Jets would represent a new future for their city.

Mike Deal / Winnipeg Free Press

Her Majesty was in the house — in spirit, courtesy of Jerrold Wiebe.

Jerrold Wiebe carried Queen Elizabeth.

"We're in the very back row," explained Wiebe, toting a much smaller portrait of the Queen than the one that famously hung in the rafters of the old Winnipeg Arena. "So we're going to hang her in her rightful place. We're bringing the Queen with us."

Even two hours to opening faceoff against the visiting and venerable Canadiens — the rebirth of the NHL in the league's smallest market — the atmosphere outside the 15,004-seat arena had the air of a New Year's Eve celebration.

"It's neat to see Winnipeg alive again," said Wiebe's wife, Jeannette. "It's feeling good that the city is waking up again."

The need to share the joy of the NHL's return was palpable. Prime Minister Stephen Harper was on hand, as were NHL commissioner Gary Bettman and the Queen, in spirit, but the return of the league was all about those who saw it leave in a heart-wrenching, long goodbye in 1996, when the former Jets left for Phoenix.

Mike Deal / Winnipeg Free Press

Wayne Glowacki / Winnipeg Free Press

ABOVE: Exhilarated fans leave the MTS Centre to a party atmosphere after the opening game.

LEFT: A large crowd follows the action on large screens at The Forks.

THE OPENING NIGHT

"When (the Jets left in 1996) I was crying like a child," offered Cory Young. "My heart just got ripped out of me. Now when you look at the pent-up enthusiasm in the community, it's phenomenal.

"I think we're walking a foot taller than we were on May 31," Young added. "It's like the Super Bowl, the Grey Cup, the world juniors and the Stanley Cup finals all rolled into one. It's binding us all together. It's an amazing thing. It makes you feel damn good."

Thousands of fans milled outside the Portage Avenue building, the vast majority decked out in Jets paraphernalia — both new and retro. A group of eight 20-something buddies were dressed in white tuxedos. Other fans went to greater extremes.

"This is the biggest buzz Winnipeg has ever had," proclaimed 22-year-old Ryan

Jonathan Hayward / The Canadian Press

Goalie Ondrej Pavelec takes to the ice on opening night. The talented netminder would quickly become a fan favourite.

Gilmour, decked out in a one-piece spandex unitard — calling himself Captain Jet, cape included. "Hockey is the fuel that runs Winnipeg."

For others, however, the Jets' return was about sentiment as much as hockey.

Mark Strople and his 25-year-old son, Braden, attended the last regular-season game of the Jets in 1996. In 2011, they were standing on Hargrave Street with the father wearing an Andrew Ladd jersey and the son sporting the number of Dustin Byfuglien.

"It just blows me away," Braden said. "Just the energy of the city. The excitement. It's taken it to a different level. The city feels better about itself. The way people view Winnipeg is a 180."

Old memories die hard. But new ones are born every minute.

The Jets' Nik Antropov puts his name in the history books by sliding the puck past Canadiens goalie Carey Price, scoring the reborn Jets' first regular-season goal.

Mikey Lintick, 26, was at the opener, too, dressed with his buddies in white tuxedos. "We wanted to welcome them back as they left, only in a classier way," he said.

Lintick remembers his last game watching the old Jets, when his mom wanted to leave early to beat the traffic with the Jets trailing 3-1. He grabbed a set of red drapes at the old Winnipeg Arena and didn't want to let go. "She (his mom) said, 'Don't worry, I'll take you to the next game'... and here I am today."

Lintick represents a generation of 20-something Winnipeggers who have been so prominent in celebrating the team's return. No surprise, he said.

"We were kids, right?" he said. "It means so much to us, and we didn't know any better (when the team left). You can't explain it. It's something deep down in your

Joe Bryksa / Winnipeg Free Press

BELOW: Fans show their spirit at the big event.

BOTTOM: Manitoba Moose mascot Mick E. Moose, a beloved holdover from the former franchise, works the crowd.

Trevor Hagan / Winnipeg Free Press

Trevor Hagan / Winnipeg Free Press

heart about remembering your childhood. Going to games with your dad. It's something that sticks with you."

Then there was Marcien Deroche, 84, who along with son, Claude, couldn't wait for the opening faceoff.

"I don't know how important this is for everybody else," said Marcien, his eyes welling with tears, "but it's sure as hell important to me. I'm glad I'm still here to watch. When I see them drop the puck, I'll be saying, 'I'm with the Jets! I'm still here and I'm 84 years old. Unbelievable!' "

It was a great day for a wedding.

Bettman with Prime Minister Stephen Harper.

Jeff Parsons / St. John's IceCaps

NHL commissioner Gary Bettman (from left) chats with former premier, current Canadian Ambassador to the U.S. Gary Doer as Mark Chipman, David Thomson talk.

Jeff Parsons / St. John's IceCaps

Bettman and Brian Burke, president and GM of the Toronto Maple Leafs, speak with the prime minister.

Jeff Parsons / St. John's IceCaps

Prime Minister Stephen Harper was on hand, as were NHL commissioner Gary Bettman, Jets co-owner David Thomson, former premier and current Canadian Ambassador to the U.S. Gary Doer, Jets legends Dale Hawerchuk and Keith Tkachuk, and a who's who of Winnipeg. It was bedlam at the barn.

"This is a great building and boy is it loud," said Tkachuk. "The old building was my first and it was special, but this is a beautiful place and this is a beautiful day."

THE OPENING NIGHT

The Jets' Brett MacLean battles with the Canadiens' Yannick Weber.

Trevor Hagan / Winnipeg Free Press

Trevor Hagan / Winnipeg Free Press

Trevor Hagan / Winnipeg Free Press

Trevor Hagan / Winnipeg Free Press

Trevor Hagan / Winnipeg Free Press

FROM LEFT:

The Jets' Evander Kane jostles for the puck with the Canadiens' Scott Gomez.

Mark Scheifele readies for a faceoff.

Jet Dustin Byfuglien launches a blast.

A fan's sign captures the evening's sentiment.

THE OPENING NIGHT

Joe Bryksa / Winnipeg Free Press

00:07:39

A missing member of the family

BETWEEN the euphoria of the NHL's return and the historic jubilation surrounding opening night, the Winnipeg Jets franchise was shaken to the core by a death in the family.

Feisty winger Rick Rypien, a 27-year-old who had first joined the Manitoba Moose organization in 2005 and then finished the 2011 season with the Moose, was found dead in his home in Crow's Nest Pass Aug. 15, 2011.

The death was a devastating blow to Jets management, in particular assistant GM Craig Heisinger and co-owner Mark Chipman, who had seen Rypien, a non-drafted player from the Regina Pats, blossom into an NHL regular with the Vancouver Canucks.

Rypien, who suffered from depression, had joined the Moose late in the 2010-11 season and excelled in the club's last playoff run. On July 2, Rypien signed with the Jets as an unrestricted free agent — heralding the return of a prodigal son of the AHL organization.

"That was one of the best days of my summer," Chipman recalled. "That was a fist-pumping moment. Beyond the announcement of joining the National Hockey League, for me that's what really brought it full circle. When we had one of our own come back full circle, that felt like the picture was complete."

Rypien epitomized the Moose/Jets organization; an undersized underdog who eventually earned a spot in the best hockey league in the world, despite the odds. While Rypien was generously listed as 5-10 and 180 pounds when he first arrived in Winnipeg as a baby-faced rookie, he earned a reputation as a fierce competitor who often fought opponents a foot taller.

At the time of his signing, Chipman was convinced Rypien would become a fan favourite.

"I mean, we were very proud of what he accomplished," Chipman said. "I personally took great pride in the fact that Craig Heisinger spotted this kid blocking shots at a practice (with the Pats) and stuck his neck out on the line to bring him in. He epitomized what we were about. He was a guy who had to earn his way into the NHL. He was relentless. He embodied a lot of the same characteristics to how Craig Heisinger got to where he is and, to a certain extent, how the organization got to (the NHL).

"He (Rypien) was the on-ice example of what we were, what we are, what we want to be."

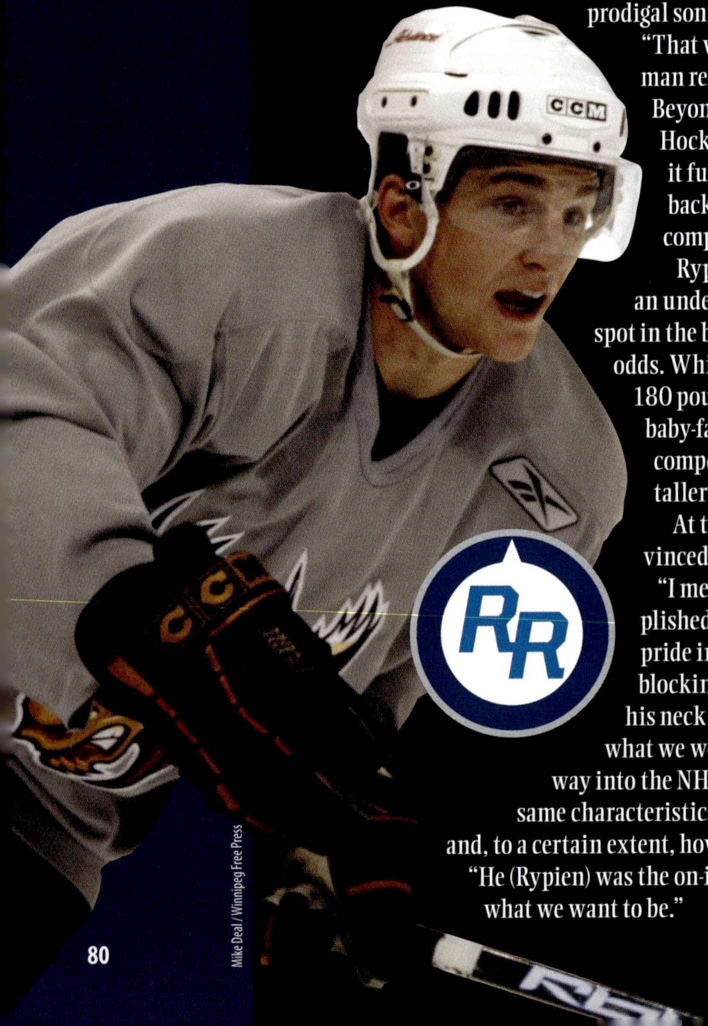

Mike Deal / Winnipeg Free Press

Jeff Parsons / St. John's IceCaps

Prior to the opening faceoff, the Jets staged a tribute to Rick Rypien, with a touching video of his highlights with the Moose and Canucks, including his first NHL goal on his first shift with Vancouver on Dec. 21, 2005. Rypien's mother, Shelley Crawford, dropped the puck for a ceremonial faceoff between Jets captain Andrew Ladd and Canadiens captain Brian Gionta.

Wayne Glowacki / Winnipeg Free Press

Boris Minkevich / Winnipeg Free Press

LEFT: The Jets' Craig Heisinger, who championed Rick Rypien after spotting him in junior hockey.

ABOVE: The 'RR' patch the Jets wore in tribute.

Rypien was going to wear No 11 with the Jets, his original number with the Moose.

Rypien's memorial was held in Blairmore, Alta., Aug. 20, with about 1,000 mourners in attendance, including several members of the Jets organization. "The system didn't fail him," Heisinger told reporters after the service. "Everybody in today's society faces a different challenge. Rick fought them like everyone else. The demon depression won out. He's at peace, we should all be."

During the season, the Jets wore a patch (RR) in his honour.

Members of the Jets watch a video tribute to Rypien.

Jonathan Hayward / The Canadian Press

GAME 1

HOME

Sunday, October 9, 2011
JETS vs. MONTREAL CANADIENS

MONTREAL 5 / WINNIPEG 1

TWO hours before opening faceoff, thousands of fans milled outside the NHL's newest arena and, at 15,004 seats, its smallest, revelling in sheer joy.

The reborn Winnipeg Jets were sloppy, nervous and mistake-happy in their 5-1 loss to the Montreal Canadiens, but still earned a prolonged standing ovation at the end.

One fan's sign told the story: "Canada's Best Comeback."

"Tonight was pretty special as far as a historical point of view," said Jets winger Chris Thorburn. "It's just unfortunate we couldn't match the fans' enthusiasm on the ice."

The Jets gift-wrapped the first two goals when Mike Cammalleri gobbled up a Johnny Oduya pass and buried it 3:05 into the contest, and with Tomas Plekanec pick-pocketing Oduya for the second marker early in the second.

Winnipeg cut the gap to 2-1 when Nik Antropov whacked home a rebound past Carey Price early in the third, but an interference call on Dustin Byfuglien that led to a Yannick Weber power-play goal sapped any momentum.

Price was steady in the Habs net, kicking out 30 of 31 shots, while Max Pacioretty and Travis Moen beat Ondrej Pavelec.

Asked afterward what good he took from the game, Jets captain Andrew Ladd said, "Not much, to be honest with you... We've got to be better going forward. We've got to get going."

BIG PICTURE

Not what Winnipeggers envisioned for the debut of the NHL's new era here. Three times during the game, Jets goalie Ondrej Pavelec was left to face — alone — Montreal shooters, and they scored on all three. Not a good omen.

LITTLE PICTURE

Pavelec faced some big-league shots — Mike Cammalleri, Tomas Plekanec, Yannick Weber, Travis Moen and Max Pacioretty all buried their chances — and the simple truth is, no Jets were shooting the puck with such accuracy on Sunday. That spells game over.

ONDREJ PAVELEC

Joe Bryksa / Winnipeg Free Press

SUMMARY

FIRST PERIOD

1. Montreal, Cammalleri 1, 3:05

Penalties — Slater Wpg (holding) 8:35, Cole Mtl (tripping) 14:26, Gill Mtl (interference) 18:49, Emelin Mtl (hooking) 19:30

SECOND PERIOD

2. Montreal, Plekanec 1 (Moen, Weber) 14:17

Penalties — Bogosian Wpg (holding) 1:44, Weber Mtl (holding) 3:22, Byfuglien Wpg (interference) 6:53, Gomez Mtl (holding) 12:15

THIRD PERIOD

3. Winnipeg, Antropov 1 (Stuart, Burmistrov) 2:27
4. Montreal, Weber 1 (Plekanec, Desharnais) 4:51 (pp)
5. Montreal, Moen 1 (Plekanec) 10:31
6. Montreal, Pacioretty 1 (Gorges) 12:32

Penalties — Subban Mtl (cross-checking), Stuart Wpg (roughing) 3:43, Byfuglien Wpg (interference) 4:28, Diaz Mtl (interference) 17:15, Subban Mtl (interference) 19:58

● **Shots on goal by**

Montreal	7	9	6	— 22
Winnipeg	8	9	14	— 31

● **Goal** — Montreal: Price (W,1-1-0); Winnipeg: Pavelec (L,0-1-0)

● **Power plays (goals-chances)** — Montreal: 1-4; Winnipeg: 0-7

● **Referees** — Rob Martell, Brad Meier. Linesmen — Vaughan Rody, Ryan Galloway

● **Attendance** — 15,004 (15,004)

CHICAGO 4 / WINNIPEG 3

A great start and some early goals still left the Jets without a win before a sellout crowd of 21,175 at the United Center.

The Chicago Blackhawks had enough kick to score a 4-3 victory.

"Turnovers are a fact in every game and they've killed us in both games," Jets coach Claude Noel said.

Chicago right-winger-turned-centre Patrick Kane had a goal and two assists.

Jets goalie Ondrej Pavelec, who faced 32 Hawks shots, was strong for his team in the final period, but by then it was too late.

The Jets were still looking for their first win of the season and looked better in Game 2, but the coach was looking for more from his troops.

"We have played two playoff teams and they have beat us," Noel said. "So regardless of the score, if we think we're going to be in the playoffs, we're going to have to find somebody we can beat. There are no accolades for losing."

BIG PICTURE

Two games, nothing close to a complete outing yet for the reborn Jets. You could call the trend positive in that there was a great start and a sturdy finish, but Winnipeg's game did not come close to 60 minutes.

LITTLE PICTURE

Jim Slater's two goals in the first eight minutes were a dream start for any visiting team in Chicago, but the advantage was nullified before the first period was over. The Blackhawks then kept the foot on the gas and established their own two-goal lead before seven minutes had gone by in the second period. From there, Winnipeg just didn't have the firepower to catch up, though Ondrej Pavelec's goaltending gave them a chance in the third period.

SUMMARY

FIRST PERIOD
1. Winnipeg, Slater 1 (Oduya) 4:24
2. Winnipeg, Slater 2 (Hainsey, Glass) 7:29
3. Chicago, Brunette 2 (P.Kane, J.Toews) 9:45 (pp)
4. Chicago, P.Kane 1 (Hossa, Carcillo) 16:50

Penalties — Enstrom Wpg (tripping) 8:35

SECOND PERIOD
5. Chicago, Hossa 1 (Leddy, P.Kane) 0:33
6. Chicago, Bolland 3 (Bickell) 6:45
7. Winnipeg, Wellwood 1 (Hainsey, MacLean) 14:34

Penalties — Montador Chi (interference) 1:28, Wellwood Wpg (tripping) 8:06, MacLean Wpg (elbowing) 12:12, Olesz Chi (high-sticking) 14:58

THIRD PERIOD
No Scoring
Penalties — None

● **Shots on goal by**

Winnipeg	9	10	11	—	30
Chicago	11	13	8	—	32

● **Goal** — Winnipeg: Pavelec (L,0-2-0); Chicago: Emery (W,1-0-0)
● **Power plays (goals-chances)** — Winnipeg: 0-2; Chicago: 1-3
● **Referees** — Steve Kozari, Brian Pochmara. Linesmen — Don Henderson, Derek Nansen
● **Attendance** — 21,175

Joe Bryksa / Winnipeg Free Press

JIM SLATER

3

GAME

AWAY

Saturday, October 15, 2011
JETS vs. PHOENIX COYOTES

PHOENIX 4 / WINNIPEG 1

THE Jets were outshot 34-19 and their special teams were a huge liability in this one-sided 4-1 loss to the Phoenix Coyotes at Jobing.com Arena.

It was the team's third loss in as many outings to start Winnipeg's comeback NHL season.

"I'm not frustrated, I'm disappointed," said coach Claude Noel. "I'm not sure what it is we're waiting for right now. It looks like our team thinks it has a free pass to fail.

"I'm not sure what the wake-up call is."

Noel relied on backup goalie Chris Mason to take the net, but Mason was scored on just 34 seconds into the game, and it went downhill from there.

"As a team, we would definitely have liked a better performance tonight," Mason said. "We're just going through a tough time."

Team captain Andrew Ladd scored his first goal of the season on a late second-period deflection.

The loss spoiled the party for thousands of Jets fans who made the trip down to Arizona for the game.

'Go Jets Go' chants were heard in and around the arena complex hours before the game, as the pro-Winnipeg contingent overwhelmed the local crowd for much of the day.

BIG PICTURE

Thirteen goals against in three games; just five for. This, as Jets coach Claude Noel said, is not a road the team wants to go down. The defensive vulnerabilities were certainly a big factor in the team's 0-3 mark to date, leaving it still the only pointless outfit in the NHL.

LITTLE PICTURE

An ugly start — a giveaway in the first minute turned into Daymond Langkow's goal — and little push-back made this result pretty apparent after the first period, when the Coyotes were ahead 2-0. And through three games, the Jets had surrendered a power-play goal in each game, and scored not one themselves.

CHRIS MASON

Joe Bryksa / Winnipeg Free Press

SUMMARY

FIRST PERIOD

1. Phoenix, Langkow 1 (Whitney, Doan) 0:34
2. Phoenix, Ekman-Larsson 2, 9:12

Penalties — Bissonnette Phx (boarding) 3:58, Phoenix bench, (too many men; served by Pyatt) 11:16, Boedker Phx (hooking) 15:10

SECOND PERIOD

3. Phoenix, Ekman-Larsson 3 (Gordon, Pyatt) 14:57
4. Winnipeg, Ladd 1 (Enstrom, Wheeler) 19:41

Penalties — Hainsey Wpg (double high-sticking) 3:43

THIRD PERIOD

5. Phoenix, Whitney 2 (Hanzal, Doan) 6:43 (pp)

Penalties — Ladd Wpg (slashing) 5:14, Stuart Wpg (high-sticking) 7:19, Kane Wpg (interference) 10:56, Aucoin Phx (hooking) 15:23

Missed penalty shot — Antropov Wpg, 9:10

● **Shots on goal by**

Winnipeg	5	9	5	—	19
Phoenix	11	10	14	—	34

● **Goal** — Winnipeg: Mason (L,0-1-0); Phoenix: Smith (W,1-1-1)

● **Power plays (goals-chances)** — Winnipeg: 0-4; Phoenix: 1-5

● **Referees** — Mike Hasenfratz, Greg Kimmerly. Linesmen — Vaughan Rody, Jay Sharrers

● **Attendance** — 17,132 (17,135)

WINNIPEG 2 / PITTSBURGH 1

IT took Kyle Wellwood just eight seconds to score the Jets' first goal as the team surged forward to turn the tide on an ugly 0-3 start before 15,004 wild fans.

The decibel level in the rink grew as the scoreless third period wore on, finally ending with a deafening roar and the fourth or fifth standing ovation of the night.

"It was awesome for us," said Jets captain Andrew Ladd. "It was nice for us to finally deliver a win for these fans who have been waiting so long to have that feeling and excitement about this team."

More than one of the standing ovations were for Jets goalie Ondrej Pavelec, who made 27 saves against some high-quality chances.

"We knew they're missing two of the best players (Sidney Crosby, Evgeni Malkin) in the NHL, probably, but they still have a really good team," Pavelec said. "We played so hard tonight and we deserved to win."

Another big factor was second-year pro Alexander Burmistrov, who set up both goals.

BIG PICTURE

The first win — sure, it came against a Penguins squad minus Sidney Crosby and Evgeni Malkin — but there are no asterisks attached to any victories in the NHL. It was the most complete performance from the Jets in the young season and the timing couldn't have been more perfect.

LITTLE PICTURE

To a man, the Jets talked about playing a simpler, grittier game. Consider that task Mission: Accomplished. The home side went hard to the net, played the dump-and-chase game effectively and — most important of all — dramatically cut down the number of turnovers.

SUMMARY

FIRST PERIOD
1. Winnipeg, Wellwood 2 (Burmistrov, Antropov) 0:08
2. Winnipeg, Glass 1 (Burmistrov) 18:27

Penalties — Wheeler Wpg (holding) 9:36, Engelland Pgh, Thorburn Wpg (fighting) 14:01

SECOND PERIOD
3. Pittsburgh, Michalek 1 (Letang, Cooke) 18:22

Penalties — Hainsey Wpg (tripping) 0:54, Park Pgh (hooking) 9:20, Neal Pgh (slashing) 11:53, Sullivan Pgh (hooking) 19:44

THIRD PERIOD
No Scoring
Penalties — Letang Pgh (boarding) 13:08, Kunitz Pgh, Glass Wpg (roughing), Lovejoy Pgh, Slater Wpg (fighting), Thorburn Wpg (hooking) 16:02, Neal (slashing) 20:00

Shots on goal by

Pittsburgh	7	14	8	—	29
Winnipeg	11	11	13	—	35

Goal — Pittsburgh: Fleury (L,3-2-0); Winnipeg: Pavelec (W,1-2-0)
Power plays (goals-chances) — Pittsburgh: 0-3; Winnipeg: 0-4
Referees — Dean Morton, Brad Watson
Linesmen — Lonnie Cameron, Thor Nelson
Attendance — 15,004 (15,004)

Trevor Hagan / Winnipeg Free Press

TANNER GLASS

5 GAME

AWAY

Wednesday, October 19, 2011
JETS vs. TORONTO MAPLE LEAFS

TORONTO 4 / WINNIPEG 3 (SO)

IF the Jets' 4-3 shootout loss to the Maple Leafs was described metaphorically, it would look something like a big, fat shiner under the squad's eye.

Playing a textbook road game for the better part of 47 minutes in front of 19,154 at the Air Canada Centre, the Jets unravelled during a 27-second span in the third period and gift-wrapped a come-from-behind victory for the Leafs.

In the process, this occasionally intriguing but often-frustrating squad fell to 1-3-1 on the season while Toronto improved to 4-0-1.

Winnipeg built a 3-1 advantage on goals by Tobias Enstrom, Alex Burmistrov and Mark Scheifele — two of the goals coming on the power play —but took two costly penalties in an ugly stretch in the third and were victimized by Joffrey Lupul and Phil Kessel. The Jets managed to avoid the knockout punch through the rest of the third and OT, but in the shootout, Lupul and Matt Frattin scored while Kyle Wellwood and Alex Burmistrov were stoned by Manitoba's James Reimer in the Leafs net.

BIG PICTURE

The Jets picked up a point on the road against one of the hottest teams of this young NHL season. But blowing a two-goal lead in the third was going to stick in some craws for a while. Some aspects of the Jets' game came alive — like the power play — but the penalty kill was iffy and the team had no answer when the Leafs finally began counterpunching in the third.

LITTLE PICTURE

It could have been remembered as a night of firsts for the Jets — first power-play goal, first goal by a defenceman and first markers for Tobias Enstrom, Alex Burmistrov and rookie Mark Scheifele.

MARK SCHEIFELE

Joe Bryksa / Winnipeg Free Press

SUMMARY

FIRST PERIOD
1. Winnipeg, Enstrom 1 (Little, Byfuglien) 9:49 (pp)
2. Toronto, Lupul 3 (Kessel, Bozak) 11:39

Penalties — Little Wpg (unsportsmanlike conduct) 5:47, Schenn Tor (hooking) 8:24

SECOND PERIOD
3. Winnipeg, Burmistrov 1 (Antropov, Wellwood) 2:27
4. Winnipeg, Scheifele 1 (Byfuglien, MacLean) 7:53 (pp)

Penalties — Komisarek Tor (interference) 3:13, Komisarek Tor (holding) 6:48, Meech Wpg (hooking) 13:20

THIRD PERIOD
5. Toronto, Lupul 4 (Liles, Kessel) 7:28 (pp)
6. Toronto, Kessel 7 (Phaneuf, Liles) 7:55 (pp)

Penalties — Bogosian Wpg (interference) 6:44, Meech Wpg (tripping) 7:42, Kessel Tor (slashing) 10:54

Overtime — No Scoring **Penalties** — None

Shootout — (Toronto wins 2-0)
Toronto (2) — Kessel, miss; Lupul, goal; Frattin, goal; Winnipeg (0) — Wellwood, miss; Burmistrov, miss

Shots on goal by

Winnipeg	9	6	11	3 —	29
Toronto	6	6	10	1 —	23

Goal — Winnipeg: Pavelec (SOL,1-2-1); Toronto: Reimer (W,4-0-1)
Power plays (goals-chances) — Winnipeg: 2-4; Toronto: 2-4
Referees — Frederick L'Ecuyer, Don VanMassenhoven. Linesmen — Brad Lazarowich, Jean Morin
Attendance — 19,514 (18,819)

OTTAWA 4 / WINNIPEG 1

ALEXANDER Burmistrov, one of the few bright lights in the Jets lineup, picked up another assist in Winnipeg's 4-1 loss to the Senators at Scotiabank Place.

The young Russian led the Jets in points with one goal and four assists through six games, but wasn't interested in platitudes following the loss.

"Right now it's more important for me to win the game. I don't really care about my points. We need to win the game," Burmistrov said afterwards.

Ottawa honoured the Jets with a video tribute, welcoming the franchise back to the league. The fans gave it some nice applause, but nowhere near the standing ovation Leafs fans gave the franchise earlier in Toronto.

Defenceman Dustin Byfuglien scored the lone goal for Winnipeg. Jason Spezza had three points (one goal, two assists) for Ottawa.

The Senators also honoured three former Jets in the building, saying hello to Norm Beaudoin, Jim Kyte and Laurie Boschman.

BIG PICTURE

The Jets rolled into Ottawa to face a team that had lost three straight and had been roughed up repeatedly in their own zone, having surrendered 30 goals in six games. By game's end, the Sens looked like the 1976-77 Montreal Canadiens.

LITTLE PICTURE

An all-too-common theme for these Jets, who were looking more and more like the Thrashers that struggled for stretches in Atlanta last year. If head coach Claude Noel were a man trying to stop a dam from leaking, he'd have run out of fingers and toes by now.

SUMMARY

FIRST PERIOD

1. Winnipeg, Byfuglien 1 (Burmistrov, Antropov) 14:39

Penalties — Burmistrov Wpg (double high-sticking) 1:29, Karlsson Ott (holding) 7:01

SECOND PERIOD

2. Ottawa, Michalek 4 (Greening, Spezza) 4:48 (pp)
3. Ottawa, Spezza 3 (Greening, Michalek) 13:20

Penalties — Bogosian Wpg (holding) 2:09, Antropov Wpg (hooking) 4:13, Gonchar Ott (hooking) 15:26

THIRD PERIOD

4. Ottawa, Alfredsson 3, 9:15
5. Ottawa, Michalek 5 (Smith, Spezza) 19:20 (en)

Penalties — Enstrom Wpg (holding) 8:16, Neil Ott (high-sticking) 8:16, Karlsson Ott (holding) 11:54, Alfredsson Ott (tripping) 14:02

Shots on goal by

Winnipeg	13	9	14	— 36
Ottawa	12	12	6	— 30

Goal — Winnipeg: Pavelec (L,1-3-1); Ottawa: Anderson (W,2-2-0)

Power plays (goals-chances) — Winnipeg: 0-4; Ottawa: 1-4

Referees — Frederick L'Ecuyer, Wes McCauley. Linesmen — Scott Driscoll, Brad Kovalchik

Attendance — 17,919 (19,153)

John Woods / Winnipeg Free Press

ALEX BURMISTROV

7

GAME

HOME

Saturday, October 22, 2011

JETS vs. CAROLINA HURRICANES

WINNIPEG 5 / CAROLINA 3

GOING down 2-0 to the Carolina Hurricanes seven minutes into the game was not a way to endear yourself to the home crowd — no matter how fanatic they are.

But then the Jets' puny-so-far power play caught fire and the home team scored five goals in a 15-minute span. Five goals in 15 minutes — how many times can you say that in a season? — and carried it through for a 5-3 victory before 15,004 ecstatic fans at the MTS Centre.

"We didn't have the first period we wanted but we came out a lot stronger and wanted to show ourselves and the fans that we're a lot better team than we showed in the first," said Jets winger Evander Kane, who scored his first goal of the season.

"We came out in the second and played real hard."

Kane, Andrew Ladd, Jim Slater, Kyle Wellwood and Alexander Burmistrov spread the scoring around as the Jets improved to 2-4-1.

Forward Jeff Skinner put up a three-point night for the Canes.

BIG PICTURE

It capped a great day in Winnipeg for sports fans, with an afternoon Blue Bomber football game drawing more than 30,000 to Canad Inns Stadium (they beat the Montreal Alouettes 26-25 to tie for first place in the East Division). Local sports fans attending the 'Douple Dip' brought their closets with them: parkas and tuques in the afternoon before stuffing them in the trunk and strolling into the comfort of the downtown rink.

LITTLE PICTURE

Jets goaltender Ondrej Pavelec was pulled after allowing two goals in the first 6:43 of the game. Chris Mason was solid the rest of the way, stopping 18 of 19 shots.

DUSTIN BYFUGLIEN

John Woods / Winnipeg Free Press

SUMMARY

FIRST PERIOD

1. Carolina, Jokinen 2 (LaRose, Skinner) 4:40
2. Carolina, Skinner 3 (LaRose, McBain) 6:43
3. Winnipeg, Burmistrov 2 (Bogosian, Wellwood) 12:32 (pp)
4. Winnipeg, Wellwood 3 (Antorpov, Entstrom) 19:58 (pp)

Penalties — Tlusty Car (tripping) 7:36, LaRose car (tripping) 10:49, Sutter Car (boarding) 14:49, Wheeler, Wpg (tripping) 16:35, Ponikarovsky, Car (elbowing) 18:28

SECOND PERIOD

5. Winnipeg, Slater 3 (Glass) 4:29
6. Winnipeg, Ladd 2 (Wheeler, Bogosian) 6:07
7. Winnipeg, Kane 1 (Antropov, Stuart) 7:30

Penalty — Enstrom, Wpg (holding) 11:42

THIRD PERIOD

8. Carolina, Ruutu 2 (Skinner) 8:58

Penalties — Bogosian Wpg (holding the stick) 4:12, Stuart Wpg (hooking) 9:18, Stewart Car (cross-checking) 12:08, Little Wpg (tripping) 13:32, Antropov Wpg (interference) 13:49, Enstrom Wpg (hooking) 15:43, Jokinen Car (high sticking double minor) 19:13

Shots on goal by

Carolina	6	6	12	—	24
Winnipeg	13	6	5	—	24

Goal (shots-saves) — Carolina: Boucher (L,0-1-1); Winnipeg: Pavelec (five shots-three saves); Mason (W,1-1-0; 6:43 of the first, 19-18)

Power plays (goals-chances) — Carolina: 2-6; Winnipeg: 0-7

Referees — Kyle Rehman, Chris Rooney. Linesmen — Ryan Galloway, Vaughan Rody

Attendance — 15,004 (15,004)

N.Y. RANGERS 2 / WINNIPEG 1

8

GAME

HOME

Monday, October 24, 2011

JETS vs. NEW YORK RANGERS

THE Jets rolled up their sleeves and got straight to the task of doing all the grunt-work required for their second consecutive win and third of the season.

And yet, despite outshooting the Rangers 28-17 and despite clanging a couple off posts and controlling the play for long stretches — particularly in the third period — at the end of the evening, the Jets were staring at a 2-1 loss and left with a handful of blisters, an aching back and diddly to show for a night's work.

The Rangers got the game-winner on a fluke and against the flow of play. With Chris Thorburn in the penalty box, the Rangers' struggling power play had the winner bounce in off Zach Bogosian on a shot by Ryan Callahan.

New York managed just three shots in the first period, but opened the scoring early in the second with the man advantage when Ruslan Fedotenko deftly tipped a point shot past Jets netminder Chris Mason.

The Jets tied the game with 5:31 left in the second when Nik Antropov pounced on a loose puck in the Rangers zone and wristed home a shot short side on goaltender Marty Biron for his second of the year.

"It was one of those nights," said Jets defenceman Johnny Oduya. "The opposition goalie played great and shut us down. What can you do other than keep working?"

The Jets' record fell to 2-5-1 on the season.

BIG PICTURE

The Jets had chances to score but only their inability to finish came through this night. The Rangers' defence, coupled with the stellar play of goaltender Marty Biron, led to the fifth outright loss of the season for Winnipeg.

LITTLE PICTURE

It was a winnable game for the home team. The Rangers sometimes contained the pressure the Jets created, and not at other times. When the Jets had the visitors reeling, they were unable to find the back of the net.

SUMMARY

FIRST PERIOD
No Scoring
Penalties — Prust NYR, Glass Wpg (fighting) 1:55, Wheeler Wpg (hooking) 4:52, Fedotenko NYR (holding the stick) 14:34, Antropov Wpg (high-sticking) 15:51

SECOND PERIOD
1. New York, Fedotenko 1 (Girardi, Del Zotto) 5:51 (pp)
2. Winnipeg, Antropov 2 (Burmistrov, Kane) 14:29
Penalties — Byfuglien Wpg (tripping) 4:51, Jones Wpg (tripping) 11:39

THIRD PERIOD
3. New York, Callahan 2 (Fedotenko, Girardi) 8:41 (pp)
Penalty — Thorburn, Wpg (tripping) 7:49

Shots on goal by

New York	3	7	7	—	17
Winnipeg	8	7	13	—	28

Goal — New York: Biron (W,1-0-0); Winnipeg: Mason (L,1-2-0)
Power plays (goals-chances) — New York: 2-5; Winnipeg: 0-1
Referees — Mike Leggo, Don VanMassenhoven
Linesmen — Steve Barton, Mike Shewchyk
Attendance — 15,004 (15,004)

Boris Minkevich / Winnipeg Free Press

TANNER GLASS

9 GAME

AWAY

Thursday, October 27, 2011
JETS vs. PHILADELPHIA FLYERS

WINNIPEG 9 / PHILADELPHIA 8

JETS head coach Claude Noel managed to keep his sense of humour after this game, only because his team came out on the winning end.

This was a game that saw the visitors blow a pair of four-goal leads, then in the third period give up three goals to fall behind 7-6 before finding a way to get to the final buzzer with more goals than the opposition.

The back-and-forth and back-again had many minds spinning.

"I thought to myself, 'Self, you're a sick man trying to make logic of this.' I just, ah, I just... it was hard," Noel mused after the game. "It was a tough night for the goaltenders, to say the least."

The victory was Winnipeg's first on the road, giving them a 3-5-1 record.

The Jets broke out to a 5-1 lead early in the second period and led 6-2 with the game almost half over. But the Flyers kept chipping away and got the score to 6-4 heading into the third. When the Flyers finally moved past the Jets at 7-6, it seemed they would steam ahead and get the win, but the visitors refused to go along.

The fun wasn't just reserved for the ice, either.

"The '80s called and they want their Flyers-Jets game back." Pierre LeBrun, ESPN columnist, tweeted out to his followers as the game progressed. Final thought to Noel, who through the madness was searching for a higher power to make some sense of the play on the ice.

"I had the rosary beads going," Noel said. "I had it all going tonight."

BIG PICTURE

Coach Claude Noel would have liked it to be a little neater but he took the win.

LITTLE PICTURE

Giving up eight goals isn't a good thing, even if you manage to score nine and get the win.

ANDREW LADD

Joe Bryksa / Winnipeg Free Press

SUMMARY

FIRST PERIOD

1. Philadelphia, Hartnell 3 (Jagr, Timonen) 4:10
2. Winnipeg, Jones 1 (Wheeler, Glass) 10:01
3. Winnipeg, Slater 4 (Thorburn, Glass) 13:39
4. Winnipeg, K.Wellwood 4 (Enstrom, Little) 18:37

Penalties — Byfuglien Wpg (slashing) 6:00, Lilja Pha (interference) 16:37

SECOND PERIOD

5. Winnipeg, Glass 2 (Enstrom, Byfuglien) 3:39
6. Winnipeg, Antropov 3 (Stapleton) 4:39 (pp)
7. Philadelphia, Giroux 6 (Timonen, Briere) 6:25 (pp)
8. Winnipeg, Kane 2 (Antropov, Burmistrov) 10:39 (pp)
9. Philadelphia, Briere 3 (Hartnell, Timonen) 14:11
10. Philadelphia, Talbot 2, 16:41

Penalties — Timonen Pha (interference) 4:36, Oduya Wpg (slashing) 5:29, Ladd Wpg (holding) 6:13, Coburn Pha (slashing) 10:00, McArdle Wpg (hooking) 12:08, Kane Wpg (delay of game) 14:33, Bogosian Wpg, Hartnell Pha (roughing) 18:18

THIRD PERIOD

11. Philadelphia, Briere 4 (Coburn, van Riemsdyk) 1:09
12. Philadelphia, Read 3 (Lilja, Voracek) 2:23
13. Philadelphia, van Riemsdyk 3 (Briere, Carle) 3:02
14. Winnipeg, Burmistrov 3 (Antropov, Kane) 3:30
15. Winnipeg, Stuart 1 (Stapleton, Wheeler) 4:31
16. Philadelphia, van Riemsdyk 4 (Timonen, Meszaros) 16:21
17. Winnipeg, Ladd 3 (Wheeler, Little) 18:54

Penalties — Voracek Pha (hooking) 5:33, Gustafsson Pha (tripping) 8:37

● **Shots on goal by**

Winnipeg —	11	8	6 —	25
Philadelphia —	13	19	16 —	48

● **Goal (shots-saves)** — Winnipeg: Pavelec (W,2-3-1)(43-36), Mason (2:33 third) (5-4); Philadelphia: Bobrovsky (15-10), Bryzgalov (L,3-4-1)(4:39 second)(10-6)

● **Power plays (goals-chances)** — Winnipeg: 2-5; Philadelphia: 1-5

● **Referees** — Brad Watson, Francis Charron. Linesmen — Anthony Sericolo, Greg Devorski

● **Attendance** — 19,588 (19,537)

TAMPA BAY 1 / WINNIPEG 0

10

GAME

AWAY

Saturday, October 29, 2011

JETS vs. TAMPA BAY LIGHTNING

ONDREJ Pavelec was the best of the Jets this night, but he wasn't perfect — and he needed to be.

Pavelec lost track of a rebound and while his eyes were searching for the puck, Lightning sniper Vincent Lecavalier whipped it past the unsuspecting goalie from a sharp angle near the corner.

That goal was the difference, as the Lightning took a 1-0 win over the Jets before 19,204 fans at the St. Pete Times Forum. Winnipeg fell to 3-6-1 on the season.

Pavelec was able to stop all but one of Tampa's 27 shots, while Lightning goalie Dwayne Roloson was a perfect 28-for-28.

"It's difficult. You let eight goals in on Thursday and get two points and in this game, you let one goal in and you get the loss," said Pavelec.

Despite the final outcome, head coach Claude Noel liked the way his team cut down on mistakes and played within their system.

The Jets were winless in their last 12 games against the Lightning dating back to the franchise's days in Atlanta.

BIG PICTURE

The Jets were much better defensively than they had been most nights in the year but weren't able to find a happy medium and provide any offence. Winnipeg was 0-2 on the power play while the Lightning were 1-4. The Jets took solace in the fact they played a solid team game and only needed a little offence to have had a better outcome.

LITTLE PICTURE

Goal-scoring remained an issue for the Jets, despite their nine-goal outburst against the Flyers earlier in the week. Winnipeg's power play was fruitless, one area where the team would have to find results as they went forward searching for wins.

SUMMARY

FIRST PERIOD
No Scoring
Penalties — Moore TB (goaltender interference) 9:59, Enstrom Wpg (tripping) 17:42

SECOND PERIOD
1. Tampa Bay, Lecavalier 5 (Stamkos, Brewer) 19:20 (pp)
Penalties — Glass Wpg (roughing) 2:14, Glass Wpg (high-sticking) 8:46, Kubina TB (interference) 14:48, Stuart Wpg (holding) 18:54

THIRD PERIOD
No Scoring
Penalties — None

Shots on goal by

Winnipeg	10	7	11	—	28
Tampa Bay	11	13	3	—	27

Goal — Winnipeg: Pavelec (L,2-4-1); Tampa Bay: Roloson (W,2-2-1)
Power plays (goals-chances) — Winnipeg: 0-2; Tampa Bay: 1-4
Referees — Tom Kowal, Francois St. Laurent
Linesmen — Brad Kovachik, Pierre Racicot
Attendance — 19,204 (19,204)

Joe Bryksa / Winnipeg Free Press

ONDREJ PAVELEC

11

GAME

AWAY

Monday, October 31, 2011
JETS vs. FLORIDA PANTHERSS

WINNIPEG 4 / FLORIDA 3 (SO)

ALREADY a goal and an assist invested in the night, Kyle Wellwood scored the game-winner in the shootout as Winnipeg hung a 4-3 loss on the Panthers at the Bank Atlantic Center.

With two of three wins on its seven-game road trip, Winnipeg improved to 4-6-1.

"Kyle Wellwood has been a good player for us and to unclog a line we've used him to move into that situation. He's a guy that a lot of guys want to play with," said Jets coach Claude Noel.

The Jets jumped out to a 2-0 lead on goals from Wellwood and Evander Kane, but that lead evaporated thanks to a lack of discipline on the Winnipeg side.

Florida's Tomas Fleischmann scored twice and defenceman Jason Garrison added one of his own to give the home side a 3-2 lead. Kane potted his second goal of the game as he tipped a Zach Bogosian shot from the point past Panthers goalie Jose Theodore with 10 seconds left on the clock.

One referee, Tom Kowal, waved it off, thinking a high stick was involved, but the other three officials on the ice deemed it good. Video review from the command centre in Toronto confirmed the majority opinion.

BIG PICTURE

Winnipeg took a 2-1 lead and then fell behind 3-2 in the third before Kane tied the game with 50 seconds left in regulation.

LITTLE PICTURE

The Jets didn't like the hit Panthers winger Jack Skille put on blue-liner Tobias Enstrom in the second period. Enstrom was hunched over and appeared defenceless when Skille tagged him. Early in the third period, Jets captain Andrew Ladd demanded Skille answer for his actions and the two scrapped, with Ladd earning a slight edge. It was later revealed Enstrom suffered a broken collarbone.

KYLE WELLWOOD, ZACH BOGOSIAN

John Woods / Winnipeg Free Press

SUMMARY

FIRST PERIOD

1. Winnipeg, Wellwood 5 (Ladd, Stuart) 3:44
2. Winnipeg, Kane 3 (Antropov, Bogosian) 9:58 (pp)
3. Florida, Garrison 5 (Campbell, Fleischmann) 19:40

Penalties — Upshall Fla (elbowing) 8:40, Byfuglien Wpg (high-sticking) 12:57

SECOND PERIOD

No Scoring

Penalties — McArdle Wpg (hooking) 5:29, Byfuglien Wpg (double roughing) 16:22

THIRD PERIOD

4. Florida, Fleischmann 4 (Weiss, Weaver) 3:13
5. Florida, Fleischmann 5 (Kulikov, Campbell) 17:50 (pp)
6. Winnipeg, Kane 4 (Wellwood, Bogosian) 19:10

Penalties — Ladd Wpg, Skille Fla (fighting) 2:10, Kulikov Fla (high-sticking) 12:54, Wheeler Wpg (holding) 16:50

Overtime — No Scoring.
Penalties — None

Shootout — Winnipeg wins 2-0
Winnipeg (2) — Stapleton, miss; Ladd, goal; Wellwood, goal
Florida (0) — Versteeg, miss; Santorelli, miss

Shots on goal by

Winnipeg	7	9	12	3 —	31
Florida	20	9	11	2 —	42

Goal — Winnipeg: Pavelec (W,3-4-1); Florida: Theodore (W,4-2-1)

Power plays (goals-chances) — Winnipeg: 1-2; Florida: 1-5

Referees — Tom Kowal, Francois St. Laurent. Linesmen — Brad Kovachik, Andy McElman

Attendance — 11,855 (17,040)

WINNIPEG 3 / N.Y. ISLANDERS 0

JETS goaltender Ondrej Pavelec put on an acrobatic display that should have earned him a job offer from the Ringling Bros.

And yet, when a media scrum approached Pavelec following his 3-0 shutout of the Islanders at the Nassau Veterans Memorial Coliseum, the man of the moment deflected praise just like each of the 34 shots he had just thwarted.

Consider these, then, Pavelec's glowing off-Broadway reviews:

"Pav's playing great right now and that's what you need to win on the road: a great goalie stealing you some points." — Jets winger Tanner Glass.

"Pavelec was outstanding. He did everything to win that game. He battled hard, he was into it and I thought he was fabulous again for us tonight." — Jets head coach Claude Noel.

The spectacular effort earned Pavelec his fifth career shutout.

Evander Kane, Johnny Oduya and Alex Burmistrov had the goals for the Jets.

BIG PICTURE

It wasn't the classic formula for winning a game — goalie plays brilliantly and ravaged defensive corps soldiers on while management works over the rosary beads and lucky charms — but it worked. And, in the process, the Jets won consecutive games for the first time this season to hit 3-1 on a road trip that had looked so daunting a week previous.

LITTLE PICTURE

There were still some defensive flaws and the goals seemed hard to come by, but this was one of those gritty wins that build a team's collective resolve. Winnipeg may have lost another D-man in Randy Jones, who limped off after blocking a shot, but reserves Mark Flood and Brett Festerling were solid and the team picked up a critical 'W' in enemy territory.

12 GAME

AWAY

Thursday, November 3, 2011
JETS vs. NEW YORK ISLANDERS

SUMMARY

FIRST PERIOD
1. Winnipeg, Kane 5 (Wellwood, Oduya) 4:21
Missed penalty shot — Kane Wpg, 9:13
Penalties — Kane Wpg, Hamonic NYI (fighting) 19:42

SECOND PERIOD
No Scoring
Penalties — Slater Wpg (roughing) 5:52, Little Wpg (tripping) 11:30, Oduya Wpg (hooking) 19:54

THIRD PERIOD
2. Winnipeg, Oduya 1 (Antropov, Kane) 16:04
3. Winnipeg, Burmistrov 4, 17:44 (en)
Penalties — None

Shots on goal by

Winnipeg	8	6	12	—	26
N.Y. Islanders	9	19	6	—	34

Goal — Winnipeg: Pavelec (W,4-4-1); N.Y. Islanders: DiPietro (L,0-1-2)
Power plays (goals-chances) — Winnipeg: 0-0; N.Y. Islanders: 0-3
Referees — Dean Morton, Dan O'Halloran
Linesmen — Jay Sharrers, Bryan Pancich
Attendance — 10,157 (16,234)

Joe Bryksa / Winnipeg Free Press

ONDREJ PAVELEC

13

GAME

AWAY

Saturday, November 5, 2011
JETS vs. NEW JERSEY DEVILS

NEW JERSEY 3 / WINNIPEG 2 (OT)

WITH five defencemen out of the lineup — three of them regulars — the Jets were fortunate to salvage a point against the Devils at the Prudential Center this night.

Especially considering how they fell behind in the game.

After watching Devils forwards Patrik Elias and Adam Henrique stake the home side to a 2-0 lead with 20 minutes to play, the Jets stormed back on goals by defenceman Mark Flood and centre Jim Slater, whose late third-period goal with 2:45 remaining sent the game into overtime.

Henrique scored the game-winner in the extra session.

"A lot of teams, when they're down 2-0 going into the third against the New Jersey Devils, don't have much success," Slater said. "We showed a lot of poise out there to get that big point that we needed."

Winnipeg, which was without Ron Hainsey, Toby Enstrom and Mark Stuart for the contest, moved its record to 5-6-2 overall.

BIG PICTURE

It's easy to lament giving up a game-winning goal in overtime — on a breakaway, no less — but considering the circumstances in which the Jets found themselves, this was a point earned. Big-time. A team that appeared all but dead and buried heading into the third period against a notoriously stingy Devils team rallied to tie before goofing in OT.

LITTLE PICTURE

It was still early in the campaign but resiliency was starting to become the Jets' trademark. Yes, there could be worse ways to describe a club.

MARK FLOOD

Ruth Bonneville / Winnipeg Free Press

SUMMARY

FIRST PERIOD
No Scoring
Penalties — Elias NJ (cross-checking) 11:54, Thorburn Wpg, Fraser NJ (fighting) 15:42

SECOND PERIOD
1. New Jersey, Elias 6 (Zubrus, Salvador) 4:08
2. New Jersey, Henrique 2 (Parise) 12:59

Penalties — Volchenkov NJ (hooking) 15:33, Byfuglien Wpg (tripping) 16:26

THIRD PERIOD
3. Winnipeg, Flood 1 (Byfuglien) 6:43
4. Winnipeg, Slater 5 (Flood, Byfuglien) 17:15

Penalties — Clarkson NJ (tripping) 10:50, Kane Wpg (hooking) 19:12

Overtime
5. New Jersey, Henrique 3 (Parise, Larsson) 1:28

Penalties — None

● **Shots on goal by**

Winnipeg	8	7	8	0 —	23
New Jersey	9	6	8	5 —	28

● **Goal** — Winnipeg: Pavelec (L,4-4-2); New Jersey: Brodeur (W,1-2-0)
● **Power plays (goals-chances)** — Winnipeg: 0-3; New Jersey: 0-2
● **Referees** — Steve Kozari, Dan O'Halloran. Linesmen — Derek Amell, Brian Murphy
● **Attendance** — 14,952 (17,625)

N.Y. RANGERS 3 / WINNIPEG 0

14 GAME

AWAY

Sunday, November 6, 2011
JETS vs. NEW YORK RANGERS

THE signs of a travel-weary Winnipeg Jets squad were all there. Dead legs. No jump. And, at times, displaying about as much energy as a sloth on an afternoon siesta.

"I thought we looked tired and didn't have much energy," Jets head coach Claude Noel said after falling to the New York Rangers in front of 18,200 at Madison Square Garden. "The size of our team was worn down in back-to-back games. I thought (Ondrej) Pavelec did a heckuva job getting us in the game and keeping us in the game.

High-speed sniper Marian Gaborik led the Rangers with two goals and an assist, including an empty-netter, while Derek Stepan scored the other and added a helper. Martin Biron stopped 23 shots for the shutout, his first in Ranger blue.

For the Jets, who fell to 5-7-2 on the season, getting out of Manhattan was more about survival than anything else. New York marked the second-last stop on a season-longest seven-game road trip for Winnipeg.

"Right now our biggest task is to find some more energy," Noel concluded.

BIG PICTURE

Maybe everyone should have seen this coming: the Jets were away from home for their longest stretch of the season, a seven-game trek that took them from Pennsylvania to Florida to New York and New Jersey. And with this being the third game in four nights, perhaps it was inevitable a listless effort such as this would happen.

LITTLE PICTURE

It's about the power play. The Jets generated chances and decent puck movement with the extra skater, but those qualities meant little if the puck couldn't find the back of the net. On a night they could have used a goal or three, Winnipeg went 0-for-4 with the man advantage.

SUMMARY

FIRST PERIOD
No Scoring
Penalties — Gaborik NYR (cross-checking) 8:07, Anisimov NYR (hooking) 15:31

SECOND PERIOD
1. New York, Stepan 2 (Gaborik, Del Zotto) 10:01 (pp)
Penalties — Stepan NYR (interference) 3:10, Ladd Wpg (holding) 6:54, Ladd Wpg (high-sticking) 9:36

THIRD PERIOD
2. New York, Gaborik 6 (Stepan, Anisimov) 8:31
3. New York, Gaborik 7 (Anisimov) 19:58 (en)
Penalties — Festerling Wpg (cross-checking) 1:14, Flood Wpg (tripping) 2:12, Stuart Wpg (high-sticking) 2:43, Boyle, NYR (high-sticking) 10:12, Burmistrov Wpg (hooking) 12:34

Shots on goal by

Winnipeg	9	7	7	—	23
New York	5	8	14	—	27

Goal — Winnipeg: Pavelec (L,4-5-2); New York: Biron (W,3-0-0)
Power plays (goals-chances) — Winnipeg: 0-4; New York: 1-6
Referees — Dave Jackson, Kyle Rehman. Linesmen — Steve Barton, Jay Sharrers
Attendance — 18,200 (18,200)

Mike Deal / Winnipeg Free Press

NIK ANTROPOV

BUFFALO 6 / WINNIPEG 5 (OT)

JETS goaltender Ondrej Pavelec looked like a man who wanted to scream, his frustration boiling over in the post-game interviews.

"We won the point in the jackpot tonight," a sarcastic Pavelec said following the tough overtime loss to the Sabres in upstate New York. "I think we are smart enough to realize that if you do stupid penalties in their zone six times, it's going to hurt you, especially against Buffalo. They've got good guys and that's exactly what happened. We just gave it to them. Same story again.

"Everybody's working hard, but like I said, stupid plays cost us the game."

Pavelec's reasons for the outburst are many: The Jets blew four leads, were down two men three times, gave up four power-play goals and essentially gift-wrapped a victory for the other side.

The game-winning goal came with the extra attacker as Thomas Vanek tipped home a blast by Jason Pominville with 25 seconds remaining. The game-tying marker came with Mark Stuart and Zach Bogosian in the box.

The Jets fell to 5-7-3 on the season.

BIG PICTURE

The Jets finished the almost-two-week adventure through Pennsylvania, New Jersey and New York with a 3-2-2 record, but the consensus in the room afterwards was this was a point lost. Bigger concern: The team had an alarming habit of leaving Ondrej Pavelec to fend for himself for long stretches.

LITTLE PICTURE

Some questionable penalties against the Jets — a third-period roughing penalty by Mark Stuart was the most egregious — but Winnipeg could not expect to win when they gave the opposition 12 power plays. Surrendering 45 shots was also not good for business.

JIM SLATER

Mike Deal / Winnipeg Free Press

SUMMARY

FIRST PERIOD
1. Winnipeg, Flood 2 (Glass, Slater) 4:48
2. Winnipeg, Little 1 (Wheeler, Ladd) 5:54
3. Buffalo, Roy 3 (Myers) 9:05 (pp)
4. Buffalo, Tropp 1 (Gerbe, Gaustad) 9:16
5. Winnipeg, Glass 3 (Wellwood, Oduya) 11:25
6. Buffalo, Pominville 6 (Gaustad) 13:06 (sh)

Penalties — Burmistrov Wpg (charging) 6:39, Antropov Wpg (cross-checking) 8:47, Leopold Buf (holding) 12:25, Kane Wpg (holding) 17:39, Bogosian Wpg (hooking) 18:14

SECOND PERIOD
7. Winnipeg, Little 2 (Byfuglien, Stapleton) 1:07 (pp)
8. Buffalo, Vanek 9 (Boyes, Roy) 15:48 (pp)

Penalties — Gerbe Buf (holding stick) 0:30, Ladd Wpg (interference) 3:52, Glass Wpg, McCormick Buf (fighting) 8:16, Gerbe Buf (tripping) 9:08, Ladd Wpg (holding) 15:26, Adam Buf (hooking) 19:18, Kane Wpg (holding) 20:00

THIRD PERIOD
9. Winnipeg, Byfuglien 2 (Wheeler) 0:48
10. Buffalo, Roy 4 (Pominville, Ehrhoff) 13:52 (pp)

Penalties — Byfuglien Wpg (holding) 3:40, Myers Buf (interference) 4:04, Oduya Wpg (cross-checking) 11:14, Bogosian Wpg (high-sticking) 12:51, M.Stuart Wpg (roughing) 13:35

Overtime — 11. Buffalo, Vanek 10 (Pominville, Gragnani) 4:35 (pp)

Penalties — Wheeler Wpg (hooking), Byfuglien Wpg (misconduct) 4:05

Shots on goal by

Winnipeg	12	12	6	1	— 31
Buffalo	19	9	14	3	— 45

Goal — Winnipeg: Pavelec (L,4-5-3); Buffalo: Miller (W,5-5-0)

Power plays (goals-chances) — Winnipeg: 1-5; Buffalo: 4-12

Referees — Dean Morton, Ian Walsh. Linesmen — Brad Kovalchik, Brad Amell

Attendance — 18,690 (18,690)

FLORIDA 5 / WINNIPEG 2

16

GAME

HOME

Thursday, November 10, 2011
JETS vs. FLORIDA PANTHERS

FORWARD Kris Versteeg scored three goals and added an assist, leading the visiting Panthers to a convincing 5-2 victory over the Jets at the MTS Centre.

Did someone say "frustration?" Yeah, there was plenty of that to go around.

Versteeg, who would make a habit of terrorizing the Jets in their own barn this season, scored the first two goals of the game. He then set up the third one, a tally off the stick of defenceman Jason Garrison in the second period, before sitting out Florida's fourth straight goal of the game.

That was it for Ondrej Pavelec. He was yanked at the intermission for backup Peter Mannino.

The Jets mounted an early third-period comeback of sorts — enough to give the illusion they would make their way all the way back from such a huge disadvantage — but it barely scratched the surface of the mountain they needed to climb.

Tim Stapleton and Andrew Ladd did the goal-scoring honours for Winnipeg. Versteeg added an empty-netter.

Jets forward Tanner Glass on the effort: "It's tough to flip the page on that one. We've got some guys that are passengers right now. Overstaying their shifts, not staying within the system. It takes 20 guys to win in this league. You can't have passengers, and for us it's about getting everyone on the same page."

BIG PICTURE
No other way to describe this one than putrid with a capital 'P-U.' The Jets served up one of their worst efforts of the young season, partially ruining what had been a relatively successful road trip with an effort that made a whole lot of warts visible again. Winnipeg's winless streak: four games (0-2-2) and counting.

LITTLE PICTURE
Jets head coach Claude Noel had been a patient man through the first 15 games of the season, speaking often of the growth and upside of a young squad still getting to know each other. Exit patience, stage left. Rumours of a whip started to surface.

SUMMARY

FIRST PERIOD
1. Florida, Versteeg 6 (Fleischmann, Weiss) 7:14
2. Florida, Versteeg 7 (Fleischmann, Campbell) 17:27 (pp)

Penalties — Ellerby Fla (hooking) 3:42, Antropov Wpg (checking to head) 16:14

SECOND PERIOD
3. Florida, Garrison 6 (Versteeg, Campbell) 4:53
4. Florida, Santorelli 2 (Campbell, Kulikov) 18:04 (pp)

Penalties — Stuart Wpg (interference) 5:25, Byfuglien Wpg (slashing) 16:43

THIRD PERIOD
5. Winnipeg, Stapleton 1 (Kane, Antropov) 2:28 (pp)
6. Winnipeg, Ladd 4 (Bogosian, Stuart) 5:40
7. Florida, Versteeg 8 (Kulikov) 18:41 (en)

Penalties — Fleischmann Fla (tripping) 1:46, Byfuglien Wpg (slashing) 11:47, Weaver Fla (high-sticking) 14:07, Burmistrov Wpg (elbowing) 19:54

● **Shots on goal by**

Florida	5	10	5	—	20
Winnipeg	4	6	17	—	27

● **Goal** — Florida: Theodore (W,6-2-2); Winnipeg: Pavelec (L,4-6-3)(15-11), Mannino (0:00 third, 4-4)
● **Power plays (goals-chances)** — Florida: 2-5; Winnipeg: 1-3
● **Referees** — Dennis LaRue, Kyle Rehman. Linesmen — Brad Lazarowich, Thor Nelson
● **Attendance** — 15,004 (15,004)

DUSTIN BYFUGLIEN

John Woods / Winnipeg Free Press

COLUMBUS 2 / WINNIPEG 1

THE Jets opened the door for the league's worst team to score in the game's first minute then fumbled away most of their top-quality offensive chances in a 2-1 defeat at Nationwide Arena.

Winnipeg fell to 5-9-3 overall with the loss while the Blue Jackets — suffering through an even worse start to the season — improved to a paltry 3-12-1.

"I think both teams played the same way," said Jets forward Kyle Wellwood about the battle between two teams well under .500. "They had chances in front of our net by themselves, too. And they scored on only two of them. It wasn't a fun game to be in and unfortunately we were on the losing end."

Columbus rookie Ryan Johansen had both goals for the Jackets, the first just 53 seconds in and the second converting a two-on-one at 4:06 of the third.

Defenceman Mark Stuart answered for the Jets with just 3:45 remaining in the game, but it was too little, too late for any comeback heroics.

"Yes, I'm fine with our team," Jets head coach Claude Noel reasoned. "I'm not sitting here going, 'Well, we lost the game.' We got down 2-0 but I sensed the players wanted very much to do well and to push this thing and we couldn't get one."

Winnipeg's loss pushed the winless skid to five games (0-3-2).

BIG PICTURE

Another night of popgun offence and the Jets came away with only disappointment against the NHL's worst team to date. Too many blown scoring chances — shots off the mark, shots off sticks, an extra pass when one wasn't needed — mark the signs of a pressing attack.

LITTLE PICTURE

Rookie Ryan Johansen's goal just 53 seconds in completely changed the tone. The Jets came into Columbus trying desperately to get the jump and inflict a little more doubt into the struggling Blue Jackets. It wasn't meant to be.

MARK STUART

Phil Hossack / Winnipeg Free Press

SUMMARY

First Period
1. Columbus, Johansen 4 (Wisniewski, Methot) 0:53
Penalties — Tlusty Clb (tripping) 7:36, LaRose Clb (tripping) 10:49, Sutter Clb (boarding) 14:49, Wheeler, Wpg (tripping) 16:35, Ponikarovsky, Clb (elbowing) 18:28

Second Period
No Scoring
Penalty — Flood Wpg (holding) 1:41, Byfuglien Wpg (delay of game) 3:41, Thorburn Wpg, Boll Clb (fighting) 9:40, Clitsome Clb (hooking) 14:17

Third Period
2. Columbus, Johansen 5 (Prospal, Nikitin) 4:06
3. Winnipeg, Stuart 2 (Byfuglien) 16:15 (sh)
Penalties — Moore Clb (holding) 0:57, Dorsett Clb (tripping) 4:50, Wheeler Wpg (hooking) 13:07, Wisniewski Clb (hooking) 13:44, Bogosian Wpg (tripping) 15:16

Shots on goal by

Winnipeg	12	10	14	—	36
Columbus	10	13	4	—	27

Goal — Winnipeg: Pavelec (L,4-7-3); Columbus: S.Mason (W,3-11-1)
Power plays (goals-chances) — Winnipeg: 0-5; Columbus: 0-4
Referees — Paul Devorski, Kevin Pollock. Linesmen — Brian Mach, Steve Miller.
Attendance — 15,581 (18,144)

WINNIPEG 5 / TAMPA BAY 2

REELING after five straight losses, the Winnipeg coaching staff retooled the forward lines and watched the team turn in its best effort to date, crushing the Lightning 5-2 at the MTS Centre.

Five different Jets scored — Evander Kane, Dustin Byfuglien, Mark Flood, Andrew Ladd and Tim Stapleton — in a contest in which 10 Winnipeg players picked up a point. It was a far cry from the output the home side had been turning in to this point and sparked an offence that had been held to one goal or less in seven of their first 17 games this season.

So that was nice to see. So was the play of a big defenceman who was under some scrutiny in the opening stretch of the season.

"This was Dustin's best game with the Jets," head coach Claude Noel said afterwards. "He's got a lot of tools. He can be a great player, not just for us but in this league. He can be outstanding."

The 6-5, 268-pound blue-liner found a mix of offence and defence that made him a threat at both ends of the ice with a goal, an assist and a plus-1 rating, as well as a couple of crunches that had Tampa players tiptoeing into the Jets defensive zone through his team-high 24 minutes of ice time.

He wasn't the only Jets player putting in a turnaround performance against Tampa Bay.

Goaltender Ondrej Pavelec, who had drawn some honest criticism from Noel in the days leading up to the game, returned to excellence in the Winnipeg net, stopping 30 of the 32 shots he faced.

BIG PICTURE

The win snapped a five-game stretch without a win (two overtime losses), and kept Winnipeg in reasonable touch with the division rivals above them. Tampa Bay, for instance, was just three points higher in the standings.

LITTLE PICTURE

Noel had been harping on wanting his team to play smarter. It did a good job in this department on this night, exposing the Lightning as sloppy or weak in their own end on multiple occasions. The first goal, by Kane, also mattered, as did the Jets' penalty killing, which rose to the challenge against Tampa Bay's talented power play.

SUMMARY

First Period
1. Winnipeg, Kane 6 (Byfuglien, Burmistrov) 4:51
2. Winnipeg, Byfuglien 3 (Kane) 13:02

Penalties — Kane Wpg (high-sticking) 9:22, Stuart Wpg (slashing) 17:21

Second Period
3. Winnipeg, Flood 3 (Stapleton, Little) 7:49 (pp)
4. Tampa Bay, St. Louis 4 (Stamkos, Lecavalier) 10:47
5. Winnipeg, Ladd 5 (Oduya, Wellwood) 12:14

Penalties — Bogosian Wpg (holding, unsportsmanlike conduct) 1:51, Downie TB (hooking) 6:40, Oduya Wpg (hooking) 16:48, Burmistrov Wpg (high-sticking) 17:31

Third Period
6. Winnipeg, Stapleton 2 (Glass) 10:04
7. Tampa Bay, Stamkos 11 (Gilroy) 10:26

Penalties — Slater Wpg (slashing), Stamkos TB (interference, slashing) 19:16

Shots on goal by

Tampa Bay	11	15	6 —	32
Winnipeg	16	9	14 —	39

Goal — Tampa Bay: Roloson (L,5-4-1)(22-18), Garon (12:14 second; 17-16): Winnipeg: Pavelec (W,5-7-3)

Power plays (goals-chances) — Tampa Bay: 0-6; Winnipeg: 1-2

Referees — Brad Meier, Ian Walsh. Linesmen — Thor Nelson, Mark Wheler

Attendance — 15,004 (15,004)

Boris Minkevich / Winnipeg Free Press

ALEX BURMISTROV, DUSTIN BYFUGLIEN

19 GAME

HOME

Thursday, November 17, 2011
JETS vs. WASHINGTON CAPITALS

WINNIPEG 4 / WASHINGTON 1

THREE goals in the second period paced the Jets to a convincing 4-1 win over the Southeast Division rival Capitals at the MTS Centre, but it was the monkey leaping off the back of one player that garnered the most attention.

Forward Blake Wheeler, counted on by many to provide some much-needed offence to a side riddled with doubt in that department, finally found the back of the net.

Eighteen games is a long time to go without scoring, right Mr. Wheeler?

"I don't even remember how to celebrate goals anymore, so I'm sure it wasn't pretty," he said, commenting on his post-goal celebration, which featured a jump of relief into the rink glass. "Hopefully, as more goals come, the celebrations get a little better."

Evander Kane scored twice and Kyle Wellwood added a single for the Jets, who improved to 7-9-3 on the season, but the night was Wheeler's.

After signing an extension in the summer under the premise he would be a forward piece worth keeping around, the Minnesota product was worried he wasn't earning his keep.

"You can't even describe how good it feels," he said. "It's the longest drought of my career by a pretty good amount. You kind of forget what it feels like when the puck goes in the net, and you want to get that feeling back."

BIG PICTURE

The master plan for the Winnipeg Jets was simple: Become a playoff squad by making the MTS Centre an absolute nightmare for visitors. Establishing that kind of reputation didn't come overnight, but the dominating win over the Caps sure as heck didn't hurt. The Jets improved to 4-3 at home.

LITTLE PICTURE

The Jets' special teams were masterful, going two-for-five on the power play and killing off all five of the Caps' power plays, including a span of 61 seconds in the second when Washington held a two-man advantage.

ZACH BOGOSIAN, ONDREJ PAVELEC, TIM STAPLETON

John Woods / Winnipeg Free Press

SUMMARY

First Period
1. Washington, Semin 4 (Chimera, Laich) 3:53
2. Winnipeg, Kane 7 (Burmistrov) 7:51

Penalties — Wideman Wash (interference) 9:08, Kulda Wpg (delay of game) 13:55

Second Period
3. Winnipeg, Kane 8 (Wellwood) 6:38
4. Winnipeg, Wheeler 1 (Little) 8:31 (pp)
5. Winnipeg, Wellwood 6 (Ladd, Stapleton) 10:54 (pp)

Penalties — Stuart Wpg (interference) 3:16, Erskine Wash (interference) 7:05, Erskine Wash, Thorburn Wpg (fighting) 8:51, Hamrlik Wash (tripping) 9:04, Ladd Wpg (tripping) 13:23, Oduya Wpg (holding) 14:22, Semin Wash (unsportsmanlike conduct) 16:02

Third Period
No Scoring

Penalties — Neuvirth Wash (tripping; served by Semin) 4:04, Glass Wpg (slashing) 9:52

Shots on goal by

Washington	10	15	7	— 32
Winnipeg	11	13	7	— 31

Goal (shots-saves) — Washington: Neuvirth (L,2-3-1)(24-20), Vokoun (15:03 second, 7-7)

Power plays (goals-chances) — Washington: 0-5; Winnipeg: 2-5

Referees — Rob Martel, Tim Peel. Linesmen — Steve Barton, Scott Driscoll

Attendance — 15,004 (15,004).

WINNIPEG 6 / PHILADELPHIA 4

20

GAME

HOME

Saturday, November 19, 2011
JETS vs. PHILADELPHIA FLYERS

THREE straight home games, three straight wins.

That was where the Jets found themselves after a high-scoring 6-4 win over the Flyers at the MTS Centre, trumpeting the fact the club was seemingly turning a corner after a slow start to the season.

"I think our group understands better how to win, how to play to win and manage the game better," head coach Claude Noel said after the win, which pushed Winnipeg's record to a game under the .500 mark (8-9-3). "We've still got some areas (to work on), but this was pretty good.

"We're playing as a group. It's a team that is enjoying winning. We were frustrated at the beginning because I think we thought we could be a little bit better than what we were. We're watching a team think 'this is how we can play.' It's a confidence thing."

Bryan Little scored two goals, Dustin Byfuglien picked up three points, and Ondrej Pavelec made 27 saves for the Jets, who jumped out to a 5-1 lead before the contest reached the halfway point.

The game also marked the return of Eric Fehr to NHL action. The Winkler product, acquired in an off-season trade with Washington, missed the first 19 games of the season recovering from shoulder surgery.

BIG PICTURE

A winning streak of three games — all in regulation time — had put the 8-9-3 Jets within striking distance of .500 and, for the moment, back into the top-eight playoff picture in the Eastern Conference. It was a pretty productive week for a club finding its way in a new environment.

LITTLE PICTURE

The Jets and Flyers seemed to be a combination to cause ulcers for coaches and fans. The teams had combined in two games for 27 goals, very un-NHL-like. This night, each squad had eight power plays. With three goals with the man advantage, the Jets won the special-teams game and the two points.

SUMMARY

First Period

1. Winnipeg, Little 3 (Wheeler, Byfuglien) 4:45 (pp)
2. Winnipeg, Little 4 (Wheeler, Kane) 7:00
3. Winnipeg, Ladd 6 (Wellwood, Byfuglien) 10:15 (pp)
4. Philadelphia, Hartnell 7 (Pronger, Giroux) 13:27 (pp)

Penalties — Philadelphia bench (too many men, served by Zolnierczyk) 3:22, Pronger Pha (slashing) 9:35, Briere Pha (unsportsmanlike conduct) 10:15, Burmistrov Wpg (tripping) 12:52, Slater Wpg (delay of game) 17:50

Second Period

5. Winnipeg, Slater 6 5:49 (sh)
6. Winnipeg, Byfuglien 4 (Ladd, Wellwood) 10:20 (pp)
7. Philadelphia, Hartnell 8 (Briere, Pronger) 16:09 (pp)

Penalties — Oduya Wpg (hooking) 3:54, Rinaldo Pha (interference) 6:00, Carle Pha (holding) Briere Pha (cross-checking) 8:36, Lilja Pha (hooking) 11:03, Shelley Pha (misconduct) Antropov Wpg (interference) 14:06, Glass Wpg (delay of game) 15:25, Zolnierczyk Pha, Glass Wpg (roughing) 16:56

Third Period

8. Philadelphia, Read 7 (Hartnell, Giroux) 8:32
9. Philadelphia, Read 8 (Giroux, Carle) 17:46
10. Winnipeg, Antropov 4 18:46 (en)

Penalties — Kane Wpg (elbowing) 2:21, Talbot Pha (hooking) 9:46, Kane Wpg (cross-checking) 11:39, Kane Wpg (interference) 14:17

Shots on goal by

Philadelphia	8	10	13	—	31
Winnipeg	18	15	7	—	40

Goal — Philadelphia: Bobrovsky (L,3-1-1); Winnipeg: Pavelec (W,7-7-3)

Power plays (goals-chances) — Washington: 2-8; Winnipeg: 3-8

Referees — Mike Hazenfratz, Wes McCauley. Linesmen — Mike Cvik, Andy McElman

Attendance — 15,004 (15,004)

John Woods / Winnipeg Free Press

NIK ANTROPOV, DUSTIN BYFUGLIEN

21
GAME
AWAY

Wednesday, November 23, 2011
JETS vs. WASHINGTON CAPITALS

WASHINGTON 4 / WINNIPEG 3 (OT)

CHASING games is not where NHL teams typically find success, as the constant push and pressure of playing from behind often leaves players out of gas at the end of the game.

That's what the Jets found in Washington, dropping a 4-3 overtime loss to the Capitals at the Verizon Center. The Jets, who battled back from three separate deficits before watching Jason Chimera score the last goal of the game (his second of the contest), fell to 8-9-4 on the season and remained winless when trailing after two periods of play (0-8-2).

That said, members of the club were finding silver linings in the effort.

"I think it's good for us because it shows us we're never out of it and that our will to win is paramount over what's taking place in the game," head coach Claude Noel said. "What I liked is that we battled back a few times."

"We handled it pretty good," Jets centre Bryan Little added. "They were turning it on and throwing some hits and I thought our guys stepped up and were throwing them right back.

"It was good, hard hockey to watch. It's hard to play in those types of games, so physical. I think we were kind of chasing them all game."

Little scored for the Jets, as did captain Andrew Ladd and Kyle Wellwood.

Goaltender Ondrej Pavelec, showing his worth relative to the number of shots he was facing night in and night out, made 33 saves against the dangerous Washington attack.

BIG PICTURE

Washington took a pretty good run at Winnipeg but the visitors took the punch and hung in there, gaining a point that might not have been so attainable earlier in this season. The Jets now had points in four straight games (4-0-1).

LITTLE PICTURE

There were three separate responses by the Jets as the Caps took three different leads throughout the course of the game. Bryan Little's goal at 12:36 of the third period brought the game even again and helped the Jets earn a point for the 60-minute deadlock.

BRYAN LITTLE

Phil Hossack / Winnipeg Free Press

SUMMARY

FIRST PERIOD
1. Washington, Semin 5 (Ovechkin, Carlson) 5:23
2. Winnipeg, Ladd 7 (Antropov, Wellwood) 13:21
3. Washington, Chimera 7 (Laich, Alzner) 13:33
4. Winnipeg, Wellwood 7 (Ladd, Bogosian) 16:30

Penalty — Stuart Wpg (interference) 5:36

SECOND PERIOD
5. Washington, Backstrom 7 (Brouwer, Orlov) 3:08

Penalties — Wheeler Wpg (tripping) 4:48, Perreault Wash (boarding) 11:34, Knuble Wash (slashing) 12:14, Antropov Wpg, Laich Wash (roughing) 12:59

THIRD PERIOD
6. Winnipeg, Little 5 (Wheeler, Flood) 12:36

Penalty— Stuart Wpg (holding stick) 2:16

OVERTIME
7. Washington, Chimera 8 (Wideman, Johansson) 1:52

Penalties — None

Shots on goal by

Winnipeg	10	9	6	0	— 25
Washington	9	14	13	1	— 37

Goal — Winnipeg: Pavelec (L,7-7-4); Washington: Vokoun (W,10-4-0).

Power plays (goals-chances) — Winnipeg: 0-2; Washington: 0-3.

Referees — Francis Charron, Kelly Sutherland. Linesmen — David Brisebois, Tim Nowak

Attendance — 18,506 (18,398)

WINNIPEG 3 / CAROLINA 1

22

GAME

AWAY

Friday, November 25, 2011
JETS vs. CAROLINA HURRICANES

FOLLOWING this win in Raleigh, head coach Claude Noel singled out one player — the one guy who defines what his image of the Jets should be.

"It's pretty clear whose team it is," Noel said after his captain, Andrew Ladd, scored for the third straight game to help power a 3-1 victory over the Hurricanes at RBC Center.

"You see the way he played. It's pretty clear that he wanted to win here. He's played here, won a Cup here, so it's pretty evident the way he's been pushing. The way that our team is with our work ethic is not by accident."

Following the Carolina win, Ladd, who signed a five-year contract in the summer, had found the score sheet in seven of his last eight games (nine points in that stretch). His game-winner against the Canes was his third of the season.

It was also the 100th goal of his young but eventful career.

"It's nice to score it on Ward-o," Ladd said after scoring on his friend, Carolina goalie Cam Ward. "I'll have to remind him of that one."

Evander Kane and Bryan Little also chipped in for the Jets.

Goaltender Chris Mason, who returned to action following a groin injury, earned his second win of the season.

BIG PICTURE

Remember how you felt about the Jets' record on Oct. 8? Twenty-two games into the season, the Jets reached their starting point. The win in Raleigh lifted the team back to the .500 mark at 9-9-4. Given that the deficit in that department was three and even four games through the first quarter, this qualified as progress.

LITTLE PICTURE

Two early penalty kills and then goals by Kane and Ladd put the Jets in a good spot through two periods, and they did enough in the third in front of goalie Chris Mason to earn the victory. The Jets were 4-0-1 in their last five games.

SUMMARY

FIRST PERIOD
1. Winnipeg, Kane 9 (Oduya) 14:46
Penalties — Bogosian Wpg (interference) 1:01, Fehr Wpg (delay of game) 4:23

SECOND PERIOD
2. Carolina, Tlusty 4 (Sutter, McBain) 5:17
3. Winnipeg, Ladd 8 (Bogosian, Antropov) 6:25
Penalties — Skinner Car (tripping) 6:43, Flood Wpg (tripping) 9:20

THIRD PERIOD
4. Winnipeg, Little 6 (Bogosian, Mason) 19:51 (en)
Penalties — Stuart Wpg (interference) 10:42

- **Shots on goal by**

Winnipeg	14	13	3	—	30
Carolina	7	4	10	—	21

- **Goal** — Winnipeg: Mason (W,2-2-0); Carolina: Ward (L,8-9-3)
- **Power plays (goals-chances)** — Winnipeg: 0-1; Carolina: 0-4
- **Referees** — Ghislain Hebert, Rob Martell. Linesmen — Matt MacPherson, Steve Barton
- **Attendance** — 15,718 (18,680)

Trevor Hagan / Winnipeg Free Press
ANDREW LADD

23

GAME

AWAY

Saturday, November 26, 2011
JETS vs. BOSTON BRUINS

BOSTON 4 / WINNIPEG 2

A two-goal lead in the first period was not enough of a buffer for the Jets as they watched the defending Stanley Cup champions come back and take a 4-2 win at the TD Garden.

Yes, depth is a wonderful thing and the Bruins are certainly a deep team.

Chris Kelly scored twice in the second period to give Boston the lead, capitalizing on assists from fellow third-liner Rich Peverley, to jump out in front in the second period. One of those was a short-handed marker, a goal that seemed to shake the foundation of Winnipeg's bench.

"We kind of got a little rattled there," Jets forward Blake Wheeler said about Kelly's goal at the 7:28 mark of the second period. "We have a few two-on-ones against in a row and penalty after penalty and you start doing that. It takes you a while to get your bearings back and in that time, there's a couple of goals against."

Added defenceman Zach Bogosian: "They have some talented players over there. They didn't win the Stanley Cup by accident. That said, I thought we battled relatively hard and we stuck in there with them. But I thought we kind of got sucked into their game plan a little and veered away from ours."

The Jets fell to 9-10-4 on the season but the outlook was positive: 13 of the next 15 games were to be in downtown Winnipeg, a stretch the club was looking forward to.

BIG PICTURE

The loss didn't dent the Jets' attitude. They were 9-10-4 through 23 games and had played an NHL-high 15 on the road. Nobody was crying for the new franchise's scheduling woes, which were about to turn around.

LITTLE PICTURE

Goals by Evander Kane and Dustin Byfuglien skated the Jets out to a 2-0 edge. That was the positive. That lead melted away with a Zdeno Chara power-play goal, and two from Chris Kelly in the second period. One was short-handed, and it gave the hometown Bruins a clear victory in the special-teams game.

ZACH BOGOSIAN

Joe Bryksa / Winnipeg Free Press

SUMMARY

FIRST PERIOD

1. Winnipeg, Kane 10 (Byfuglien, Wheeler) 9:31
2. Winnipeg, Byfuglien 5 (Slater, Jaffray) 10:10
3. Boston, Chara 4 (Krejci, Seidenberg) 16:38 (pp)

Penalties — Boston bench (too many men; served by Seguin) 4:26, Byfuglien Wpg (interference) 16:00, Bogosian Wpg (interference) 18:23, Corvo Bos (holding) 19:23

SECOND PERIOD

4. Boston, Kelly 8 (Peverley) 7:28 (sh)
5. Boston, Kelly 9 (Pouliot, Peverley) 16:26

Penalties — Horton Bos (tripping) 5:52, Marchand Bos (hooking) 10:45, Bogosian Wpg (delay of game) 11:52, Burmistrov Wpg (boarding) 13:32, Fehr Wpg (hooking, unsportsmanlike conduct) 18:11

THIRD PERIOD

6. Boston, Marchand 8, 18:51 (en)

Penalties — None

Shots on goal by

Winnipeg	12	14	16	—	42
Boston	15	11	10	—	36

- **Goal** — Winnipeg: Pavelec (L,7-8-4); Boston: Thomas (W,11-4-0)
- **Power plays (goals-chances)** — Winnipeg: 0-4; Boston: 1-6
- **Referees** — Gord Dwyer, Chris Rooney. Linesmen — Derek Amell, Anthony Sericolo
- **Attendance** — 17,565 (17,565)

OTTAWA 6 / WINNIPEG 4

TWO quick goals in the third period should have been enough to put the Jets in the win column, but game control had been an issue with this team all year.

Just when you thought they had things secured, they fumbled it away.

Goals from Ottawa forwards Jason Spezza, Zach Smith and Nick Foligno (into an empty net) erased the good feeling in the MTS Centre and left the Jets wondering what could have been following the 6-4 loss to the Senators.

"I think it's more disappointing that we had an opportunity to kick off a good homestand and we kind of let it slip away," said Jets winger Evander Kane, who scored those two goals in the first 2:41 of the third. "We played well for a time, but we didn't play a full 60 minutes."

Blake Wheeler and Alex Burmistrov also scored for Winnipeg.

The frustration wasn't reserved just for the dressing room, either. Head coach Claude Noel — for the most part playing it cool and calm through the first 23 games — wasn't interested in finding positives after this loss.

"It's a game where you have to be able to manage 15 minutes of your brain, that's what you have to do," he said. "As I watched it, I had no comfort, no matter what, in that game. There was no period of time I was comfortable."

BIG PICTURE

It had all the makings of a dandy little story — the Jets rally from a goal down in the third for the first time this season — but, in the end, some of the same flaws plagued the home side in their 11th loss of the season. The Jets blew a 4-3 third-period lead and gave up the game-winner while a man down as the Senators scored three times in the final 10:25.

LITTLE PICTURE

The Jets fell two games below .500 with the loss, their second of the season to the Senators. Two other factors were at play here: The defeat snapped a three-game winning streak at the MTS Centre and didn't exactly get the Jets off to a great start on their extended homestand.

SUMMARY

FIRST PERIOD

1. Ottawa, Michalek 13 (Alfredsson, Foligno) 15:55

Penalties — Spezza Ott (slashing) 3:13; Byfuglien Wpg (roughing) 18:34

SECOND PERIOD

2. Winnipeg, Wheeler 2 (Little, Byfuglien) 7:06
3. Winnipeg, Burmistrov 5 (Glass, Fehr) 15:07
4. Ottawa, Smith 5 (Condra) 15:42
5. Ottawa, Michalek 14 (Phillips, Condra) 19:16

Penalties — Konopka Ott (hooking) 8:49, Condra Ott (tripping) 10:09, Oduya Wpg (tripping) 17:05

THIRD PERIOD

6. Winnipeg, Kane 11 (Bogosian) 1:24
7. Winnipeg, Kane 12 (Flood, Little) 2:41 (pp)
8. Ottawa, Spezza 9 (Karlsson, Phillips) 9:35
9. Ottawa, Smith 6 (Gonchar, Daugavins) 13:45 (pp)
10. Ottawa, Foligno 7 (Winchester, Greening) 18:52 (en)

Penalties — Foligno Ott (tripping) 1:53, Glass Wpg (slashing) 4:07, Butler Ott (hooking) 6:36, Oduya Wpg (hooking) 13:05, Wheeler Wpg, Daugavins Ott (unsportsmanlike conduct) 18:52

Shots on goal by

Ottawa	12	8	14	—	34
Winnipeg	14	13	16	—	43

Goal — Ottawa: Anderson (W,11-7-1); Winnipeg: Pavelec (L,7-9-4)

Power plays (goals-chances) — Winnipeg: 1-5; Ottawa: 1-4

Referees — Stephane Auger, Chris Lee. Linesmen — Steve Miller, Bryan Pancich

Attendance — 15,004 (15,004)

Mike Deal / Winnipeg Free Press

BLAKE WHEELER

WINNIPEG 1 / PHOENIX 0

THE best way to chase the ghosts of a past franchise: Beat them in the city in which they once skated.

That was the take-away from the Jets' 1-0 win over the Coyotes — those Jets of old, if you remember — at the MTS Centre.

After 15 years between NHL clubs to call their own, Winnipeg watched goaltender Ondrej Pavelec make 33 saves for the shutout victory and witnessed a team — the new Jets, not the old Jets — start the process of figuring out how to win tight games.

"That was huge," said winger Blake Wheeler. "We've kind of learned that the two biggest things when you have a lead in the third period are: One, make them come 200 feet at you and get the puck in deep, and two, stay out of the penalty box.

"It's a big win and obviously with all the sentimental stuff with the crowd, it's great to see the old Jets come back here and the new Jets take care of them."

Bryan Little had the lone goal in the game, depositing a shot off the post into the net seven minutes into the first period.

Finally, a mention to Coyotes captain Shane Doan, the lone connective tissue that remained between Winnipeg and Phoenix. The home team paid special tribute to the former Jet, a recognition that drew a standing ovation from 15,004 in the crowd.

But Doan was still a ghost in these parts, and he earned boos the rest of the night.

BIG PICTURE

The current version of the Jets beat the old version of the Jets in the very city where the original Jets used to toil. Somewhere down the road here, the history of the old club won't matter anymore and the old Jets will be just another game on the schedule.

LITTLE PICTURE

The Jets (10-11-4) snapped a two-game losing streak and started the month of December off on the right foot. After a disappointing loss to Ottawa Tuesday and with 11 of the next 13 games at home, Winnipeg needed to get on the winning track and take advantage of the schedule.

MARK STUART, ALEX BURMISTROV

Phil Hossack / Winnipeg Free Press

SUMMARY

FIRST PERIOD
1. Winnipeg, Little 7 (Kane, Wheeler) 6:53
Penalties — Little Wpg (slashing) 18:16

SECOND PERIOD
No Scoring
Penalties — Kulda Wpg (hooking) 7:55, Schlemko Phx (hooking) 19:01

THIRD PERIOD
No Scoring
Penalties — Langkow Phx (tripping) 2:19, Morris Phx (hooking) 11:52

Shots on goal by

Phoenix	11	16	6	—	33
Winnipeg	10	9	12	—	31

Goal — Phoenix: Smith (L,12-5-3); Winnipeg: Pavalec (W,8-9-4)
Power plays (goals-chances) — Phoenix: 0-2; Winnipeg: 0-3
Referees — Tom Kowal, Justin St. Pierre
Linesmen — Steve Miller, Jay Sharrers
Attendance — 15,004 (15,004)

WINNIPEG 4 / NEW JERSEY 2

THE unlikeliest of heroes came through for the Jets at the most opportune time.

Defenceman Mark Stuart, a player more accustomed to banging and crashing in front of his own net, scored the winning goal with just over six minutes left in the 4-2 win over the Devils at the MTS Centre.

Stuart pinched down from his spot at the point and flung the puck towards the New Jersey goal, hoping for a bounce off a shin pad or a rebound chance for one of the forwards, specifically Evander Kane. Instead, he found the inside of the net.

"I kinda ran out of room and had to throw it at the net. It was a lucky bounce... but I'll take it," the veteran defenceman said afterwards.

"Stu made a really nice move around their guy and shot it from a bad angle and it was just bouncing," said Kane, who scored twice in the game. "I was just trying to dig... I don't know if I got my stick on it or not, but it went in and that was the main thing.

"It was a great play by him."

BIG PICTURE

It might not be worthy of a huge headline in Boston, Vancouver or Detroit, but the Jets (11-11-4) reaching the .500 mark spoke volumes of their growth and represented a forward step for this crew. There were still some significant growing pains, but the Jets were now 6-2-1 in their last nine and 5-1 in their last six at home.

LITTLE PICTURE

Head coach Claude Noel is loath to anoint any one trio as his No. 1 line but the work of Kane, Bryan Little and Blake Wheeler clearly earned them that designation. Kane had two more against the Devils, his 13th and 14th, Little had two assists and Wheeler one as that trio combined for two goals and five points.

26 GAME

HOME

Saturday, December 3, 2011
JETS vs. NEW JERSEY DEVILS

SUMMARY

FIRST PERIOD
1. Winnipeg, Kane 13 (Byfuglien, Little) 1:42
2. New Jersey, Henrique 6 (Parise, Kovalchuk) 5:53

Penalties — Zubrus NJ (holding) 14:46, Slater Wpg (slashing) 18:43

SECOND PERIOD
3. New Jersey, Elias 9 (Larsson) 17:17 (pp)
4. Winnipeg, Burmistrov 6 (Little) 18:24 (sh)

Penalties — Thorburn Wpg (hooking) 5:22, Clarkson NJ (interference) 9:24, Jaffray Wpg (holding) 16:24, Ladd Wpg (tripping) 16:38

THIRD PERIOD
5. Winnipeg, Stuart 3 (Wheeler, Bogosian) 13:13
6. Winnipeg, Kane 14, 19:28 (en)

Penalties — Sestito NJ, Jaffray Wpg (fighting) 4:10, Sykora NJ (unsportsmanlike conduct), Oduya Wpg (roughing) 11:45

Shots on goal by

New Jersey	6	12	7	—	25
Winnipeg	6	7	7	—	20

Goal — New Jersey: Hedberg (L,7-5-1); Winnipeg: Pavelec (W,9-9-4)

Power plays (goals-chances) — New Jersey: 1-4; Winnipeg: 0-2

Referees — Ghislain Hebert, Chris Lee. Linesmen — Lonnie Cameron, Jay Sharrers

Attendance — 15,004 (15,004)

Trevor Hagan / Winnipeg Free Press

CELEBRATING A MARK STUART GOAL

GAME 27

HOME

Tuesday, December 6, 2011
JETS vs. BOSTON BRUINS

WINNIPEG 2 / BOSTON 1

THE defending Stanley Cup champions still had possession of the storied old chalice and still sported the proverbial heavyweight title belt around their waist.

But these upstart Jets did something nobody else in the National Hockey League had done in over a month: They beat the Beantowners and snapped the 15-game points streak they held prior to landing in Winnipeg.

"It was really pretty impressive to watch us play," Jets coach Claude Noel said, his club having won three straight. "It's funny when you go through these stretches how much confidence helps. I think we believe we can get this thing done. We're playing smart, we're following the details and getting the job done."

With the game tied 1-1, centre Bryan Little beat Bruins netminder Tuukka Rask through the five-hole at the 4:50 mark of the third period to count the game-winner.

And as for goaltender Ondrej Pavelec, he was excellent. Thirty-nine saves worth of excellent.

Winnipeg (12-11-4) moved over the .500 mark for the first time this season.

BIG PICTURE

They knocked off the hottest team in the NHL, not so bad. Thanks to three straight wins, the Jets now sat alone in second spot in the Southeast Division with 28 points, one ahead of Washington and four up on struggling Tampa Bay. Florida (34 points) still remained on top; Winnipeg was starting to rise.

LITTLE PICTURE

The Jets (12-11-4) continued to find the right formula in downtown Winnipeg as well. Three straight wins at the MTS Centre and eight home wins overall.

ONDREJ PAVELEC, ARTURS KULDA

John Woods / Winnipeg Free Press

SUMMARY

FIRST PERIOD
1. Winnipeg, Ladd 9 (Oduya, Pavelec) 18:22
Penalties — Slater Wpg (slashing) 3:40

SECOND PERIOD
No Scoring
Penalty — Klingberg Wpg (holding) 3:17, Stapleton Wpg (hooking) 13:41, Bergeron Bos (hooking) 15:45, Krejci Bos (slashing) 18:16

THIRD PERIOD
2. Boston, Johansen 5 (Prospal, Nikitin) 4:06
3. Winnipeg, Stuart 2 (Byfuglien) 16:15 (sh)
Penalties — Krejci Bos, Bogosian Wpg (roughing) 4:44, Pouliot Bos (tripping) 9:17

Shots on goal by

Boston	10	17	13	—	40
Winnipeg	11	10	14	—	35

Goal — Boston: Rask (L, 4-4-1); Winnipeg: Pavelec (W, 10-9-4)
Power plays (goals-chances) — Boston: 0-3; Winnipeg: 0-3
Referees — Dan O'Rourke, Brian Pochmara. Linesmen — David Brisebois, Thor Nelson
Attendance — 15,004 (15,004)

WINNIPEG 4 / CAROLINA 2

IT wasn't the most complicated game plan, nor particularly unique or inventive.

But the Jets found an early lead and kept the foot on the gas pedal throughout, giving the home side a 4-2 win over Carolina at the MTS Centre.

The blueprint for success: Score early, score often, shut down.

"That's a huge win, especially after the big win against Boston," said goaltender Chris Mason after watching his club jump out to a 4-0 lead after two periods.

"Sometimes you come into these games thinking a little too high of yourself and I thought the guys did an excellent job of staying even-keel. Their work ethic was there and we stuck to our game plan."

Mason gave up two third-period goals (one to Justin Faulk, the other to Brandon Sutter), but the game was never really in danger of getting away from the Jets.

Four different scorers — Dustin Byfuglien, Evander Kane, Tim Stapleton and Bryan Little — found the range for Winnipeg.

The Jets were on a four-game win streak (the longest of the season) and had won seven of the last eight at home.

Overall, the Jets moved to a 13-11-4 mark on the season.

BIG PICTURE

The Jets had wins in eight of their last 11 games to move into ninth in the Eastern Conference, just one spot out of a playoff berth. Winnipeg was now 13-11-4 with 30 points.

LITTLE PICTURE

Another fast start that turned into a dominant performance. The Jets were beginning to play with confidence and smarts — two byproducts of playing in front of the friendly crowd at the MTS Centre.

28 GAME

HOME

Friday, December 9, 2011
JETS vs. CAROLINA HURRICANES

SUMMARY

FIRST PERIOD
1. Winnipeg, Byfuglien 6 (Wheeler) 0:34
2. Winnipeg, Kane 15 (Wheeler) 5:04

Penalties — Gleason Car, Thorburn Wpg (fighting) 7:25, Jokinen Car (slashing) 9:16, Thorburn Wpg (hooking) 18:19

SECOND PERIOD
3. Winnipeg, Stapleton 3 (Wellwood, Byfuglien) 10:16 (pp)
4. Winnipeg, Little 9 (Kane, Wheeler) 11:28 (pp)

Penalties — LaRose Car (cross-checking) 7:55, Allen Car (elbowing) 8:18, Wheeler Wpg (goaltender interference) 9:07, Faulk Car (hooking) 9:42, LaRose Car, Jones Wpg (unsportsmanlike conduct) 11:46

THIRD PERIOD
5. Carolina, Faulk 1 (Spacek, Staal) 8:24
6. Carolina, Sutter 6 (Gleason, Spacek) 12:13 (pp)

Penalties — Kane Wpg (roughing) 2:20, Klingberg Wpg (hooking) 10:36

Shots on goal by

Carolina	7	8	10	—	25
Winnipeg	19	12	6	—	37

- **Goal** — Carolina: Ward (L,9-13-3)(30-26), Murphy (11:28 second, 7-7); Winnipeg: Mason (W,3-2-0)
- **Power plays (goals-chances)** — Carolina: 1-3; Winnipeg: 2-4
- **Referees** — Eric Furlatt, Kyle Rehman. Linesmen — Mike Cvik, Don Henderson
- **Attendance** — 15,004 (15,004)

Mike Deal / Winnipeg Free Press

BRYAN LITTLE

DETROIT 7 / WINNIPEG 1

LET'S start with the good news: Centre Bryan Little staked the Jets out to an early lead — something all road teams aspire to do — scoring 35 seconds into the game.

That was it. All the good news for Winnipeg contained in one sentence.

The bad news came with the reality that Detroit flat-out embarrassed the Jets after the first goal, scoring seven straight toward a 7-1 win at Joe Louis Arena.

Pity goaltender Ondrej Pavelec, who let in the converted touchdown worth of goals on 26 shots.

Afterwards, Jets coach Claude Noel contemplated watching the game film. Or burning it.

"I don't know if I need to see it twice — I've seen it," he said. "I'll sit on the plane and try to decide where we go next, how we'll deal with this.

"You want to do the right thing. I'm not sure how I'll make that assessment. I've seen some of it between periods. It was awful."

BIG PICTURE

So much for a four-game winning streak. Dropping to 13-12-4, the Jets got quite a jolt, measuring up meekly against one of the NHL's elite teams. Defending was the biggest issue for Winnipeg coach Claude Noel, and that was a concern since it was some of the foundation upon which the team's rise from well below .500 was based.

LITTLE PICTURE

Playing the night before in Winnipeg, the Jets crawled into their Motown hotel beds about 4 a.m. ET. Detroit coach Mike Babcock cited that as an opportunity for his team before the game, of which the Winged Wheel took full advantage.

JOHNNY ODUYA

Mike Deal / Winnipeg Free Press

SUMMARY

FIRST PERIOD
1. Winnipeg, Little 10 (Wheeler, Kane) 0:35
2. Detroit, Bertuzzi 3 (Franzen, Lidstrom) 6:47
3. Detroit, Zetterberg 6 (V.Filppula, Kronwall) 14:56

Penalties — None

SECOND PERIOD
4. Detroit, Hudler 5 (Franzen, Datsyuk) 4:03
5. Detroit, Conner 1 (Cleary, Helm) 4:43
6. Detroit, V. Filppula 10 (Datsyuk, White) 9:31
7. Detroit, Miller 3 (B.Stuart, Bertuzzi) 12:41

Penalties — Little Wpg (tripping) 7:42, Bertuzzi Det (hooking) 7:59, Ericsson Det (holding) 12:59, M.Stuart Wpg (interference) 16:43, Antropov Wpg (slashing) 18:52

THIRD PERIOD
8. Detroit, Hudler 6 (Zetterberg) 1:12

Penalties — None

Shots on goal by

Winnipeg	9	9	12	— 30
Detroit	12	13	4	— 29

Goal (shots-saves) — Winnipeg: Pavelec (L,10-10-4)(26-19), Mason (1:12 third)(3-3); Detroit: Howard (W,17-6-1)
Power plays (goals-chances) — Winnipeg: 0-2; Detroit: 0-3
Referees — Gord Dwyer, Marc Joannette. Linesmen — Brian Mach, Scott Driscoll
Attendance — 20,066 (20,066)

WINNIPEG 2 / MINNESOTA 1

30
GAME
HOME

Tuesday, December 13, 2011
JETS vs. MINNESOTA WILD

NOW would be a good time to check in and see how this key part of the Jets schedule — the 12 home games in the month of December — was working out according to plan.

So far, so good, it appeared, after the local hockey concern rattled off a 2-1 win over the Wild at a raucous MTS Centre. For those scoring this success at home, the Jets had won all five home games this month.

Moving out past that, they'd earned two points in eight of the last nine at the Portage Avenue barn.

The home cooking — helped along by the excitable fans — was starting to get to the Jets. In a good way, though.

"What I like the most is the emotional level we're getting to," said coach Claude Noel.

Once again, Winnipeg leaned heavily on a couple of things: Goaltender Ondrej Pavelec was the game's first star after kicking out 34 of 35 shots. The club also found some life from the home crowd, of course, which provided a needed jolt of life during physical lulls.

BIG PICTURE

A game removed from getting pounded in Detroit, the Jets bounced back with a hard, intense game at home, knocking off the top team in the NHL. Winnipeg improved to a 14-12-4 overall record.

LITTLE PICTURE

After the Wild converted their five-on-three, the Jets turned up the temperature and produced the tying goal within four minutes. They had an apparent goal later in the period waved off but took advantage of a third-period power play when Bryan Little scored the game-winner with five minutes to play.

SUMMARY

● **FIRST PERIOD**
No Scoring
Penalties — Latendresse Minn (interference) 14:23, Byfuglien Wpg (roughing) 18:52, Brodziak Minn (boarding) 19:33

● **SECOND PERIOD**
1. Minnesota, Latendresse 5 (Koivu, Heatley) 4:39 (pp)
2. Winnipeg, Bogosian 1, 8:37
Penalties — Thorburn Wpg (interference) 2:49, Glass Wpg (tripping) 4:11, Stoner Minn, Glass Wpg (fighting) 10:19, Schultz Minn (tripping) 18:52

● **THIRD PERIOD**
3. Winnipeg, Little 11 (Byfuglien, Wheeler) 15:00 (pp)
Penalties — Stoner Minn (delay of game) 13:00, Bogosian Wpg (boarding, game misconduct) 18:54

● **Shots on goal by**

Minnesota	7	15	13	—	35
Winnipeg	10	9	8	—	27

● **Goal** — Minnesota: Backstrom (L,11-6-2), Winnipeg: Pavelec (W, 11-10-4)
● **Power plays (goals-chances)** — Minnesota: 1-4; Winnipeg: 0-4
● **Referees** — Chris Rooney, Justin St. Pierre. Linesmen — Brad Lazarowich, Don Henderson
● **Attendance** — 15,004 (15,004)

John Woods / Winnipeg Free Press
EVANDER KANE

31

GAME

HOME

Thursday, December 15, 2011
JETS vs. WASHINGTON CAPITALS

WASHINGTON 1 / WINNIPEG 0

MARK it down: The Jets will rue the day they gave away points to the Capitals.

The slick-skating Alex Ovechkin — a guy you may have heard of — took a feed from centre Nicklas Backstrom and after a slight hesitation, slipped a quick shot through the pads of Jets goaltender Ondrej Pavelec with 1:14 left in the game to give Washington a 1-0 win.

Ouch, the Jets said afterward, knowing they had squandered at least a point to a division rival.

This one really smarted. Speaking of intelligence...

"We didn't play smart, that's the disappointing part and I'm extremely mad right now," coach Claude Noel said. "I didn't think we played the right way. I didn't think we played to win the game; we played not to lose in the third. That was the disappointing part for me.

"It's a bad two points we gave that team. It's stupid. We deserve exactly what we got."

The goal was just Ovechkin's 10th of the season.

BIG PICTURE

Still staring up at an Eastern Conference playoff spot, the Jets served up a sloppy effort in a 1-0 loss to the Caps they would end up cursing at season's end. The loss also ended a five-game winning streak at home.

LITTLE PICTURE

The Jets were a miserable 0-for-5 on the power play and in a game this tight, that was critical. Too much fancy stickhandling and not enough clogging the front of the net and looking for a workmanlike goal cost them.

MARK FLOOD

Phil Hossack / Winnipeg Free Press

SUMMARY

FIRST PERIOD
No Scoring
Penalty — Knuble Wash (high-sticking) 10:07

SECOND PERIOD
No Scoring
Penalties — Perreault Wash (tripping) 6:56, Washington bench (too many men; served by Perreault) 11:12, Oduya Wpg (slashing) 17:39

THIRD PERIOD
1. Washington, Ovechkin 10 (Johansson, Backstrom) 18:46
Penalty— Stuart Wpg (roughing) 7:12, Laich Wash (holding) 11:33

Shots on goal by

Washington	7	12	9	— 28
Winnipeg	14	8	4	— 26

Goal — Washington: Neuvirth (W,4-5-1); Winnipeg: Pavelec (L,11-11-4)
Power plays (goals-chances) — Washington: 0-2; Winnipeg: 0-4
Referees — Chris Rooney, Brad Meier. Linesmen — Brad Lazarowich, Shane Heyer
Attendance — 15,004 (15,004)

WINNIPEG 5 / ANAHEIM 3

IN a season full of moments that would overshadow the final outcome, a 5-3 Jets win, the return of Teemu Selanne ranked right up there.

The Ducks star picked up two assists in his return to the city where he started his NHL career.

That his production didn't quite equal the number of standing ovations and bursts of applause he received every time he touched the puck or saw his mug on the Jumbotron, didn't really matter or diminish the occasion.

"Emotion was very high," Selanne, 41, said after playing 19:04 in his first game in Winnipeg in almost 16 years. "I tried to stay focused but I was still very emotional. Just a great feeling. Even the warm-up, all the signs and the (No.) 13 Winnipeg Jets jerseys.

"I felt like everybody was watching me."

Named the game's third star, Selanne tossed a couple of sticks over the glass as a parting gift.

"The end result wasn't what we wanted to give Teemu tonight, but we were pretty impressed with the way the crowd responded to him," Ducks captain Ryan Getzlaf said. "It says everything that we already know about him."

BIG PICTURE

The Jets had goals from five different players — Kyle Wellwood, Blake Wheeler, Alex Burmistrov, Andrew Ladd and Zach Bogosian — to lift their record to 15-13-4 on the year.

LITTLE PICTURE

The Jets had an extra challenge, having to navigate the arena's emotion for the return of the Finnish Flash. The crowd was on both sides, and the night full of distraction worked out for Winnipeg — Selanne had an impact in the game and the Jets won. Imagine if he had scored.

SUMMARY

FIRST PERIOD

1. Winnipeg, Wellwood 8 (Antropov, Bogosian) 4:54
2. Winnipeg, Wheeler 3 (Byfuglien, Enstrom) 6:19 (pp)
3. Anaheim, Hagman 5 (Selanne, Brookbank) 14:34
4. Anaheim, Perry 13 (Getzlaf, Ellis) 18:26

Penalties — Perry Ana (high-sticking) 5:58, Stuart Wpg (boarding, roughing), Parros Ana (roughing) 10:08, Visnovsky Ana (slashing) 15:32

SECOND PERIOD

5. Winnipeg, Burmistrov 7 (Kane, Bogosian) 0:31
6. Winnipeg, Ladd 10 (Byfuglien, Wellwood) 18:20

Penalties — Parros Ana, Stuart Wpg (fighting) 2:06

THIRD PERIOD

7. Winnipeg, Bogosian 2 (Thorburn) 2:49
8. Anaheim, Perry 14 (Getzlaf, Selanne) 10:26 (pp)

Penalties — Thorburn Wpg (tripping) 10:18, Thorburn Wpg (tripping) 12:29, Antropov Wpg (tripping) 19:27

Shots on goal by

Anaheim	10	11	15	— 36
Winnipeg	10	13	8	— 31

Goal — Anaheim: Ellis (L,1-5-0); Winnipeg: Mason (W,4-2-0)
Power plays (goals-chances) — Anaheim: 1-4; Winnipeg: 1-2
Referees — Mike Hasenfrantz, Dennis LaRue.
Linesmen — Derek Nansen, Vaughan Rody
Attendance — 15,004 (15,004)

Mike Deal / Winnipeg Free Press

JIM SLATER, TEEMU SELANNE

33 GAME

HOME

Tuesday, December 20, 2011
JETS vs. NEW YORK ISLANDERS

N.Y. ISLANDERS 3 / WINNIPEG 2 (SO)

AT this point of the season, at any point of the schedule, really, it was all about points.

That's what was on the mind of the Jets after giving one of those valuable points away following a 3-2 shootout loss to the Islanders at the MTS Centre. The Isles, well behind the Jets in the standings, had shootout goals from P.A. Parenteau and Frans Nielsen in the post-game tiebreak, leaving the home side frustrated about the charitable nature of their own group.

"It could have gone a different way again," said Jets goalie Ondrej Pavelec, a front-and-centre player for his team once again. "We'll see at the end of the season. The point is important."

In the Eastern Conference, Ottawa and Toronto were tantalizingly close, holding down the last two spots with 36 points. Winnipeg, with 35 points, had been behind the line every day of the season so far, in large part due to a poor start of 0-3-0 and 5-9-3.

"It was a point on a night where we could have used two," said coach Claude Noel. "We'll take the point."

Nik Antropov and Andrew Ladd scored for Winnipeg, who moved to 15-13-5 overall.

BIG PICTURE

On a night in which they could have moved above the eighth-place playoff line with a victory, it's the one that got away that would hurt the most. And so it goes. Both Washington and Ottawa won and Buffalo and New Jersey lost, leaving the Jets looking up at a pile of teams above them.

LITTLE PICTURE

We would like to comment on developments about the Jets' power-play but, alas, they never had one. The only other time they didn't enjoy a man advantage, oddly enough, came against the Islanders.

ALEX BURMISTROV

John Woods / Winnipeg Free Press

SUMMARY

FIRST PERIOD

1. N.Y. Islanders, Parenteau 5 (Moulson, Tavares) 8:17
2. Winnipeg, Antropov 5 (Oduya) 18:00

Penalties — Okposo NYI, Stuart Wpg (roughing) 3:54

SECOND PERIOD

3. N.Y. Islanders, Grabner 10 (Hamonic, MacDonald) 3:53
4. Winnipeg, Ladd 11 (Antropov, Wellwood) 9:46

Penalties — Kane Wpg (goaltender interference) 18:40

THIRD PERIOD

No Scoring

Penalties — Oduya Wpg (hooking) 16:01

Overtime

No Scoring

Penalties — None

Shootout

N.Y. Islanders win 2-0

Winnipeg (0) — Wheeler, miss; Wellwood, miss; N.Y. Islanders (2) — Parenteau, goal; Nielsen, goal

Shots on goal by

N.Y. Islanders	13	9	9	2	—	33
Winnipeg	8	11	14	5	—	38

Goal — N.Y. Islanders: Montoya (19-17), Nabokov (W,2-5-0)(18:40 second, 19-19); Winnipeg: (L,11-11-5)

Power plays (goals-chances) — N.Y. Islanders; 0-2; Winnipeg: 0-0

Referees — Stephen Walkom, Brad Watson. Linesmen — Steve Barton, Don Henderson

Attendance — 15,004 (15,004)

WINNIPEG 4 / MONTREAL 0

34 GAME

HOME

Thursday, December 22, 2011
JETS vs. MONTREAL CANADIENS

FACING a team crippled with turmoil both on and off the ice, the Jets made short work of the Canadiens, beating the bleu, blanc et rouge by a 4-0 score.

Winnipeg, which got goals from Tanner Glass, Tim Stapleton and two from Blake Wheeler, improved to 16-13-5 on the season and moved into an eighth-place tie with New Jersey in the Eastern Conference.

Montreal, already in the midst of a full-fledged sports/political/language controversy for promoting anglophone Randy Cunneyworth to interim head coach after the firing of Jacques Martin, was on a five-game losing skid and sinking fast.

Winnipeg wanted to jump on the visitors quickly, and they did just that.

"We talked about that... we wanted to have a good start," Glass said. "You know the kind of struggles they've been going through over there and you want to keep your foot on the gas and make it as tough a night on them as we can.

"Plus, we know with our crowd if we get an early one, it's going to be a long night in this building."

Ondrej Pavelec earned his third shutout of the season.

BIG PICTURE

Winnipeg's seventh win of December helped push the team to a high-water mark for the season — into a tie for eighth place in the NHL's Eastern Conference with 37 points. The smaller matter of revenge for Montreal's win here on opening night wasn't lost on some spectators, either.

LITTLE PICTURE

The Jets did what needed to be done when an opponent has had the challenge of playing on the previous night (Montreal lost 5-1 in Chicago 24 hours earlier). Winnipeg jumped out to a lead before four minutes were played, and what little spirit the Habs came in with was broken.

SUMMARY

FIRST PERIOD

1. Winnipeg, Wheeler 4 (Byfuglien, Enstrom) 3:18 (pp)
2. Winnipeg, Glass 4 (Antropov, Wellwood) 13:13

Penalties — Gill Mtl (double high-sticking) 2:43

SECOND PERIOD

3. Winnipeg, Wheeler 5 (Hainsey, Pavelec) 0:39

Penalties — Byfuglien Wpg (interference) 1:47, Thorburn Wpg (double high-sticking) 9:36, Stuart Wpg (interference) 15:10, Enstrom Wpg (holding) 18:49

THIRD PERIOD

4. Winnipeg, Stapleton 4 (Wheeler, Bogosian) 17:36

Penalties — None

Shots on goal by

Montreal	6	16	5	—	27
Winnipeg	13	8	13	—	34

Goal — Montreal: Price (L,12-12-7); Winnipeg: Pavelec (W,12-11-15)

Power plays (goals-chances) — Montreal: 0-5; Winnipeg 0-2

Referees — Dan O'Halloran, Stephen Walkom. Linesmen — Steve Barton, Mike Cvik

Attendance — 15,004 (15,004)

Trevor Hagan / Winnipeg Free Press

ANTTI MIETTINEN

35

GAME

HOME

Friday, December 23, 2011
JETS vs. PITTSBURGH PENGUINS

PITTSBURGH 4 / WINNIPEG 1

THE task of playing three games in four nights finally caught up with the Jets, right before the Christmas break, as they dropped a 4-1 decision to the high-flying Penguins.

The final score dampened some of the enthusiam of the month-long home-heavy schedule — 7-2-1 in the last 10 at the MTS Centre — but there wasn't much hand-wringing over the result.

"I would rather look at the big picture," Jets coach Claude Noel said. "To me, it was a typical three (games) in four nights game. I'm not going to sit here and criticize my team.

"We've had a good month."

That's exactly what the Jets had — a good month. December's home gains pushed their record to two games above .500 at 16-14-5, a goal they set following a miserable start to the year.

"We made some strides as a group," left-winger Tanner Glass said. "The last little bit we left some points on the table we could have snagged. But we grew as a group. With a young team, we're trying to make strides, learn about ourselves and learn about playing the right way."

BIG PICTURE

The Jets headed into the holiday break with the sour taste of a loss. And, in the process, they lost some ground in the jam-packed Eastern Conference. Ottawa, New Jersey, Toronto and Washington all picked up points.

LITTLE PICTURE

The shots-on-goal stat is often deceiving but, on this night, the numbers were telling as Pittsburgh outshot the Jets 39-19. The Jets did whiff on some glorious opportunities, particularly early, but lacked finish and didn't generate enough.

ERIC FEHR

Mike Deal / Winnipeg Free Press

SUMMARY

FIRST PERIOD
1. Pittsburgh, Vitale 2 (Picard) 13:59
Penalties — Sullivan Pgh (tripping) 12:48, Byfuglien Wpg (slashing) 16:58

SECOND PERIOD
2. Winnipeg, Burmistrov 8 (Wheeler, Kane) 9:11
Penalties — Sullivan Pgh (tripping) 12:48, Byfuglien Wpg (slashing) 16:58

THIRD PERIOD
3. Pittsburgh, Neal 20 (Malkin, Kunitz) 0:22
4. Pittsburgh, Staal 13 (Kunitz, Sullivan) 4:14 (pp)
5. Pittsburgh, Dupuis 10 (Kennedy) 4:54
Penalties — Malkin Pgh (slashing), Burmistrov (roughing) 2:00, Byfuglien Wpg (interference) 2:55, Antropov Wpg (tripping) 13:42, Niskanen Pgh (tripping) 18:23

Shots on goal by

Pittsburgh	14	12	13	— 39
Winnipeg	5	7	7	— 19

Goal — Pittsburgh: Fleury (W,18-7-2); Winnipeg: Pavelec (L,12-12-5)
Power plays (goals-chances) — Pittsburgh: 1-4; Winnipeg: 0-3
Referees — Stephane Auger, Kelly Sutherland. Linesmen — Brian Mach, Thor Nelson
Attendance — 15,004 (15,004)

WINNIPEG 4 / COLORADO 1

36

GAME

AWAY

Tuesday, December 27, 2011
JETS vs. COLORADO AVALANCHE

IT was a strange sight to hit refresh on NHL.com's standings page and see the Jets posted above the playoff border in the Eastern Conference.

The Jets pounded the Avalanche 4-1 at the Pepsi Center to vault into eighth place in the East with 39 points.

Winnipeg had all kinds of company around this desired position — just as they would the rest of the season — but if the Stanley Cup playoffs started after this game...

"It means a lot to us to finally get above the line," Jets coach Claude Noel said. "For us it's good, but our focus will be winning the next game at home, and then we'll go from there.

"Hopefully we can stay above the line. That's going to be the key for us."

Left-winger Evander Kane snapped a cold streak with a pair of goals after going without one for seven straight games.

Tim Stapleton and Jim Slater added the others for Winnipeg, who secured the win with a strong third period (they outshot the Avalanche 18-8, despite holding a 3-0 lead).

Goaltender Ondrej Pavelec was once again sensational, stopping 32 of 33 shots for his 13th win of the season.

BIG PICTURE

The Jets won their eighth game in 12 tries and moved their record to 17-14-5 on the season, edging their way into 8th place in the Eastern Conference. The win was Winnipeg's fifth on the road this season.

LITTLE PICTURE

It was about improving that road record, which now sat at 5-8-4 for Winnipeg. Finding wins away from the MTS Centre was important for the Jets' playoffs aspirations; they needed to make some hay in the white jerseys to have a chance.

SUMMARY

FIRST PERIOD

1. Winnipeg, Kane 16 (Wheeler, Burmistrov) 16:37

Penalties — None

SECOND PERIOD

2. Winnipeg, Stapleton 5 (Ladd, Enstrom) 1:21 (pp)
3. Winnipeg, Kane 17 (Thorburn, Stapleton) 14:52

Penalties — O'Byrne Col (holding) 0:40, Stuart Wpg, McLeod Col (fighting) 2:38

THIRD PERIOD

4. Winnipeg, Slater 7 (Glass) 3:41
5. Colorado, Porter 2 (Van der Gulik, McLeod) 14:48

Penalties — Wheeler Wpg (slashing) 0:29, Glass Wpg, O'Brien Col (fighting) 15:58

Shots on goal by

Winnipeg	6	12	18	—	26
Colorado	11	14	8	—	33

Goal — Winnipeg: Pavelec (W,13-12-5); Colorado: Giguere (L,8-5-0)

Power plays (goals-chances) — Winnipeg: 1-1; Colorado: 0-1

Referees — Dennis LaRue, Mike Leggo. Linesmen — Vaughan Rody, Thor Nelson

Attendance — 18,007 (18,007)

Boris Minkevich / Winnipeg Free Press

EVANDER KANE

37

GAME

HOME

Thursday, December 29, 2011
JETS vs. LOS ANGELES KINGS

WINNIPEG 1 / LOS ANGELES 0 (OT)

IT took a little longer than expected, but the home magic eventually found its way to Evander Kane's stick.

The young gun jumped on a bouncing puck in the Los Angeles crease and buried it at the 1:09 mark of the overtime session, giving the home side a 1-0 win over the Kings at the MTS Centre.

"It's a great feeling scoring an overtime goal," Kane said after scoring his 18th goal of the year. "The game is over and you're able to win it for your team, but it was a great effort by all the guys. Our penalty kill deserves a lot of credit; they did a great job.

"It was a great team effort."

The penalty kill Kane mentioned? They snuffed out a Kings 5-on-3 chance, a tense moment of the game for Winnipeg that lasted for one minute and 52 seconds in the second period and that helped the home side reach the extra frame.

Goaltender Chris Mason picked up his first shutout of the season and 22nd of his career, making 31 saves.

BIG PICTURE

They needed to have a big December, people said. They needed to capitalize on the home-heavy schedule if they wanted to make some noise in the Eastern Conference, others pointed out. No problem. The win gave Winnipeg an 8-2-1 record at the MTS Centre in December and an 18-14-5 record overall.

LITTLE PICTURE

So this was what it felt like for the Jets to win two straight. That modest streak had eluded Winnipeg in the four previous chances to build off success before Thursday, but that worry was now over. Did someone say three in a row?

EVANDER KANE, BLAKE WHEELER

Trevor Hagan / Winnipeg Free Press

SUMMARY

FIRST PERIOD
No Scoring
Penalties — Burmistrov Wpg (tripping) 17:29

SECOND PERIOD
No Scoring
Penalty — Johnson LA (roughing), Kane Wpg (double roughing) 7:35, Bogosian Wpg (holding)

THIRD PERIOD
No Scoring
Penalties — Johnson LA (holding) 3:45, Mitchell LA (tripping) 5:00, Flood Wpg (interference) 14:45

OVERTIME
1. Winnipeg, Kane 18 (Hainsey, Wheeler) 1:09
Penalties — None

Shots on goal by

Los Angeles	13	12	16	0 —	40
Winnipeg	9	8	8	2 —	27

Goal — Los Angeles: Bernier (0,2-4-1); Winnipeg: Mason (W,5-2-0)
Power plays (goals-chances) — Los Angeles: 0-5; Winnipeg: 0-2
Referees — Dennis LaRue, Kelly Sutherland. Linesmen — Lonnie Cameron, Bryan Pancich
Attendance — 15,004 (15,004)

WINNIPEG 3 / TORONTO 2

38

GAME

HOME

Saturday, December 31, 2011
JETS vs. TORONTO MAPLE LEAFS

THREE goals in the second period proved to be enough offence as the Jets rang in the New Year with a 3-2 win over the Maple Leafs at the MTS Centre.

Zach Bogosian, Andrew Ladd, and Blake Wheeler provided the offence for Winnipeg, which wrapped up a successful December with a 9-2-1 record at home. Overall, Winnipeg moved to five games above the .500 mark — a lofty status players started to appreciate as the calender flipped.

As each game passed, there was a lot more on the line.

"Look how tight it was out there," defenceman Zach Bogosian said. "It's a one-goal game. Who knows if one of those goals doesn't go in? You can look back at the end of the season (at these), but you just have to make sure you're moving forward.

"I think we're a better team than we were in the first two months of the season."

Goaltender Ondrej Pavelec made 24 saves for his 14th win of the season. He stopped all 12 pucks directed on his net in a busy third, as the Leafs searched for the equalizer.

BIG PICTURE

From one game below the .500 mark to five above, it was a pretty good month for Winnipeg. The Jets moved to 19-14-5 and into a tie for sixth place in the Eastern Conference, their highest ranking of the year to date.

LITTLE PICTURE

Goals by Zach Bogosian and Blake Wheeler came with the man advantage and Ladd's second-period marker came seconds after a Leafs penalty expired. Winnipeg was officially two-for-six on the power play, and it made all the difference.

SUMMARY

FIRST PERIOD

1. Toronto, MacArthur 11 (Gunnarsson, Phaneuf) 13:59 (pp)

Penalties — Aulie Tor (hooking) 3:28, Ladd Wpg (high-sticking) 13:49

SECOND PERIOD

2. Winnipeg, Bogosian 3 (Enstrom, Miettinen) 2:51 (pp)
3. Winnipeg, Ladd 12 (Wellwood, Oduya) 5:26
4. Toronto, Kessel 21 (Connolly, Phaneuf) 7:07
5. Winnipeg, Wheeler 6 (Hainsey, Miettinen) 10:50 (pp)

Penalties —Phaneuf Tor (high-sticking) 1:16, Franson Tor (holding) 3:22, Crabb Tor (charging) 9:18, Kadri Tor (hooking) 16:17, Burmistrov Wpg (holding) 18:51

THIRD PERIOD

No Scoring

Penalties — Ladd Wpg (slashing) 1:26, Connolly Tor (hooking) 15:54

Shots on goal by

Toronto	8	4	12	—	24
Winnipeg	15	13	7	—	35

Goal — Toronto: Reimer (L,7-4-4); Winnipeg: Pavelec (W,14-12-5)

Power plays (goals-chances) — Toronto: 1-3; Winnipeg: 2-6

Referees — Dean Morton, Tim Peel. Linesmen — Lonnie Cameron, Bryan Pancich

Attendance — 15,004 (15,004)

Mike Deal / Winnipeg Free Press

TIM STAPLETON

39

GAME

AWAY

Wednesday, January 4, 2012
JETS vs. MONTREAL CANADIENS

MONTREAL 7 / WINNIPEG 3

THE road monster, the one that constantly terrorized the Jets in 2011, came back.

Montreal forward Lars Eller, who had four goals all season prior to this one, doubled his scoring output and led the Canadiens to a convincing 7-3 win over Winnipeg at the Bell Centre.

It was just as scary as the score suggested.

"I don't think it was fun for anybody, but we weren't prepared to do the things we were doing for the last month and it showed," Jets coach Claude Noel said after his team dropped to an uninspiring 5-9-4 on the road. "You can't play with half the players, meaning some guys were in and some guys were not.

"At the end of the day, you can't fake this thing. Great, we got ourselves back in the game (3-2 Habs after two periods) and then boom, they got three goals in a matter of no time."

Fifty seconds in the third period, to be exact. That sealed the game for Montreal and Eller iced the cake later in the frame with a penalty-shot score.

The Danish player registered five points in the game.

BIG PICTURE

The Jets fell flat on their faces as they started a road-heavy month of January. The Jets remained stuck in ninth in the Eastern Conference, still at 43 points. Montreal trailed by six points.

LITTLE PICTURE

The Habs scored three times in 50 seconds early in the final period to wipe out Winnipeg's hope and leaving the Jets without a single victory this season (0-12-2) when they were trailing after two periods.

BLAKE WHEELER

Mike Deal / Winnipeg Free Press

SUMMARY

FIRST PERIOD
1. Winnipeg, Stapleton 6 (Kane, Wheeler) 3:41
2. Montreal, Gorges 2 (Desharnais, Cole) 13:24
3. Montreal, Eller 5, 14:07

Penalties — Ladd Wpg (roughing) 17:56

SECOND PERIOD
4. Montreal, Kaberle 1 (Moen, Eller) 5:32
5. Winnipeg, Wheeler 7 (Bogosian, Enstrom) 17:51 (pp)

Penalties — Slater Wpg (slashing) 13:28, Gorges Mtl (holding) 16:34, Diaz Mtl (interference) 19:05

THIRD PERIOD
6. Montreal, Eller 6 (Moen, Kostitsyn) 2:41
7. Montreal, Plekanec 9 (Cammalleri, Cole) 3:03
8. Montreal, Eller 7 (Moen, Kostitsyn) 3:31
9. Montreal, Eller 7, 11:00 (penalty shot)
10. Winnipeg, Ladd 13 (Hainsey, Antropov) 13:03

Penalties — Thorburn Wpg, Gill Mtl (fighting) 17:21, Stuart Wpg (high-sticking), Darche Mtl (roughing) 18:39

Shots on goal by

Winnipeg	7	9	11	—	27
Montreal	12	5	14	—	31

Goal (shots-saves) — Winnipeg: Pavelec (L,15-12-5; 18-24), Mason (13:11 third, 7-8); Montreal: Price (W,14-14-7)

Power plays (goals-chances) — Winnipeg: 1-2; Montreal: 0-3

Referees — Marc Joanette, Marcus Vinnerborg. Linesmen — Andy McElman, Brian Murphy

Attendance — 21,273 (21,273)

GAME 40

AWAY

Thursday, January 5, 2012

JETS vs. TORONTO MAPLE LEAFS

TORONTO 4 / WINNIPEG 0

THAT sound you heard was the wind that followed the teams blowing by the Jets.

Tied for sixth in the NHL's Eastern Conference just days prior, Winnipeg fell back to 10th after an inept 4-0 loss to the Maple Leafs at the Air Canada Centre.

Leafs goalie Jonas Gustavsson picked up his second career shutout with 24 saves. If he had three difficult ones to make all night, it would have been a generous assessment.

"He did his job, but I don't think we made it too difficult on him," said Jets netminder Chris Mason, who was left to defend back-door plays and high-quality slot shots.

"I thought we made it easy on their whole team."

The Jets were now 5-10-4 on the road. The club remained winless in the second half of back-to-back games (0-5-1) and when they trailed after 40 minutes, Winnipeg was a miserable 0-13-2.

Captain Andrew Ladd wasn't pleased with the recent turn of events for his team.

"I think the best thing to do is get pissed off," said Ladd. "We can't be happy with how we've been on the road."

BIG PICTURE

Eleven goals surrendered in two nights on the road and the Jets, who were tied for sixth in the Eastern Conference the previous week, were now 10th. Just like that.

LITTLE PICTURE

The Jets' Chris Thorburn hit the crossbar early in the game and then Toronto's Phil Kessel followed it up with the game's first goal five minutes in. His 23rd goal of the season had the Leafs on their way to a second straight win.

SUMMARY

FIRST PERIOD

1. Toronto, Kessel 23 (Lupul, Connolly) 5:00.

Penalties — None

SECOND PERIOD

2. Toronto, Connolly 12 (Crabb, Phaneuf) 1:22

Penalties — Glass Wpg (tripping) 1:22, Stuart Wpg (cross-checking) 8:48

THIRD PERIOD

3. Toronto, Grabovski 12 (Kulemin, Gunnarsson) 3:38

4. Toronto, MacArthur 12 (Grabovski, Franson) 10:37 (pp)

Penalties — Ladd Wpg (roughing) 9:19, Lombardi Tor (tripping) 12:22

Shots on goal by

Minnesota	6	9	9	—	24
Winnipeg	8	7	10	—	25

Goal — Winnipeg: Mason (L,5-3-0); Toronto: Gustavsson (W,11-7-0)

Power plays (goals-chances) — Winnipeg: 0-1; Toronto: 1-3

Referees — Brian Pochmara, Eric Furlatt. Linesmen — Steve Barton, David Brisebois

Attendance — 19,513 (18,819)

Mike Deal / Winnipeg Free Press

CHRIS MASON

41 GAME

AWAY

Saturday, January 7, 2012
JETS vs. BUFFALO SABRES

WINNIPEG 2 / BUFFALO 1 (OT)

BOUNCING back strongly from two miserable road outings earlier in the week, the Jets got a goal from defenceman Johnny Oduya at 57 seconds of overtime to defeat the Sabres 2-1 at First Niagara Center.

It pushed the Jets to 45 points through 41 games, a mark of 20-16-5.

"We're in a dogfight and we're over .500," Jets coach Claude Noel said after watching his team rally after a pair of four-goal defeats on the road. "There are some things we're doing (well) and we're happy to be where we are, I think.

"We're in the hunt. That's what we need to be."

Oduya created the winning play from the beginning, gobbling up a turnover in the neutral zone. He got it to the right wing to Kane, who crossed the blue-line and drew three of the four Sabres on the ice, leaving Oduya with plenty of room to receive the return pass and lift a shot into the top corner of the net.

"It kind of surprised our whole bench," the coach said. "Johnny came down and made it look like he was a sniper, up there with the peanut butter."

BIG PICTURE

The Jets were alive and the fans pulled back on the panic. Winnipeg had 45 points with its 20th win of the season as they hit the halfway point of the 82-game trek.

LITTLE PICTURE

The Jets fired 41 shots at the Buffalo goal, giving a glimpse of what coach Claude Noel thought the group was capable of. At the other end, goaltender Ondrej Pavelec made 31 saves for the victory.

JOHNNY ODUYA

Mike Deal / Winnipeg Free Press

SUMMARY

FIRST PERIOD
No Scoring
Penalty — Stuart Wpg (hooking) 2:16, Enroth Buf (hooking; served by Boyes) 14:45

SECOND PERIOD
1. Buffalo, Myers 3 (Pominville, Gragnani) 11:08 (pp)
2. Winnipeg, Wheeler 8 (Enstrom, Little) 19:55 (pp)
Penalties — Kaleta Buf (interference) 0:23, Wheeler Wpg (hooking) 10:04, Antropov Wpg (interference) 14:11, Vanek Buf (hooking) 18:55, Leopold Buf (throwing stick) 19:10

THIRD PERIOD
No Scoring
Penalty— Enstrom Wpg (hooking) 7:21

OVERTIME
3. Winnipeg, Oduya 2 (Kane) 0:57
Penalties— None

Shots on goal by

Winnipeg	11	18	11	1	— 41
Buffalo	10	14	8	0	— 32

Goal — Winnipeg: Pavelec (W,15-13-5); Buffalo: Enroth (L,8-7-3)
Power plays (goals-chances) — Winnipeg: 1-4; Buffalo: 1-4
Referees — Eric Furlatt, Francois St. Laurent. Linesmen — Scott Cherrey, Tim Nowak
Attendance — 18,690 (18,690)

BOSTON 5 / WINNIPEG 3

IF you've got the right stuff for two periods and then lose, do you actually have the right stuff?

That's the key question that came out of the TD Garden, where the Jets put three leads up on the scoreboard and were ahead 3-2 through 40 minutes, only to see the defending Stanley Cup champion Bruins roar back in the third for a 5-3 victory.

"It's a disappointing game," Jets coach Claude Noel said. "You played pretty solid for 40 minutes. You miss an assignment on the opening faceoff the first shift of the third and you're fricking tied."

The tying goal by Boston's Nathan Horton — scored eight seconds into the final period — did not sit well with the coach.

"What's going to take place? They're down by one. What do you think's going to happen? Well, emotionally they're going to push and physically they're going to push. They've got weight they can do that with, and they did."

Winnipeg ended the road trip with a 1-3 record.

BIG PICTURE

It was a tough road trip; being outscored 17-8 is never a good time. The Jets remained in ninth in the East, one point back of eighth-place Pittsburgh.

LITTLE PICTURE

Jets goals by Andrew Ladd, Blake Wheeler and Eric Fehr had the visitors in the lead through two periods, at 3-2. But Nathan Horton, Tyler Seguin and Benoit Pouliot scored within the first 6:41 of the third, all on a variety of soft plays by the Jets, to decide the affair.

SUMMARY

FIRST PERIOD

1. Winnipeg, Ladd 14 (Bogosian, Enstrom) 16:53
2. Boston, Horton 13 (Lucic, Krejci) 19:20

Missed penalty shot — Thorburn Wpg, 5:57
Penalties — Ladd Wpg (holding) 1:42

SECOND PERIOD

3. Winnipeg, Wheeler 9 (Enstrom, Bogosian) 0:31
4. Boston, Thornton 4, 5:16 (penalty shot, sh)
5. Winnipeg, Fehr 1 (Stapleton) 11:11

Penalties — Thornton Bos (illegal check to head minor) 3:05, Ference Bos (hooking) 4:38, Stuart Wpg, Thornton Bos (fighting) 10:17, Ference Bos (goaltender interference) 16:30

THIRD PERIOD

6. Boston, Horton 14 (Krejci, Lucic) 0:08
7. Boston, Seguin 17 (Bergeron) 3:06
8. Boston, Pouliot 8 (Bergeron, Peverley) 6:41 (pp)

Penalties — Ladd Wpg (interference) 5:25, McQuaid Bos (interference) 10:31, Jones Wpg (tripping) 13:05

Shots on goal by

Winnipeg	14	10	8	—	32
Boston	13	7	22	—	42

Goal — Winnipeg: Pavelec (L,15-14-5); Boston: Rask (W,10-4-1)
Power plays (goals-chances) — Winnipeg: 0-4; Boston: 1-3
Referees — Greg Kimmerly, Stephen Walkom
Linesmen — Steve Barton, Brian Murphy
Attendance — 17,565 (17,565)

Trevor Hagan / Winnipeg Free Press
ONDREJ PAVELEC

43

GAME

HOME

Thursday, January 12, 2012
JETS vs. SAN JOSE SHARKS

SAN JOSE 2 / WINNIPEG 0

ANDREW Ladd, the man who represented the Jets dressing room, offered this honest assessment.

"The frustration comes out of us still turning pucks over, still trying to make something out of nothing," the captain said matter-of-factly after his club dropped a 2-0 decision to the Sharks.

"It's killing us, really. How many times have we stressed about getting pucks deep and doing those smart things? How many turnovers did we have? Way too many.

"At some point we have to figure out, do we want to be a playoff team or are we content with being this win one here, win one there-type team?"

These are the questions the Jets asked themselves at this juncture, having dropped four of the last five games and watched the playoff line — the definitive eighth-place position in the conference — drift further and further away.

Winnipeg (20-18-5) would manage 24 shots against the Sharks and had now been held to one goal or less in 14 games this season — going 2-12 in those contests.

BIG PICTURE

The Jets remained stalled at 45 points and still outside the playoff picture in the Eastern Conference, though it was just by one point. The winning ways needed to start happening again.

LITTLE PICTURE

Things began to go south at 13:36 of the second when Logan Couture came down the slot and wasn't impeded near enough when the puck arrived in front of Jets goalie Ondrej Pavelec. Brad Winchester scored early in the third. Sharks goalie Antti Niemi had an easy night.

EVANDER KANE, ALEX BURMISTROV

Trevor Hagan / Winnipeg Free Press

SUMMARY

FIRST PERIOD
No Scoring
Penalties — Winchester SJ (charging) 2:29, Demers SJ (holding), Wellwood Wpg (unsportsmanlike conduct, diving) 8:28

SECOND PERIOD
1. San Jose, Couture 18 (Burns) 13:36
Penalties — Burns SJ (interference) 3:34, Wheeler Wpg (slashing) 14:16

THIRD PERIOD
2. San Jose, Winchester 5 (Desjardins, Murray) 2:33
Penalties — Ladd Wpg (hooking) 11:54

Shots on goal by

San Jose	14	9	14	—	37
Winnipeg	10	8	6	—	24

Goal — San Jose: Niemi (W,19-7-5); Winnipeg: Pavelec (L,15-15-5)
Power plays (goals-chances) — San Jose: 0-2; Winnipeg: 0-2
Referees — Dan O'Rourke, Kevin Pollock. Linesmen — David Brisebois, Pierre Champoux
Attendance — 15,004 (15,004)

NEW JERSEY 2 / WINNIPEG 1

44

GAME

HOME

Saturday, January 14, 2012
JETS vs. NEW JERSEY DEVILS

HAD the simple act of flipping a calendar dramatically changed something for the Jets?

After winning four of their last five games in a stirring December, January brought five losses in six games, including the 2-1 disappointment against the Devils at the MTS Centre.

The effort is there, the club said.

"They're doing the best that they can right now with what we have," coach Claude Noel said. "What I like is the fact that we wanted to play a game with more will, regardless of the score. We were up for a good portion of the game, but even though they tied it, we rallied back and battled hard to the end.

"I'm certainly not going to beat up on my team."

Kurtis Foster and Patrick Elias scored less than three minutes apart midway through the third to deliver New Jersey's victory. To this point, the Jets had been outscored 50-27 in the final periods, second-worst behind only Columbus.

Tanner Glass had this to say on recent events: "You've got to stay positive. That's how you get out of these things."

BIG PICTURE

There's no sugar-coating it: Winnipeg had lost five of their last six. The Jets were to play their next 14 against conference rivals, and if they couldn't stop the bleeding ASAP, they would fade fast from the post-season discussion.

LITTLE PICTURE

No Dustin Byfuglien, no Zach Bogosian and Blake Wheeler left in the second after taking a shot to the throat. It's hard for any club to survive without its two best D-men and its leading scorer.

SUMMARY

FIRST PERIOD

1. Winnipeg, Ladd 15 (Oduya) 18:31

Penalties — Carter NJ (roughing, fighting) Stuart Wpg (fighting) 3:26, Fehr Wpg (elbowing) 14:55

SECOND PERIOD

No Scoring

Penalties — Teneby NJ (interference) 12:28

THIRD PERIOD

2. New Jersey, Foster 2 (Zubrus) 9:45
3. New Jersey, Elias 16 (Larsson, Sykora) 12:43

Missed penalty shot — Elias, NJ 18:24

Penalties — Burmistrov Wpg (high-sticking) 5:25, Hainsey Wpg (holding on a breakaway, penalty shot) 18:24

Shots on goal by

New Jersey	7	9	8	—	24
Winnipeg	6	6	11	—	23

Goal — New Jersey: Brodeur (W,13-10-1); Winnipeg: Pavelec (L,15-16-5)

Power plays (goals-chances) — New Jersey: 0-2; Winnipeg: 0-2

Referees — Ian Walsh, Paul Devorski

Linesmen — Brian Murphy, Derek Nansen

Attendance — 15,004 (15,004)

Ruth Bonneville / Winnipeg Free Press

EVANDER KANE

WINNIPEG 2 / OTTAWA 0

GOALS by Jim Slater and Tobias Enstrom accounted for all the scoring as the injury-riddled Jets skated past the Senators 2-0 at Scotiabank Place.

Winnipeg was without defencemen Dustin Byfuglien and Zach Bogosian, as well as forward Blake Wheeler, but despite the short-handed lineup, the Jets found a way.

"That's really big," Jets captain Andrew Ladd said after the game. "We've done a great job all year of having guys coming in for the injured guys and playing really well and to a teammate, every guy in here had a great game."

The Jets improved to a 21-19-5 record, good for 47 points on the season. Winnipeg also snapped a three-game losing streak.

"To me, it's a real test, how you deal with adversity," head coach Claude Noel said. "You have to move forward. I thought the guys faced adversity head-on and the only way around is through. That's what we did: We went right through it.

"We made (Ottawa) earn every inch. There was no free ice out there for them. It was good to see a consistent effort through our 20 guys."

BIG PICTURE

This was a much-needed win for the Jets, as it ended a three-game losing skid. More importantly, the win kept Winnipeg in the playoff picture — an image that had started to get fuzzy of late.

LITTLE PICTURE

Goaltender Chris Mason stopped all 25 shots directed at his net but the Jets played a near-perfect road game, as they shut down the Sens' attack all evening. Impressive work, considering the Jets were without defencemen Dustin Byfuglien and Zach Bogosian.

JIM SLATER

Trevor Hagan / Winnipeg Free Press

SUMMARY

FIRST PERIOD
1. Winnipeg, Slater 8 (Thorburn) 0:49
Penalties — Kane Wpg (roughing), Stuart Wpg, Carkner Ott (fighting), Neil Ott (double roughing) 17:45

SECOND PERIOD
2. Winnipeg, Enstrom 2 (Wellwood, Ladd) 6:48
Penalties — Neil Ott (hooking) 7:23

THIRD PERIOD
No Scoring
Penalties — Enstrom Wpg (interference) 3:23, Condra Ott (high-sticking) 8:01, Oduya Wpg (tripping) 19:41

Shots on goal by

Winnipeg	13	12	10	— 35
Ottawa	3	8	14	— 25

Goal — Winnipeg: Mason (W,6-3-0); Ottawa: Anderson (L,23-13-4)
Power plays (goals-chances) — Winnipeg: 0-3; Ottawa: 0-2
Referees — Dean Morton, Marc Joanette. Linesmen — Jonny Murray, Lonnie Cameron
Attendance — 19,927 (19,153)

NEW JERSEY 5 / WINNIPEG 1

46

GAME

AWAY

Tuesday, January 17, 2012
JETS vs. NEW JERSEY DEVILS

PETR Sykora's goal 92 seconds into the second period turned out to be the winning goal as the Devils beat the Jets 5-1 in Newark, N.J.

The loss dropped the Jets' record to 0-7 in the second half of back-to-back games, a disturbing stat that had players searching for answers.

"I just think it's mental toughness," goaltender Chris Mason said. "The way that we travel and everything... guys get tired sometimes, but you've got to do it. There's no excuse. I don't know why we haven't been good; we've been terrible in our second games. You can't do that and expect to make the playoffs. You've got to win some of those games.

"It's tough, but everyone in the league has to do it."

Mason, frustrated all night, surrendered four goals on 15 shots. He was lifted for Ondrej Pavelec in the second period.

Defenceman Tobias Enstrom scored the lone goal for the Jets, who mustered up just 21 shots on Devils goaltender Martin Brodeur.

BIG PICTURE

A stat that continued to be the cold, hard evidence as to the Jets' offensive struggles: The loss to New Jersey was the 16th game this season in which the club managed just one goal or less. Winnipeg, not surprisingly, was 2-14 in those games.

LITTLE PICTURE

The game was essentially in question for Winnipeg when a seeing-eye point shot by Petr Sykora found its way past Chris Mason just 92 seconds into the second period. That put the Jets down 2-0 and put the defensively sound Devils at the controls for the remainder of the contest.

SUMMARY

● **FIRST PERIOD**
1. New Jersey, Kovalchuk 18 (Parise) 18:59
Penalties — Slater Wpg (interference) 5:48

● **SECOND PERIOD**
2. New Jersey, Sykora 11 (Tallinder, Elias) 1:32
3. New Jersey, Clarkson 16 (Elias) 4:48
4. New Jersey, Kovalchuk 19 (Clarkson, Foster) 7:38 (pp)
Penalties — Kane Wpg (high-sticking) 5:34, Antropov Wpg (elbowing) 7:07, Oduya Wpg (slashing) 12:14

● **THIRD PERIOD**
5. Winnipeg, Enstrom 3 (Antropov, Wellwood) 8:18
6. New Jersey, Elias 17 (Volchenkov, Sykora) 11:31
Penalties — Zubrus NJ (tripping) 13:08

● **Shots on goal by**

Winnipeg	6	7	8	—	21
New Jersey	9	7	4	—	20

● **Goal** — Winnipeg: Mason (L,6-4-0)(15-11), Pavelec (8:46 second) (5-4); New Jersey: Brodeur (W,14-10-1)
● **Power plays (goals-chances)** — Winnipeg: 0-1; New Jersey: 1-4
● **Referees** — Ian Walsh, Paul Devorski. Linesmen — Brian Murphy, Derek Nansen
● **Attendance** — 14,129 (17,625)

Trevor Hagan / Winnipeg Free Press

TOBIAS ENSTROM

47 GAME

HOME

Thursday, January 19, 2012
JETS vs. BUFFALO SABRES

WINNIPEG 4 / BUFFALO 1

BACK away from the panic button, put down those sharp knives and make room on the bandwagon, Jets fans — the local side had its mojo again.

For one night, at least.

Tobias Enstrom scored a power-play goal at the 12:55 mark of the second period that led Winnipeg to a 4-1 win over Buffalo at the MTS Centre. The victory brought some much-needed positivity to a side that was struggling to light the lamp in recent games.

The Jets' power play scored twice against the Sabres, a marked improvement after failing to score in the previous five games.

"It's always great to get a win coming home from the road," said Enstrom, who had goals in three straight games. "To bounce back with a win like this feels good. It's fun to score goals, but the most important thing is winning and we've got some important games coming up here."

Andrew Ladd and Nik Antropov each had a goal and an assist, while Kyle Wellwood (two assists), Ondrej Pavelec (25 saves) and Mark Stuart (four blocked shots, three hits) also turned in solid efforts.

BIG PICTURE

The victory moved the Jets to 49 points, still in 10th place in the Eastern Conference but to within three points of both a playoff spot and the Southeast Division lead.

LITTLE PICTURE

The two power-play goals were nice, as was the third. Winnipeg played a safe, no-nonsense style in the final frame and scored two goals (courtesy of Tim Stapleton and Nik Antropov) on just three shots in the period.

MARK STUART

Phil Hossack / Winnipeg Free Press

SUMMARY

FIRST PERIOD

1. Winnipeg, Ladd 18 (Hainsey, Wellwood) 11:34

Penalties — McCormick Buf, Stuart Wpg (fighting) 4:29

SECOND PERIOD

2. Buffalo, Stafford 8 (Gerbe) 4:18

3. Winnipeg, Enstrom 4 (Little, Wheeler) 12:55 (pp)

Penalty — Buffalo bench (too many men; served by Stafford) 11:41, Hecht Buf (interference) 13:31, Stapleton Wpg (hooking) 14:26, Gerbe Buf, Wheeler Wpg (unsportsmanlike conduct) 20:00

THIRD PERIOD

4. Winnipeg, Stapleton 7 (Antropov, Ladd) 3:46 (pp)

5. Winnipeg, Antropov 6 (Wellwood, Oduya) 18:40

Penalties — Roy Buf (tripping) 3:00, Antropov Wpg (roughing) 9:28, McCormick Buf (interference) 11:58

Shots on goal by

Buffalo	10	7	9 —	26
Winnipeg	19	11	3 —	33

Goal — Buffalo: Miller (L,11-14-2); Winnipeg: Pavelec (W,16-16-5)

Power plays (goals-chances) — Buffalo: 0-2; Winnipeg: 2-3

Referees — Ghislain Hebert, Tim Peel. Linesmen — Shane Heyer, Derek Nansen

Attendance — 15,004 (15,004)

FLORIDA 4 / WINNIPEG 3 (SO)

"FREE pizzas" was a term Jets head coach Claude Noel used to describe turnovers and poor defensive play by his club.

He delivered the line a few times following the Jets' 4-3 shootout loss to the Panthers.

"The hard part of the game for me was the fact we gave them three free goals. For me, that was really disappointing," Noel said. "We had clear possession of the puck three times in our D-zone with really not a lot of pressure and we served up three pizzas that ended up in our net.

"We haven't given a team three opportunities in a game like that this year. Why does that happen in a game, in this game? I have no idea and neither do the players. They don't play that way, they don't think that way, they don't motivate themselves that way... 'Hey, let's go out and really give up some free pizzas tonight.' And when it happens, trust me, you drag it with you."

Nik Antropov scored two goals for the Jets, who fell to a 22-20-6 overall record. Alex Burmistrov scored the other marker for Winnipeg.

Kris Versteeg scored two goals and added an assist for the visitors.

BIG PICTURE

The one point earned from the shootout loss put the Jets two back of eighth-place Washington and only one behind ninth-place Toronto. Winnipeg — 2-1-1 in the last four outings — had 50 points in 48 games.

LITTLE PICTURE

Two third-period comebacks helped the Jets get that point but they remained winless when trailing after two periods (0-15-3). Florida winger Mikael Samuelsson ended the shootout in the seventh round.

SUMMARY

FIRST PERIOD
1. Florida, Versteeg 18 (Goc) 5:40
2. Florida, Santorelli 6 (Barch, Versteeg) 19:44

Penalties — Antropov Wpg (elbowing) 6:21, Bergenheim Fla (roughing) 7:14, Goc Fla (tripping) 8:14, Barch Fla (Fla (roughing) 11:19

SECOND PERIOD
3. Winnipeg, Antropov 7 (Wellwood) 5:06 (pp)

Penalties —Bergenheim Fla (hooking) 3:51, Slater Wpg (tripping) 7:01, Enstrom Wpg (tripping) 16:54, Bergenheim Fla (boarding) 18:44

THIRD PERIOD
4. Winnipeg, Antropov 8 (Ladd, Wellwood) 5:54
5. Florida, Versteeg 19 6:51
6. Winnipeg, Burmistrov 9 (Enstrom, Miettinen) 13:45

Penalties — None

Overtime
No scoring
Penalties — None

Shootout
Florida wins 3-2
Florida (3) — Weiss, miss; Versteeg, goal; Kopecky, miss; Santorelli, goal; Fleischmann, miss; Goc, miss; Samuelsson, goal. Winnipeg (2) — Little, miss; Wellwood, goal; Ladd, miss; Wheeler, goal; Antropov, miss; Miettinen, miss; Burmistrov, miss

Shots on goal by

Florida	10	7	2	3 —	22
Winnipeg	15	15	10	4 —	44

Goal — Florida: Clemmensen (W,6-2-4); Winnipeg: Pavelec (L,16-17-5)
Power plays (goals-chances) — Florida: 0-3; Winnipeg: 1-5
Referees — Chris Lee, Frederick L'Ecuyer. Linesmen — Michel Cormier, Derek Nansen
Attendance — 15,004 (15,004)

Mike Deal / Winnipeg Free Press
BLAKE WHEELER

49

GAME

AWAY

Monday, January 23, 2012
JETS vs. CAROLINA HURRICANES

CAROLINA 2 / WINNIPEG 1

A lack of firepower came back to bite the Jets in the 2-1 loss to the Hurricanes at RBC Center.

Tim Brent's first-period goal was the difference as Winnipeg, who badly outshot Carolina 30-16, could not find enough offence to at least grab a valuable point.

Canes goalie Cam Ward was sharp, the Jets admitted after the game.

"The one thing I thought Ward was really good at was that he was really aggressive," said Jets coach Claude Noel. "He came out. We almost needed to get pucks on the other side of him by redirecting pucks with somebody in front and somebody off to the side but that's an easier thing said than done.

"He made some big saves... we did everything but score."

Kyle Wellwood scored the lone goal for the Jets. The veteran had a chance to tie the score with two minutes left in the game but fired the puck high on a breakaway.

"I was hoping he'd start leaning down and thought I'd have a shot," Wellwood said. "I somehow got so much under it that it went almost over the glass. That's disappointing."

BIG PICTURE

Another stall, another lost opportunity against a lower-ranked team. The Jets dropped to 7-13-4 on the road and 22-21-6 overall, a record that showed the inconsistency of the club's overall play.

LITTLE PICTURE

Brent's goal from a bad angle at 8:28 of the first shouldn't have been a game-changer. But the Jets, offensively challenged on many nights, didn't have enough against a good goalie (Ward) to come back from a two-goal hole.

JOHNNY ODUYA

Mike Deal / Winnipeg Free Press

SUMMARY

FIRST PERIOD
1. Carolina, Skinner 14 (Gleason) 3:55
2. Carolina, Brent 6 (Stewart) 9:28
Penalties — Ruutu Car (boarding) 0:51

SECOND PERIOD
3. Winnipeg, Wellwood 9 (Enstrom, Antropov) 13:47
Penalties — Jokinen car (tripping) 6:36, Oduya Wpg (interference) 16:14

THIRD PERIOD
No Scoring
Penalties — Slater, Wpg (holding) 10:35, Tlusty Car (tripping) 20:00

Shots on goal by

Winnipeg	6	10	14	—	30
Carolina	7	7	2	—	16

Goal — Winnipeg: Mason (L,6-5-0); Carolina: Ward (W,18-17-8)
Power plays (goals-chances) — Winnipeg: 0-2; Carolina: 0-2
Referees — Don Van Massenhoven, Francois St. Laurent. Linesmen — Scott Cherrey, Darren Gibbs
Attendance — 16,045 (18,680)

N.Y. RANGERS 3 / WINNIPEG 0

FOLLOWING a 3-0 loss to the Rangers at Madison Square Garden, the Jets, shut out again through this January swoon, grew tired of the outcomes.

The wins weren't coming as fast as some players would like.

"This is a results business and trying doesn't mean anything," forward Blake Wheeler said. "We can talk about trying all we want but it doesn't do anything. At a certain point in time, we've got to learn how to translate trying into winning.

"It just seems like when you go through stretches like this, it doesn't matter what you do. You just can't put it in the net. That's just the way hockey goes sometimes. Most of the time you might get one or two guys having that problem, but right now we've got a good majority having that problem."

The Jets were without four regulars against New York (Dustin Byfuglien, Evander Kane, Alex Burmistrov and Tim Stapleton).

Head coach Claude Noel continued to preach positivity.

"Don't lose hope. We will have hope," he said. "There's no doubt about that. We'll get back on track here with our injuries and we'll get things going. We'll try to mend ourselves and go from there."

BIG PICTURE

The Jets reached the .500 mark on Dec. 3 and surged to five games over that mark by Dec. 31. Following this loss to the Rangers, Winnipeg was back at even par, holding a 22-22-6 record.

LITTLE PICTURE

Following the shutout, the Jets had scored just 17 goals in their last 11 games. It was the third time Winnipeg had been blanked in those 11 games and the sixth time this season. The Rangers had goals in each period, from Ryan Callahan, John Mitchell and Brad Richards.

SUMMARY

FIRST PERIOD
1. N.Y. Rangers, Callahan 17 (Stralman, Boyle) 4:05
Penalties — Thorburn Wpg, Rupp NYR (fighting) 6:14

SECOND PERIOD
2. N.Y. Rangers, Mitchell 5 (Del Zotto, Stepan) 13:22
Penalties — Slater Wpg (interference) 0:36, Thorburn Wpg, Rupp NYR (fighting) 5:33, Fehr Wpg (holding) 10:53, Girardi NYR (boarding) 16:43

THIRD PERIOD
3. N.Y. Rangers, Richards 16 (Callahan) 16:22
Penalties — Fehr Wpg (high-sticking) 3:49, Wheeler Wpg (high-sticking) 6:29, Gaborik NYR (interference) 17:05

Shots on goal by

Winnipeg	6	6	10	— 22
New York	11	6	12	— 31

Goal — Winnipeg: Pavelec (L,16-17-6); N.Y. Rangers: Lundqvist (W,22-10-4)
Power plays (goals-chances) — Winnipeg: 0-2; N.Y. Rangers: 0-4
Referees — Eric Furlatt, Rob Martell. Linesmen — Scott Cherrey, Anthony Sericolo
Attendance — 18,200 (18,200)

Joe Bryksa / Winnipeg Free Press

ONDREJ PAVELEC

GAME 51

AWAY

Tuesday, January 31, 2012

JETS vs. PHILADELPHIA FLYERS

WINNIPEG 2 / PHILADELPHIA 1 (SO)

THE Jets gutted out a 2-1 shootout win against the Flyers but the real story circled around Chris Thorburn, who finally ended a lengthy personal drought.

Thorburn went 60 games (dating back to the 2010-11 season) without a goal.

"You know what? I haven't had that feeling in a while," Thorburn said after scoring the Jets' only goal in regulation. "I tell you what, there's not many feelings like that. I actually turned to the corner for my celebration and no one came to me. It kind of felt odd. It was great, it was awesome.

"It's a sense of relief, but at the same time it gives me the confidence to know I can do it. I can get a good shot away and give myself a chance to score. It's not like I haven't been getting chances. Lately, I've been getting a lot of chances, I just haven't been able to find the back of the net."

When it was suggested it was a goal-scorer's goal, Thorburn grinned:

"Thank you. I appreciate that."

Bryan Little scored the only goal in the shootout to give Winnipeg the win.

Goaltender Ondrej Pavelec made 27 saves and stopped all three Flyers forwards in the shootout.

The Jets finished the month with a 4-8-1 record.

BIG PICTURE

Grabbing points — any points — was critical for a Jets team trying to make a post-all-star-game sprint to the post-season. The importance of the fact they picked up a win in Philly — especially given their road and shootout record — couldn't be overstated.

LITTLE PICTURE

Scoring continued to be a problem. One goal in 60 minutes was not the recipe for success for any team. The Jets were fortunate to remain in the playoff hunt following the January swoon.

CHRIS THORBURN

John Woods / Winnipeg Free Press

SUMMARY

FIRST PERIOD
1. Philadelphia, Schenn 4 (Carle, Jagr) 15:11 (pp)
Penalty — Jagr Pha (tripping) 11:04, Thorburn Wpg (roughing) 13:32.

SECOND PERIOD
2. Winnipeg, Thorburn 1 (Antropov, Hainsey) 2:06
Penalties — Meszaros Pha (holding stick) 15:46

THIRD PERIOD
No scoring.
Penalty— Thorburn Wpg, Sestito Pha (fighting) 11:43, Philadelphia bench (too many men; served by Jagr) 15:42

Overtime — No scoring. Penalties — None

Shootout
Winnipeg wins 1-0
Winnipeg (1) — K.Wellwood, miss; Wheeler, miss; Little, goal.
Philadelphia (0) — Couturier, miss; Giroux, miss; Jagr, miss.

Shots on goal by

Winnipeg	7	9	4	4 —	24
Philadelphia	6	7	13	2 —	28

Goal — Winnipeg: Pavelec (W,17-17-6); Philadelphia: Bryzgalov (L,18-10-5)
Power plays (goals-chances) — Winnipeg: 0-3; Philadelphia: 1-1
Referees — Paul Devorski, Brian Pochmara. Linesmen — Lonnie Cameron, Brian Murphy
Attendance — 19,874 (19,537)

52 GAME

AWAY

Thursday, February 2, 2012
JETS vs. TAMPA BAY LIGHTNING

WINNIPEG 2 / TAMPA BAY 1 (OT)

KYLE Wellwood played the hero at the 3:14 mark of overtime, scoring the deciding goal that gave the Jets a 2-1 win over the Lightning at the Tampa Bay Times Forum.

It was the second extra-time 2-1 victory by Winnipeg in as many games. A tough way to live, the players admitted, but one that seemed to be working.

"We have to have the same mentality," Jets winger Blake Wheeler said. "Never quit, never say die is our motto right now. We're going to play you hard for 60 minutes and if you beat us, then hats off to you, but it's going to be tough."

Coach Claude Noel wasn't too concerned with the lack of offence from his club (Winnipeg had just three regulation goals in the last four games).

"I'm not really too concerned with our scoring too much," Noel said. "Can you keep it up? Right now, it's about winning; we're winning some games and that's a good thing."

BIG PICTURE

The Jets picked up a point on the Lightning and moved five points ahead of them in the Eastern Conference standings. More importantly, Winnipeg moved to within four points of eighth-place Toronto, two behind ninth-place Washington and three back of Southeast Division leaders Florida.

LITTLE PICTURE

Netminder Ondrej Pavelec, who had let in just two goals in his last two games, stopped 30 shots for his 18th win of the season.

SUMMARY

FIRST PERIOD
No Scoring.
Penalties — Winnipeg bench (too many men; served by Gagnon) 1:54, Enstrom Wpg (diving), Downie TB (hooking) 4:09, Gilroy TB (cross-checking) 6:52

SECOND PERIOD
1. Winnipeg, Wheeler 10 (Slater, Ladd) 19:44
Penalties — Winnipeg bench (too many men; served by Gagnon) 1:54, Enstrom Wpg (diving), Downie TB (hooking) 4:09, Gilroy TB (cross-checking) 6:52

THIRD PERIOD
2. Tampa Bay, Hedman 3 (St. Louis, Stamkos) 10:34
Penalties — Ladd Wpg (slashing) 15:50

Overtime
3. Winnipeg, Wellwood 10 (Wheeler, Byfuglien) 3:14
Penalties — None

Shots on goal by

Winnipeg	7	7	8	2 —	24
Tampa bay	6	15	10	0 —	31

Goal — Winnipeg: Pavelec (W,18-17-6); Tampa Bay: Garon (L,15-13-3)
Power plays (goals-chances) — Winnipeg: 0-2; Tampa Bay: 0-2
Referees — Greg Kimmerly, Stephen Walkom
Linesmen — Steve Kozari, Frederick L'Ecuyer. Linesmen — Derek Amell, Derek Nansen
Attendance — 16,923 (19,204)

Mike Deal / Winnipeg Free Press

KYLE WELLWOOD

53

GAME

AWAY

Friday, February 3, 2012
JETS vs. FLORIDA PANTHERS

FLORIDA 2 / WINNIPEG 1

ANOTHER game, another 2-1 decision that involved the Jets.

This time against the Panthers, however, Winnipeg came up on the short end of the score, an outcome that led to head coach Claude Noel finally blowing his top.

The lack of production wore on him.

"Our team right now can't give up 20 minutes of free friggin' play and expect that you're going to be able to win the game," an angry and frustrated Noel said afterward. "And I know... don't ask me the same dumb question again, 'Are you concerned about the one-goal (games).' Do I like the one goal we get every game? No. Would I like to see it change? Yes. Do I coach that way? No. But that's what we have and there's still a way to win the games.

"There's no easy way. You've got to pound it through, you've got to get greasy goals and you've got to play 60 minutes. I look at effort and I look at accountability and different things. Our guys are giving us what we got, what they can. We don't have the Crosbys of the world and the Malkins. We've got what we've got and I'm fine with that. Our guys are working."

Bryan Little scored the only goal for the Jets, who fell to 24-23-6 overall.

BIG PICTURE

Even the most gifted defensive NHL team would be hard-pressed to find success averaging one goal per game. The Jets had too many passengers against the Panthers, especially in the first. As Claude Noel put it, he had half a team in the opening 20 minutes.

LITTLE PICTURE

Winnipeg was burned by Kris Versteeg, who scored again against the Jets. A first-period goal gave the Panthers forward eight points in four games.

ANDREW LADD

Mike Deal / Winnipeg Free Press

SUMMARY

FIRST PERIOD
1. Florida, Versteeg 20 (Samuelsson, Campbell) 15:46 (pp)
Penalties — Burmistrov Wpg (slashing) 15:05, Bergenheim Fla (roughing) 18:10

SECOND PERIOD
2. Winnipeg, Little 12 (Ladd) 11:29
3. Florida, Bergenheim 8 (Goc, Garrison) 14:27
Penalties — Burmistrov Wpg (boarding) 4:22, Thorburn Wpg, Barch Fla (fighting) 10:59

THIRD PERIOD
No Scoring
Penalties — Enstrom Wpg (tripping) 13:22

Shots on goal by

Winnipeg	6	8	7	—	21
Florida	10	12	8	—	30

Goal — Winnipeg: Mason (L,6-6-0); Florida: Clemmensen (W,8-2-5)
Power plays (goals-chances) — Winnipeg: 0-1; Florida: 1-3
Referees — Steve Kozari, Dennis LaRue. Linesmen — Steve Barton, Bryan Pancich
Attendance — 16,773 (17,040)

MONTREAL 3 / WINNIPEG 0

54
GAME
AWAY

Sunday, February 5, 2012
JETS vs. MONTREAL CANADIENS

GOALS from Max Pacioretty, Alexei Emelin, and Tomas Plekanec led the Canadiens to a 3-0 win over the Jets at the Bell Centre.

Montreal goaltender Carey Price made 23 saves for the shutout, but he had an easy afternoon. Winnipeg's offence once again struggled to generate any sustained attack.

"Obviously it's frustrating getting the chances we're getting and not being able to put anything in the net," Jets captain Andrew Ladd said. "That's where the frustration level comes from. We get those chances and we have to bear down. It seems like we're fanning on pucks or the puck's jumping... we get a goal there and maybe momentum shifts and it re-energizes us. But we just can't seem to do that right now."

But what did anyone expect? The Jets lineup featured two guys called up from the AHL in Aaron Gagnon and Spencer Machacek — neither with an NHL goal this season — and two others who had yet to score in Antti Miettinen and Ron Hainsey.

Only Kyle Wellwood, Bryan Little, Blake Wheeler and Andrew Ladd had double-digits in goals to this point. The Habs, by comparison, had seven.

"It's frustrating... we can't score goals," Wheeler said.

BIG PICTURE

The Jets played 54 games and had 28 remaining, but with more efforts like this, they would have been out of the picture before April. Listless and lifeless, they failed to close the gap on Washington and idle Florida in the Southeast Division.

LITTLE PICTURE

Winnipeg went 0-for-3 on the power play against Montreal. On this six-game road trip that began before the all-star break, they went 0-for-13.

SUMMARY

FIRST PERIOD

1. Montreal, Pacioretty 19 (Weber, Palushaj) 18:02

Penalties — Byfuglien Wpg (goaltender interference) 3:31, Kostitsyn Mtl (goaltender interference) 9:03

SECOND PERIOD

2. Montreal, Emelin 2 (Plekanec, Darche) 7:20
3. Montreal, Plekanec 11 (Kaberle, Subban) 11:28

Penalties — Darche Mtl (interference) 1:05, Wheeler Wpg (roughing), Kostitsyn Mtl (tripping) 10:12, Wheeler Wpg, Subban Mtl (fighting) 16:05

THIRD PERIOD

No scoring

Penalties —Montreal bench (too many men) 13:25, Stuart Wpg (tripping) 15:03, Bourque Mtl (tripping) 17:58, Byfuglien Wpg (19:07)

- **Shots on goal by**

Winnipeg	7	8	8	—	23
Montreal	11	11	1	—	23

- **Goal** — Winnipeg: Pavelec (L,18-18-6); Montreal: Price (W,18-19-8)
- **Power plays (goals-chances)** — Winnipeg: 0-5; Montreal: 1-3
- **Referees** —Dan O'Rourke, Justin St. Pierre. Linesmen — Don Henderson, Andy McElman
- **Attendance** — 21,273 (21,273)

Mike Deal / Winnipeg Free Press

BLAKE WHEELER

55

GAME

HOME

Tuesday, February 7, 2012
JETS vs. TORONTO MAPLE LEAFS

WINNIPEG 2 / TORONTO 1

THE Jets scored more than one actual goal for only the second time in seven games and beat the Toronto Maple Leafs 2-1 before 15,004 fans at the MTS Centre.

Chris Thorburn and Bryan Little scored for Winnipeg, which improved to 25-24-6 on the season.

"We needed this, especially at home," Jets winger Blake Wheeler said. "It's against a team we're trying to chase. Getting the win is huge but getting it in regulation is better, keeping them off the board."

The Jets held the Leafs to just 18 shots on goaltender Ondrej Pavelec, only the fourth time all season Toronto generated less than 20 shots. Winnipeg put 29 shots towards Leafs netminder Jonas Gustavsson.

"It wasn't a Picasso, but it was a win," Jets coach Claude Noel said. "We're happy about that. Our power play struggled but I thought we looked tired coming off a road trip. I didn't think we gave them a whole ton, but we did some good things. It was a good win for us."

BIG PICTURE

Silly to call it a 'must-win', what with so much hockey yet to be played, but the Jets couldn't afford to slip further from the Eastern Conference/Southeast Division picture and the two points allowed them to keep pace with Washington and Florida.

LITTLE PICTURE

The two goals constituted an eruption for Winnipeg; more impressive was the defensive effort. The Jets limited the Leafs, fifth in the NHL in scoring, to just one goal and 18 shots.

DUSTIN BYFUGLIEN

John Woods / Winnipeg Free Press

SUMMARY

FIRST PERIOD

1. Toronto, Kessel 30 (Lupul) 11:06
2. Winnipeg, Thorburn 2 (Bogosian, Slater) 14:16

Penalty — Antropov Wpg (cross-checking) 6:43

SECOND PERIOD

3. Winnipeg, Little 13 (Wheeler, Oduya) 9:47

Penalty — Kessel Tor (slashing) 2:00

THIRD PERIOD

No scoring

Penalties — Crabb Tor, Oduya Wpg (fighting) 1:54, Burmistrov Wpg (high-sticking) 10:17, Crabb Tor (holding) 13:10

Shots on goal by

Toronto	6	7	5	— 18
Winnipeg	9	8	12	— 29

Goal — Toronto: Gustavsson (L,16-11-1); Winnipeg: Pavelec (W,19-18-6)

Power plays (goals-chances) — Toronto: 0-2; Winnipeg: 0-2

Referees — Mike Leggo, Brad Meier. Linesmen — Mike Cvik, Mark Wheler

Attendance — 15,004 (15,004)

WINNIPEG 3 / WASHINGTON 2 (SO)

56

GAME

AWAY

Thursday, February 9, 2012
JETS vs. WASHINGTON CAPITALS

TWO goals in the last three minutes — plus a little bit of luck thrown in for good measure — pushed the Jets to a 3-2 shootout victory over the Capitals at a stunned Verizon Center.

Down 2-0 and in serious danger of falling further out of the playoff picture in the Eastern Conference, Evander Kane and Dustin Byfuglien found the back of the net for Winnipeg in the waning moments. Overtime solved nothing, and Blake Wheeler and Bryan Little scored in a shootout.

Byfuglien's goal, coming with two minutes and three seconds remaining, was fortunate.

His blast into the Washington zone clipped a defenceman's stick and caught goaltender Thomas Vokoun out of position; some much-needed puck luck for a Jets club that hadn't had much of late.

"It's what a team always needs, good luck and some bounces," Byfuglien said. "I thought we've worked hard lately and haven't really got a nice bounce. We got one tonight."

Jets netminder Ondrej Pavelec was excellent in the Winnipeg net. He stopped 32 shots — plus two out of the three Caps chances in the shootout — for his 20th win.

BIG PICTURE
The two points pulled the Jets to within three of the Southeast Division lead, at that point shared by both Washington and Florida at 61 points. The Jets also moved closer to the eighth spot in the Eastern Conference, four back of the Toronto Maple Leafs.

LITTLE PICTURE
Kane scored his 19th goal. This was noteworthy as it snapped a personal 11-game scoring drought. On a team suffering for offence, his breakthrough was welcomed.

SUMMARY

FIRST PERIOD
No Scoring
Penalties — None

SECOND PERIOD
No Scoring
Penalties — Bogosian Wpg (holding) 12:28

THIRD PERIOD
1. Washington, Ovechkin 23 (Semin, Wideman) 9:46 (pp)
2. Washington, Semin 14 (Ovechkin, Wideman) 12:30 (pp)
3. Winnipeg, Kane 19 (Ladd, Byfuglien) 17:45 (pp)
4. Winnipeg, Byfuglien 7, 17:57 (pp)

Penalties — Halpern Wash (hooking) 5:02, Enstrom Wpg (slashing) 9:36, Little Wpg (double high-sticking) 12:18, Hamrlik Wash (slashing) 15:55, Laich Wash (broken stick) 17:0

Overtime
No Scoring
Penalties — Byfuglien Wpg (tripping) 4:42, Glass Wpg (slashing) 5:00

Shootout
Winnipeg wins 2-1
Winnipeg (2) — Wheeler, goal; Little, goal. Washington (1) — Ovechkin, goal; Semin, miss; Perreault, miss

Shots on goal by

Winnipeg	4	11	11	1	— 27
Washington	12	12	8	2	— 34

Goal — Winnipeg: Pavelec (W,20-18-6); Washington: Vokoun (L,22-13-2)
Power plays (goals-chances) — Winnipeg: 2-3; Washington: 2-5
Referees — Stephen Walkom, Rob Martell. Linesmen — Dan Schachte, Matt MacPherson
Attendance — 18,506 (18,398)

Mike Deal / Winnipeg Free Press
EVANDER KANE

PITTSBURGH 8 / WINNIPEG 5

THE Jets scored five goals for the first time in 25 games but were no match for the Penguins, who subdued them easily, 8-5, at Consol Energy Center.

NHL scoring leader Evgeni Malkin had five points in the game. The Jets, meanwhile, had no answers during or after the contest.

"It wasn't just one thing or one guy or the 'D' or the forwards, it was everything," winger Blake Wheeler said. "We haven't been able to score goals and all of a sudden we score five and give up eight. It's frustrating and it's a mystery in that sense."

Jets defenceman Ron Hainsey was a little more concise in the post-game evaluation.

"Let's get past the BS," he said. "We got outplayed, didn't do enough to win. It would be really hard to go over the whole thing. You just cut through most of the BS (and say) we just gave up way too much close to our net and gave up eight goals. Very difficult to overcome."

Zach Bogosian said he felt bad for goalie Ondrej Pavelec, who stayed in for all eight against.

"That's not the game we wanted to have and it's obviously embarrassing. And to leave your goaltender out to dry like that is embarrassing."

BIG PICTURE

The Jets registered five goals, which counted for something. Kyle Wellwood, Alex Burmistrov, Tim Stapleton, Dustin Byfuglien and Bryan Little all scored for Winnipeg. Though he gave up eight, Pavelec still made 31 saves.

LITTLE PICTURE

The Jets allowed the Pens too many odd-man rushes and pretty plays. Evgeni Malkin had five points (1G, 4A) and Chris Kunitz had four (1G, 3A). Together with James Neal, that line was deadly.

ALEX BURMISTROV

Mike Deal / Winnipeg Free Press

SUMMARY

FIRST PERIOD
1. Winnipeg, Wellwood 11 (Enstrom, Byfuglien) 5:17
2. Winnipeg, Burmistrov 10 (Miettinen, Stapleton) 8:04
3. Pittsburgh, Jeffrey 3 (Staal, Letang) 12:11
4. Pittsburgh, Neal 29 (Malkin) 16:42

Penalties — Letang Pgh (holding stick) 17:54

SECOND PERIOD
5. Pittsburgh, Kunitz 15 (Malkin, Fleury) 3:12 (pp)
6. Pittsburgh, Letang 6 (Malkin, Kunitz) 9:53
7. Winnipeg, Stapleton 8 (Wheeler) 14:19
8. Pittsburgh, Malkin 30 (Kunitz, Neal) 17:08

Penalties — Thorburn Wpg (roughing) 2:01, Enstrom Wpg (tripping) 11:33

THIRD PERIOD
9. Winnipeg, Byfuglien 8 (Little, Wheeler) 4:35
10. Pittsburgh, Park 5 (Orpik, Adams) 4:54
11. Pittsburgh, Staal 16 (Dupuis, Cooke) 7:48
12. Winnipeg, Little 14 (Hainsey, Bogosian) 10:02
13. Pittsburgh, Letang 7 (Malkin, Kunitz) 17:16 (pp)

Penalties — Ladd Wpg (slashing) 16:57

Shots on goal by

Winnipeg	10	4	11	—	25
Pittsburgh	14	15	10	—	39

Goal — Winnipeg: Pavelec (L,20-19-6); Pittsburgh: Fleury (W,29-13-3)

Power plays (goals-chances) — Buffalo: 0-2; Winnipeg: 2-3

Referees — Eric Furlatt, Stephane Auger. Linesmen — Derek Amell, Mark Shewchyk

Attendance — 18,602 (18,387)

N.Y. ISLANDERS 3 / WINNIPEG 1

THE numbers were disappointing.

As the Jets stumbled again against a club below them in the standings — a 3-1 loss to the Islanders at the MTS Centre this time around — a truth was evident.

The team wasn't going to win a whole lot of games scoring one goal.

"It hasn't been easy for us lately," forward Tanner Glass said afterwards. "Guys are working hard and trying to get to those areas and battling and I know the guys who are offensive guys are frustrated. But they're working really hard. It's tough to say what we've got to do to get out of it. All we can do is come to the rink and keep working."

The loss to the Isles marked the 21st time this season (in 58 games) — and the ninth time in the 20 games since the calendar turned to 2012 — the Jets scored one measly goal.

"Of course I would be more happy if we scored some more goals, but you have to deal with it," Jets goaltender Ondrej Pavelec said. "You have to be patient and hopefully it's going to change. Those games, at the end of the year, would be a big difference."

Winnipeg fired 38 shots at Evgeni Nabokov. Chris Thorburn was the only Jet to beat the Russian netminder; his first-period goal opened the scoring in the contest.

Big picture
Another missed opportunity for the Jets. This loss came on a night in which Ottawa, seventh in the East, pulled further ahead with a win over Tampa while Toronto, eighth in the conference, lost to Calgary.

Little picture
Down 2-1 early in the third, the Jets were handed two power-play chances but did little with them. Head coach Claude Noel talked about winning the puck battles with the man advantage, but it was the visitors who came out victorious in most of those situations.

58 GAME

HOME

Tuesday, February 14, 2012
JETS vs. NEW YORK ISLANDERS

SUMMARY

FIRST PERIOD
1. Winnipeg, Thorburn 3 (Slater, Glass) 17:50

Penalties — None

SECOND PERIOD
2. N.Y. Islanders, Moulson 25 (Tavares) 3:55 (pp)

Penalties — Wheeler Wpg (tripping) 3:32, Grabner NYI (slashing), Bogosian Wpg (cross-checking) 8:26, Parenteau NYI (diving), Antropov Wpg (interference) 14:17, Tavares NYI (delay of game) 18:03

THIRD PERIOD
3. N.Y. Islanders, Parenteau 12 (Jurcina, Rolston) 1:36
4. N.Y. Islanders, Martin 7 (Parenteau) 19:07 (en)

Penalties — Rolston NYI (tripping) 5:50, Parenteau NYI (cross-checking) 11:26

Shots on goal by

New York	10	7	8	—	25
Winnipeg	16	10	12	—	38

Goal — N.Y. Islanders: Nabokov (W,14-14-0); Winnipeg: Pavelec (L,20-20-6)

Power plays (goals-chances) — N.Y. Islanders: 1-1; Winnipeg: 0-3

Referees — Greg Kimmerly, Stephen Walkom. Linesmen — Don Henderson, Vaughan Rody

Attendance — 15,004 (15,004)

John Woods / Winnipeg Free Press

ANDREW LADD

59
GAME
AWAY
Thursday, February 16, 2012
JETS vs. MINNESOTA WILD

WINNIPEG 4 / MINNESOTA 3 (SO)

EVANDER Kane scored two goals, added an assist and scored the winner in a shootout, as he led the Jets to a 4-3 win over the Wild at Xcel Energy Center.

Kane's goals — his 20th and 21st to this point of the season — helped Winnipeg get to the extra breakaway session and once there, he finished off his pseudo-hat trick.

A fan threw a hat on the ice to mark the occasion — though it came down from the stands BEFORE his shootout attempt.

"I was thinking that it was good that somebody was thinking that I was going to score," Kane said after the game. "I knew what I wanted to do and I stuck to it. I'm a shooter and I was able to pick the corner."

Jets goaltender Chris Mason made 22 stops in regulation time and three more during the shootout.

"This is really big," Mason said. "We're all aware we haven't been as good as we wanted to be on the road, so any time we can pick one up and start building confidence is huge."

The Jets (27-26-6) played before thousands of Jets fans who made the eight-hour drive to the Twin Cities.

"It's always fun to go on the road and know your team travels well and see them make the game not so fun for the home crowd, maybe stir things up a little bit," Jets forward Blake Wheeler said.

BIG PICTURE

The shootout win pulled Winnipeg to 60 points, four points back of Toronto in the eighth spot of the Eastern Conference and only five back of division-leading Florida.

LITTLE PICTURE

Evander Kane's two goals gave him a team-leading 21 on the year. More importantly, he showed signs of being the difference-maker everyone projected him to be at the start of the season.

EVANDER KANE

Mike Deal / Winnipeg Free Press

SUMMARY

FIRST PERIOD
1. Minnesota, Setoguchi 13 (Koivu, Heatley) 7:50
2. Winnipeg, Kane 20 (Wheeler, Byfuglien) 18:47

Penalties — Koivu Minn (hooking) 0:25, Thorburn Wpg (high-sticking) 11:17

SECOND PERIOD
3. Winnipeg, Kane 21 (Wellwood, Burmistrov) 3:00
4. Minnesota, Setoguchi 14 (Prosser, Scandella) 12:15 (pp)

Penalties — Stapleton Wpg (high-sticking) 10:32, Byfuglien Wpg (roughing), Peters Minn (unsportsmanlike conduct) 13:08, Winnipeg bench (too many men; served by Stapleton) 14:41

THIRD PERIOD
5. Minnesota, Koivu 10 (Spurgeon, Setoguchi) 1:03
6. Winnipeg, Burmistrov 11 (Byfuglien, Kane) 3:03

Penalties — Lundin Minn (interference) 6:15, Slater Wpg (roughing), Glass Wpg, Powe Minn (fighting), Clutterbuck Minn (unsportsmanlike conduct, roughing) 8:48

Overtime
No Scoring
Penalties — None

Shootout
Winnipeg wins 2-1
Winnipeg (2) — Wheeler, goal; Wellwood, miss; Little, miss; Kane, goal.
Minnesota (1) — Cullen, miss; Koivu, miss; Christensen, goal; Heatley, miss

Shots on goal by

Winnipeg	8	11	6	2	—	27
Minnesota	6	3	14	2	—	25

Goal — Winnipeg: Mason (W,7-6-0); Minnesota: Backstrom (L,14-15-6)

Power plays (goals-chances) — Winnipeg: 0-3; Minnesota: 1-3

Referees — Greg Kimmerly, Chris Lee. Linesmen — Darren Gibbs, Mike Cvik

Attendance — 19,060 (18,064)

WINNIPEG 4 / BOSTON 2

TWO third-period goals from centre Bryan Little lifted the Jets to a 4-2 win over the Bruins at the MTS Centre.

The win improved the 10th-place Jets to 28-26-6, one point behind Washington — who knocked off Florida — and two back of idle Toronto in the Eastern Conference standings. It also kicked off a stretch of eight straight games in downtown Winnipeg for the hockey club.

"It seemed like in the third we found another gear," Little said after scoring the game-winning goal. "And after we got that lead I thought we played our best hockey. We shut them down, we did a good job of managing the puck and not making mistakes.

"To beat a team like Boston... these points mean a lot to us in the standings. We need to keep winning these games at home."

Alex Burmistrov and Blake Wheeler also scored for the Jets. Goaltender Ondrej Pavelec was instrumental in the victory over the defending Stanley Cup champs, making 31 saves — 13 of those coming in a scoreless first period.

"It's going to be a huge two weeks for us," Pavelec said. "It's nice to be home. We feel comfortable here, but it's going to be tough. It's going to be a huge two weeks for us. We're finally going to be home for eight games and we need to win."

BIG PICTURE

The Jets began an eight-game homestand with a win and enjoyed a 17-9-2 record in downtown Winnipeg to this point. Home cooking was a big factor in keeping the club close to the playoff line.

LITTLE PICTURE

All the talk before the game was how the Jets were 0-9 in the second half of back-to-back contests this season. Not only was that monkey off their backs, the club had some momentum thanks to a two-game win streak.

SUMMARY

FIRST PERIOD
No Scoring
Penalties — None

SECOND PERIOD
1. Winnipeg, Burmistrov 12 (Stuart) 1:59
2. Boston, Caron 3 (Kelly) 6:10
3. Winnipeg, Wheeler 11 (Byfuglien, Kane) 15:50

Penalties — Kane Wpg (elbowing) 13:20

THIRD PERIOD
4. Boston, Krejci 12 (Seguin, Lucic) 0:49
5. Winnipeg, Little 15 (Wheeler, Ladd) 4:16
6. Winnipeg, Little 16 (Wheeler, Enstrom 6:20

Penalties — Little Wpg (hooking) 1:43, Hennessy Bos, Stuart Wpg (roughing) 9:38, Kelly Bos (charging) 10:33

Shots on goal by

Boston	13	8	12	—	33
Winnipeg	4	9	12	—	25

Goal — Boston: Rask (L,11-8-2); Winnipeg: Pavelec (W,21-20-6)
Power plays (goals-chances) — Boston: 0-2; Winnipeg: 0-2
Referees — Justin St. Pierre, Dan O'Halloran. Linesmen — Lonnie Cameron, Steve Miller
Attendance — 15,004 (15,004)

Ruth Bonneville / Winnipeg Free Press

CHRIS THORBURN

61

GAME

HOME

Sunday, February 19, 2012
JETS vs. COLORADO AVALANCHE

WINNIPEG 5 / COLORADO 1

TAKE a bow, Blake Wheeler.

The big winger had four assists in the Jets' dominating 5-1 win over the Avalanche at the MTS Centre, production that gave him 46 points (11 goals and 35 helpers) at this juncture of the season. Remember, Wheeler went 18 games without scoring to open the year.

"I really am not wrapped up in the individual-statistics thing," Winnipeg's point leader said. "Our whole line's playing really well. When we were put together after the all-star break, we made a conscious effort to try and make this thing work, similar to how we did last year in Atlanta. I think we're going really well right now. We're trying to win puck battles and keep things simple, and it's turning into some good chances for us and translating into some big goals."

The Jets scored 12 goals in their last three games, with the Top 6 forward group of Wheeler, Andrew Ladd, Bryan Little, Evander Kane, Alex Burmistrov and Kyle Wellwood accounting for all 12 and racking up 29 points combined.

"That's good. That's more fun," head coach Claude Noel said. "But what you have to be careful of is you start thinking you're a five-, six-goal team every night. You're always fearful of overconfidence. It seems every time I feel good about things, I'm fearful about something else."

BIG PICTURE

The Jets scored two third-period power-play goals (they were 2-for-5 on the night) and ended a four-game drought that saw the unit go 0-for-9.

LITTLE PICTURE

The Little-Ladd-Wheeler line combined for three goals and eight points and the second line of Kane-Burmistrov-Wellwood scored twice and finished with five points. That was huge production from the Top 6 forward group.

BIG WIN VS AVS

John Woods / Winnipeg Free Press

SUMMARY

FIRST PERIOD
No Scoring
Penalty — Stastny Col (double high-sticking) 14:28

SECOND PERIOD
1. Winnipeg, Kane 22 (Burmistrov, Wellwood) 1:45
2. Winnipeg, Little 17 (Ladd, Wheeler) 3:30
3. Colorado, Landeskog 15 (Johnson) 10:42 (pp)
4. Winnipeg, Wellwood 12 (Kane, Wheeler) 11:28

Penalties — Thorburn Wpg (hooking) 6:11, Byfuglien Wpg (hooking) 8:52, Antropov Wpg (interference) 17:31

THIRD PERIOD
5. Winnipeg, Ladd 17 (Wheeler, Byfuglien) 5:40 (pp)
6. Winnipeg, Little 18 (Wheeler, Byfuglien) 15:41 (pp)

Penalty — Duchane Col (hooking) 0:27, McLeod Col (holding) 4:16, Kane Wpg (double roughing) 7:45, Quincey Col (cross-checking) 9:31, McLeod Col (interference, fighting) Thorburn Wpg (fighting) 14:52

Shots on goal by

Colorado	6	20	6	—	32
Winnipeg	6	8	11	—	25

Goal — Colorado: Varlamov (L,15-18-2); Winnipeg: Pavelec (W,22-20-6)
Power plays (goals-chances) — Colorado: 1-5; Winnipeg: 2-5
Referees — Tom Kowal, Brian Pochmara. Linesmen — Lonnie Cameron, Scott Cherrey
Attendance — 15,004 (15,004)

PHILADELPHIA 5 / WINNIPEG 4 (OT)

IF you wanted a picture of what it looks like to have your heart torn from your chest and be kicked in the private parts all at once, the Jets provided a decent portrait following a 5-4 overtime loss to the Flyers at the MTS Centre.

"It's obviously a pretty crappy feeling," captain Andrew Ladd said. "You're in control of the game, you've got a chance to pick two big points up and you only end up with one. I guess 'disappointment' is the word."

Flyers forward Wayne Simmonds scored with 10 seconds left in the third period to tie the game and Jaromir Jagr won it with 43.6 seconds remaining in the extra session. The Jets allowed the two points to shrink to one and failed to move into first place in the Southeast Division.

"What do you want to say after a game like that? What do you want to do? How demoralized do you want to get? What do you want to do... go home and put the knives and ropes away? There's another day tomorrow, we've got another game coming up. We're going to have to pick our bootstraps up and play," Jets head coach Claude Noel said.

Goaltender Ondrej Pavelec was excellent in the Jets net. He stopped 50 of 55 shots, including 17 of 18 in a hectic third period.

BIG PICTURE

The point earned put the Jets at 65 points and right in the middle of the playoff hunt. Literally, right in the middle. Winnipeg moved into a tie with Southeast Division-leading Florida and into a tie with Toronto for eighth spot in the conference.

LITTLE PICTURE

Andrew Ladd scored twice; Evander Kane and Dustin Byfuglien had singles for the Jets. Claude Giroux, Scott Hartnell and Maxime Talbot had the other goals for the Flyers.

62 GAME

HOME

Tuesday, February 21, 2012
JETS vs. PHILADELPHIA FLYERS

SUMMARY

FIRST PERIOD
1. Winnipeg, Byfuglien 9 (Stapleton, Little) 12:31 (pp)
2. Philadelphia, Giroux 23 (Hartnell, Carle) 15:50

Penalties — Burmistrov Wpg (high-sticking) 8:59, Talbot Pha (cross-checking) 12:04

SECOND PERIOD
3. Philadelphia, Hartnell 28 (Simmonds, Timonen) 1:08 (pp)
4. Winnipeg, Ladd 18 (Wheeler, Stapleton) 7:52 (pp)
5. Winnipeg, Ladd 19 (Little, Byfuglien) 8:56
6. Philadelphia, Talbot 17 (Meszaros, Grossman) 11:14

Penalties — Enstrom Wpg (interference) 0:57, Coburn Pha (hooking) 6:34

THIRD PERIOD
7. Winnipeg, Kane 23 (Stapleton) 4:57 (pp)
8. Philadelphia, Simmonds 22 (van Riemsdyk, Giroux) 19:50

Penalties — Briere Pha (tripping) 3:59, Read Pha (roughing), Slater Wpg (double roughing) 11:39

Overtime
9. Philadelphia, Jagr 16 (Briere) 4:16

Penalties — None

Shots on goal by

Philadelphia	15	16	18	6 —	55
Winnipeg	10	10	5	1 —	26

Goal — Philadelphia: Bryzgalov (W,21-11-6); Winnipeg: Pavelec (L,22-21-6)

Power plays (goals-chances) — Philadelphia: 1-3; Winnipeg: 3-3

Referees — Brad Meier, Kelly Sutherland. Linesmen — Scott Cherrey, Shane Heyer

Attendance — 15,004 (15,004)

John Woods / Winnipeg Free Press

ANDREW LADD

63

GAME

HOME

Thursday, February 23, 2012
JETS vs. TAMPA BAY LIGHTNING

WINNIPEG 4 / TAMPA BAY 3

THANKS to a 4-3 win over the Lightning, the Jets, a team that battled to get above the playoff line, finally took the leap they had been trying to make all season.

The victory put Winnipeg (30-26-7, 67 points) into sole possession of first place the Southeast and into third place in the conference as a division leader. Though other clubs had multiple games in hand on the Jets, players were pleased with their standing at this point.

"It's nice to be above (the playoff line), but we understand we still have a long way to go," captain Andrew Ladd. "We're not going to be happy until the season's over and we're above the line. We need to keep taking advantage of playing at home here and playing some good hockey.

"We're scoring goals, our power play is clicking, but at the end of the day we've got 19 games left and we've got to keep going."

Ladd scored two goals and added an assist in the contest and extended his point streak to four games (5G, 3A). Blake Wheeler and Dustin Byfuglien both registered two-point nights.

The Jets went 2-for-3 on the power play but had their consecutive PPG streak stopped at seven when they failed to convert an opportunity in the third period.

Big picture

The Jets grabbed points in five straight games (4-0-1) and had scored at least three goals over that span. The club continued to roll at the MTS Centre: 19 wins in 31 games in downtown Winnipeg.

Little picture

There were some tense moments at the end of the game when the Lightning, who trailed 4-1, scored two quick goals in a 45-second blink of the eye during the last minute of play. Eventually, the Jets ran the visitors out of time.

ONDREJ PAVELEC, RON HAINSEY

Phil Hossack / Winnipeg Free Press

SUMMARY

FIRST PERIOD
1. Winnipeg, Ladd 20 (Little, Wheeler) 7:11
2. Winnipeg, Glass 5 (Thorburn, Flood) 14:59

Penalties — None

SECOND PERIOD
3. Winnipeg, Ladd 21 (Kane, Byfuglien) 1:36 (pp)
4. Winnipeg, Byfuglien 10 (Wheeler, Ladd) 2:48 (pp)

Penalties — Hedman TB (delay of game) 0:14, Malone TB (interference) 2:39, Byfuglien Wpg (roughing) 8:15, Hedman TB, Wheeler Wpg (roughing) 13:49

THIRD PERIOD
5. Tampa Bay, Stamkos 43 (Malone, Purcell) 11:00 (pp)
6. Tampa Bay, Purcell 16 (Stamkos) 19:06
7. Tampa Bay, St. Louis 19 (Purcell, Stamkos) 19:51 (pp)

Penalties — Wheeler Wpg (cross-checking) 0:12, Stapleton Wpg (tripping) 3:08, Kane Wpg (slashing) 10:13, Gilroy TB (tripping) 16:14, Malone TB (roughing), Glass Wpg (cross-checking; served by Stapleton), Glass Wpg (roughing) 19:43

Shots on goal by

Tampa Bay	9	6	10	—	25
Winnipeg	16	10	8	—	34

Goal — Tampa Bay: Garon (L,19-16-4)(18-14), Roloson (2:48 second; 16-16); Winnipeg: Pavelec (W,23-20-7)

Power plays (goals-chances) — Tampa Bay: 2-5; Winnipeg: 2-3

Referees — Ghislain Hebert, Kelly Sutherland. Linesmen — Shane Heyer, Thor Nelson

Attendance — 15,004 (15,004)

ST. LOUIS 3 / WINNIPEG 2 (SO)

CLAUDE Noel didn't mince words after he watched his club drop a hard-fought 3-2 shootout loss to the Blues at the MTS Centre.

"I thought Blake Wheeler was the best player on the ice for both teams, by far," Noel said. "He was really good. He was dangerous all the time and he's a hard man to control when he skates like that. He's got reach... he dings one off the post, scores two... that's a heckuva 'A' game for me.

"What I really liked, is when you see the growth of a young player like him coming into his own, that's the fun part when you watch that."

Wheeler, who, as mentioned, scored both Winnipeg goals, extended his point streak to six games (3G, 10A) and had the crowd chanting his name — "Whee-ler! Whee-ler!" — in the shootout (he was the only Jet to score on Jaro Halak).

"That was awesome," Wheeler said. "No matter how many times you've gone in those things, you're always a little nervous going in there. But I heard them chanting my name and had a pretty good feeling going in."

BIG PICTURE

Winnipeg was five games into a crucial eight-game homestand and things looked good. Eight out of a possible 10 points kept the Jets in the playoff conversation with fewer than 20 games to play.

LITTLE PICTURE

Halak was the difference. In the shootout, Wheeler scored first, but the Blues netminder shut the door on Bryan Little, Evander Kane and Andrew Ladd. St. Louis got shootout goals by Andy McDonald and David Perron.

SUMMARY

FIRST PERIOD
1. St. Louis, Backes 18 (Oshie, McDonald) 7:43
2. St. Louis, Perron 12 (Berglund, Oshie) 19:14

Penalties — None

SECOND PERIOD
3. Winnipeg, Wheeler 12 (Kane, Byfuglien) 7:19
4. Winnipeg, Wheeler 13 (Ladd, Byfuglien) 15:14

Penalties — Burmistrov Wpg (hooking) 4:49, Reaves StL (tripping) 8:53, St. Louis bench (too many men; served by Stewart) 11:06

THIRD PERIOD
No Scoring
Penalties — None

Overtime
No Scoring
Penalties — None

Shootout
St. Louis wins 2-1
Winnipeg (1) — Wheeler, goal; Little, miss; Kane, miss; Ladd, miss; St. Louis (2) — McDonald, goal; Oshie, miss; Shattenkirk, miss; Perron, goal

Shots on goal by

St. Louis	6	4	6	0 —	23
Winnipeg	16	17	8	0 —	23

Goal — St. Louis: Halak (W,18-10-5); Winnipeg: Mason (SOL,7-6-1

Power plays (goals-chances) — St. Louis: 0-1; Winnipeg: 0-2

Referees — Stephane Auger, Don Van Massenhoven. Linesmen — Michael Cormier, Brad Lazarowich

Attendance — 15,004 (15,004)

Trevor Hagan / Winnipeg Free Press

EVANDER KANE

EDMONTON 5 / WINNIPEG 3

THE Jets appeared flat, listless, dull — use any descriptor that suggests sleepy disinterest — in a 5-3 loss to the Oilers at the MTS Centre, a score that flattered the home side.

Edmonton scored four times in the third period and pulled out the positive result. The Jets, meanwhile, couldn't find any explanation for the poor showing.

"It stings, coming off a good homestand so far (now 3-1-2)," Kyle Wellwood said. "I wouldn't say we were looking ahead, but we didn't have our best game. There's reasons you look at it and say why. It could have been the trade deadline and guys feeling comfortable and not giving enough effort."

Earlier in the day, the NHL trade deadline came and went. The Jets made one deal, as they shipped defenceman Johnny Oduya to Chicago for draft picks.

"I guess we felt too good about ourselves coming out for the third period," Nik Antropov said, "and that's why they made us pay for it. We came out flat. They played a pretty good game, so you've got to give them credit for that."

Wellwood, Antropov and Alex Burmistrov scored for Winnipeg.

BIG PICTURE

This was a missed opportunity. Winnipeg (68 points) remained in a playoff spot but they had played more games than anyone else. Both Washington (67 points) and Toronto (65 points) had three games in hand on the Jets.

LITTLE PICTURE

The Oilers handed the Jets their first regulation loss in seven games, a stretch where Winnipeg picked up 10 of a possible 12 points.

CHRIS THORBURN

John Woods / Winnipeg Free Press

SUMMARY

FIRST PERIOD
No scoring
Penalty — None

SECOND PERIOD
1. Winnipeg, Wellwood 13 (Antropov, Burmistrov) 15:45 (pp)
2. Edmonton, Whitney 2 (Hall, Dubnyk) 18:13 (pp)
3. Winnipeg, Burmistrov 13 (Byfuglien) 19:27

Penalty — Byfuglien Wpg (holding the stick) 5:21, Hall Edm (hooking) 14:00, Kane Wpg (roughing) 17:51, Hall Edm (unsportsmanlike conduct), Little Wpg (roughing) 18:29

THIRD PERIOD
4. Edmonton, Jones 14 (Nugent-Hopkins, Hemsky) 1:54 (pp)
5. Edmonton, Petrell 4 2:29
6. Edmonton, Hall 23 (Petrell) 9:24
7. Edmonton, Eberle 28 (Smyth, Smid) 17:34
8. Winnipeg, Antropov 9 (Kane, Byfuglien) 18:50 (pp)

Penalties — Wheeler Wpg (high-sticking) 0:34, Petrell Edm (closing hand on puck) 13:54, Jones Edm (interference) 17:52

Shots on goal by

Edmonton	12	4	9	—	25
Winnipeg	7	10	13	—	30

Goal — Edmonton: Dubnyk (W,13-15-1); Winnipeg: Pavelec (L,23-21-7)
Power plays (goals-chances) — Edmonton: 2-3; Winnipeg: 2-3
Referees — Don VanMassenhoven, Tim Peel. Linesmen — Brad Lazarowich, Mark Wheler
Attendance — 15,004 (15,004)

WINNIPEG 7 / FLORIDA 0

THE Jets throttled the Panthers 7-0 in a one-sided thumping that had the MTS Centre rattling from the rafters to its very foundation.

The win pushed Winnipeg's record to 31-27-8 and vaulted them back into the playoff race.

As the players turned in a solid outing on the ice, the fans were also in top form. A "We want first place! We want first place!" chant in the third period — a period that saw Winnipeg score five times — was particularly noteworthy.

"You could tell there was an extra little buzz around the city with everything on the line," winger Blake Wheeler said. "I think they want first place — they made that clear tonight, too — and that was great. Our team definitely had that feeling in our locker-room and to go out there on the ice and get the same feeling from the fans was a huge lift for us and it helped us, especially early on."

Evander Kane led the Jets with four points on two goals and two assists. The other scores came from Kyle Wellwood, Bryan Little, Jim Slater and Nik Antropov, while Ondrej Pavelec kicked out 33 shots for his fourth shutout of the season.

BIG PICTURE

The win gave the Jets a 4-1-2 record in this eight-game homestand. The romp over the first-place Panthers pushed Winnipeg two points away from the division lead, over idle Washington and back into eighth spot in the conference.

LITTLE PICTURE

How impressive was the offence this night? Thirteen skaters — five players short of the whole bench — registered at least a point against Florida.

SUMMARY

FIRST PERIOD

1. Winnipeg, Kane 25, 4:01
2. Winnipeg, Slater 9 (Stuart, Thorburn) 6:03

Penalties — Fleischmann Fla (hooking) 0:30

SECOND PERIOD

No Scoring

Penalties — Stapleton Wpg (hooking) 3:56

THIRD PERIOD

3. Winnipeg, Wellwood 14, (Stuart, Kane) 1:49
4. Winnipeg, Little 19 (Wheeler, Jones) 4:35
5. Winnipeg, Antropov 10 (Bogosian, Enstrom) 8:06 (pp)
6. Winnipeg, Kane 26 (Wellwood, Burmistrov) 8:18
7. Winnipeg, Wheeler 14 (Kane, Stapleton) 17:58

Penalties — Jovanovski Fla (slashing) 6:46, Gudbranson Fla (roughing), Stuart Wpg (double roughing, misconduct) 10:51, Antropov Wpg (holding) 15:21, Skille Fla (cross-checking) 19:21

Shots on goal by

Florida	7	17	9	—	33
Winnipeg	13	8	10	—	31

Goal (shot-saves) — Florida: Theodore (L,17-12-6)(24-20), Clemmensen (4:35 third, 7-4; Winnipeg: Pavelec (W,24-21-7)

Power plays (goals-chances) — Florida: 0-3; Winnipeg: 1-3

Referees — Greg Kimmerly, Dennis LaRue. Linesmen — Brian Mach, Vaughan Rody

Attendance — 15,004 (15,004)

Phil Hossack / Winnipeg Free Press

BRYAN LITTLE

67

GAME

HOME

Monday, March 5, 2012
JETS vs. BUFFALO SABRES

WINNIPEG 3 / BUFFALO 1

BLAKE Wheeler beat goaltender Ryan Miller on a breakaway eight minutes into the third that snapped a tie game and gave the Jets a 3-1 victory over the Sabres.

The goal, which clanged off the crossbar and into the net, nearly blew the roof off the MTS Centre.

"The scouting report has kind of been that Miller's unbeatable (of late), but if you're going to beat him, you've got to try to go over the shoulder," Wheeler said. "You always feel fortunate scoring on a goalie like him. He's probably the best in the league right now. It felt good when it went in.

"Hopefully there's bigger ones to come."

Winnipeg concluded its eight-game homestand with a record of 5-1-2. Overall, the Jets improved to 32-27-8, good for 72 points and the eighth spot in the Eastern Conference.

"We did a great job of taking advantage of this homestand," centre Bryan Little said. "We did a great job of getting points we needed. We didn't play easy teams. Hopefully we can take that on the road with us."

Netminder Ondrej Pavelec made 23 saves in the Jets net.

BIG PICTURE

The win kept the Jets in eighth place in the conference, now three points clear of Washington and four ahead of the Sabres and Tampa Bay. Just as important, first-place Florida remained two points ahead of the Jets.

LITTLE PICTURE

The Jets had given up the tying goal with 34.8 seconds left in the second, but the critical, game-changing play came on the Wheeler goal. It was highlight-of-the-year material.

CELEBRATING A TERRIFIC HOMESTAND

John Woods / Winnipeg Free Press

SUMMARY

FIRST PERIOD
1. Winnipeg, Ladd 21 (Little) 13:45
Penalties — None

SECOND PERIOD
2. Buffalo, Tropp 2 (Ellis, Boyes) 19:25
Penalty — Slater Wpg (boarding) 5:58, Ladd Wpg (hooking) 8:33, Myers Buf (tripping) 14:01

THIRD PERIOD
3. Winnipeg, Wheeler 15 (Little) 8:02
4. Winnipeg, Thorburn 4 (Little, Enstrom) 10:54
Penalties — Roy Buf (hooking) 18:44, Kaleta Buf, Byfuglien Wpg (roughing) 19:53

● **Shots on goal by**

Buffalo	7	9	8	—	24
Winnipeg	10	8	13	—	31

● **Goal** — Buffalo: Miller (L,22-18-5); Winnipeg: Pavelec (W,25-21-7)
● **Power plays (goals-chances)** — Buffalo: 0-2; Winnipeg: 0-2
● **Referees** — Eric Furlatt, Gord Swyer. Linesmen — David Brisbois, Mike Cvik
● **Attendance** — 15,004 (15,004)

VANCOUVER 3 / WINNIPEG 2

A late goal by Canucks forward Sami Pahlsson — a seeing-eye shot that found its way through a screen — sank the Jets 3-2 in their first visit to Western Canada.

Pahlsson's goal came with just 5:43 left in regulation time.

"I didn't see it at all," Jets goalie Ondrej Pavelec said of Pahlsson's winning shot under the crossbar. "No way. It was over my shoulder. We did a turnover in their zone and then they come up to our zone and got the middle. It was too late to do something about it.

"We could have won the game, but too many mistakes."

Winnipeg held a 2-1 lead early in the third on a Blake Wheeler goal, but the Canucks came back at the visitors hard. They pressed the issue with the Jets and tied it up with an Alex Edler score.

"You've got to give them credit because they really turned things up in the third after we scored the second goal, but it was a byproduct of us not pushing the force like we really can," Wheeler noted.

The Jets fell to 32-28-8, and 11-18-4 on the road.

BIG PICTURE

As a result of the late defeat, the Jets dropped to ninth spot in the Eastern Conference after Washington pulled out a late comeback and won in overtime.

LITTLE PICTURE

Pavelec deserved a better outcome against the Canucks. He faced 45 shots, stopping all 20 pucks directed his way in the first, as the Jets were badly outplayed at the start.

SUMMARY

FIRST PERIOD
No Scoring
Penalties — Clitsome Wpg (high-sticking) 8:52

SECOND PERIOD
1. Vancouver, Kesler 20, 1:44 (sh)
2. Winnipeg, Wellwood 15 (Kane) 15:22
Penalties — Edler Vcr (tripping) 0:37, Gragnani Vcr (tripping) 6:08, Kesler Vcr (slashing) 9:52

THIRD PERIOD
3. Winnipeg, Wheeler 16 (Ladd) 3:34
4. Vancouver, Edler 10 (Salo, Higgins) 6:28
5. Vancouver, Pahlsson 3 (Bieksa, Hansen) 14:17
Penalties — None

Shots on goal by

Winnipeg	11	9	11	—	32
Vancouver	20	12	13	—	45

Goal — N.Y. Islanders: Nabokov (W,14-14-0); Winnipeg: Pavelec (L,20-20-6)
Power plays (goals-chances) — Winnipeg: 0-3; Vancouver: 0-1
Referees — Tom Kowal, Dave Jackson. Linesmen — Lonnie Cameron, Greg Devorski
Attendance — 18,860 (18,860)

Mike Deal / Winnipeg Free Press
KYLE WELLWOOD

69

GAME

AWAY

Friday, March 9, 2012

JETS vs. CALGARY FLAMES

CALGARY 5 / WINNIPEG 3

AFTER dropping a 5-3 decision to the Flames at the Scotiabank Saddledome, the pressure of the moment was starting to creep into the Jets.

The playoff race, a losing streak, inconsistent play — those were the things that wore on head coach Claude Noel, who snapped at reporters following the game.

The question: How disappointed was Noel at the fact his club failed to earn a point in this quick road swing through Western Canada?

"How would you like me to answer that?" he spat. "Do you want me to say medium, large? How would you like me to say that? How disappointed are you? Is there a level there? Is it a 10 out of 10? Would you like to say six out of 10? I mean, how disappointed do you need to be?"

Winnipeg was stuck in ninth place. At 32-29-8, with a terrible road record of 11-19-4, the Jets could only hope other clubs would falter as they had.

"We're going to be watching and hoping they lose," said Jets centre Jim Slater. "We're going to have to have a little bit of help, but we still play our own division quite a bit down the stretch here."

Winnipeg had just 13 games left, with seven of those road dates.

BIG PICTURE

Dustin Byfuglien, dealing with an injury for the better part of the season, didn't take the warm-up but played in the game. The defenceman logged big minutes on the blue-line and the club continued to do everything possible to keep him in the lineup.

LITTLE PICTURE

Evander Kane, Blake Wheeler and Tobias Enstrom scored, but by the time Winnipeg found the back of the net it was already 3-0 Calgary. Alex Tanguay had four points for the Flames.

BLAKE WHEELER

Mike Deal / Winnipeg Free Press

SUMMARY

FIRST PERIOD

1. Calgary, Giordano 7 (Jokinen, Tanguay) 3:54 (pp)
2. Calgary, Iginla 28 (Jokinen, Giordano) 6:47 (pp)
3. Calgary, Stajan 4 (Iginla, Tanguay) 12:51
4. Winnipeg, Kane 27 (Little, Enstrom) 17:31
5. Winnipeg, Wheeler 17 (Clitsome, Stuart) 19:33

Penalties — Flood Wpg (delay of game) 3:27, Glass Wpg (boarding) 6:02

SECOND PERIOD

6. Calgary, Tanguay 11 (Iginla, Stajan) 12:53

Penalties — Antropov Wpg, Glencross Cal (roughing) 15:20

THIRD PERIOD

7. Calgary, Glencross 24 (Tanguay, Jokinen) 11:28 (pp)
8. Winnipeg, Enstrom 5 (Slater, Byfuglien) 13:48

Penalties — Baertschi Cal (charging) 5:56, Ladd Wpg (high-sticking) 10:30, Giordano Cal (delay of game) 14:14

Shots on goal by

Winnipeg	16	12	17	—	45
Calgary	14	9	4	—	27

Goal — Winnipeg: Pavelec (L,25-23-7); Calgary: Kiprusoff (W,30-19-8)

Power plays (goals-chances) — Winnipeg: 0-2; Calgary: 3-3

Referees — Dean Morton, Dave Jackson. Linesmen — Greg Devorski, Jay Sharrers

Attendance — 19,289 (19,289)

WINNIPEG 5 / DALLAS 2

HOME is where the heart is.

That expression aptly described why the Jets, who pumped the Stars 5-2 at the MTS Centre, remained in the playoff picture with 13 games to play.

Flat-out miserable on the road with an 11-19-4 mark, the Jets improved their home record to 22-10-4, which sat among the best in the NHL. Winnipeg won three straight at home and in its last nine (6-1-2) had filled the net with 37 goals — an average of 4.11 per game.

"It's great playing at home, but we've got to win on the road, too," said centre Jim Slater.

Andrew Ladd scored two goals for the Jets, while Nik Antropov, Evander Kane and Eric Fehr chipped in with singles.

Goaltender Ondrej Pavelec stopped 28 of 30 shots.

"We played really good," said Pavelec. "We were disciplined, we played really well and scored goals. Everything we did was right and now we have to keep going and take advantage of the home games.

"I don't know what it is... at home we start right away and defend really well right from the first faceoff. And that's how you win games."

BIG PICTURE

How big was the win over the Stars? The Jets used the two points to move to within four of eighth-place Washington in the Eastern Conference. The Caps were the next opponent.

LITTLE PICTURE

It probably didn't do anything to take the sour out of his season, but Fehr's goal midway through the second was just his first in front of the home faithful. The Winkler product was a healthy scratch for seven straight games prior to the Dallas game.

SUMMARY

FIRST PERIOD

1. Winnipeg, Antropov 11 (Miettinen, Clitsome) 2:21

Penalties — None

SECOND PERIOD

2. Winnipeg, Kane 28 (Burmistrov, Wellwood) 1:19
3. Winnipeg, Fehr 2, 8:29
4. Winnipeg, Ladd 22 (Little, Wheeler) 9:15
5. Winnipeg, Ladd 23 (Byfuglien, Wheeler) 16:12 (pp)
6. Dallas, Eriksson 24 (Ribeiro) 16:29

Penalties — Fiddler Dal (tripping) 5:34, Ribeiro Dal (unsportsmanlike conduct), Hainsey Wpg (cross-checking) 10:44, Robidas Dal (delay of game) 15:59

THIRD PERIOD

7. Dallas, Eriksson 25 (Ryder, Goligoski) 16:16

Penalties — Burish Dal (roughing, unsportsmanlike conduct, game misconduct), Fiddler Dal (unsportsmanlike conduct), Glass Wpg (roughing, misconduct) 17:13

Shots on goal by

Dallas	9	13	8	—	30
Winnipeg	10	13	5	—	28

- **Goal** — Dallas: Bachman (L,8-4-1); Winnipeg: Pavelec (W,26-23-7)
- **Power plays (goals-chances)** — Dallas: 0-0; Winnipeg: 1-3
- **Referees** — Chris Rooney, Mike Leggo. Linesmen — Brian Murphy, Bryan Pancich
- **Attendance** — 15,004 (15,004)

Phil Hossack / Winnipeg Free Press

TIM SLATER

71

GAME

HOME

Friday, March 16, 2012

JETS vs. WASHINGTON CAPITALS

WINNIPEG 3 / WASHINGTON 2

DUSTIN Byfuglien, the biggest guy on the ice, scored the winning goal in the 3-2 Jets win over the Capitals at the MTS Centre.

The hulking defenceman crashed the Washington crease and redirected an Evander Kane pass midway through the third period. It was a big goal, as it moved the Jets to within two points of the Caps in the race for the final playoff spot in the Eastern Conference.

Both teams had 11 games left to play.

"Buff likes to get out there and make a difference," said coach Claude Noel. "And he was. He was resting in the crease... Evander Kane made a heck of a play.

"He fed Buff there and what can you say? Buff wants to have impact on games and does."

Andrew Ladd and Nik Antropov had the other goals for Winnipeg, but the night belonged to Byfuglien. He wasn't available for comment in the post-game — getting treatment, the Jets said — but others had lots to say.

"He seems to find a different level, a different level of excitement, a different level of compete," forward Blake Wheeler said. "You get a guy like that, big as he is and talented as he is with his mind in the right place, you can't stop him."

BIG PICTURE

The playoff race was red-hot, sure, but the questions about "big games" grew old. "Every day for the past month it's been the exact same questions: How big the game is, what It's like at home — it's seems like it's the same thing," Jets centre Bryan Little said.

LITTLE PICTURE

Winnipeg improved to a 23-10-4 overall record at home, one off the franchise mark for home victories in a season.

DUSTIN BYFUGLIEN

Trevor Hagan / Winnipeg Free Press

SUMMARY

FIRST PERIOD

1. Winnipeg, Ladd 24 (Wheeler, Byfuglien) 11:08
2. Washington, Laich 15 (Johansson) 11:30

Penalty — Chimera Wash (hooking) 1:30, Hainsey Wpg (hooking) 8:09

SECOND PERIOD

3. Winnipeg, Antropov 12 (Stapleton, Miettinen) 16:10

Penalties — Brouwer Wash (hooking) 1:17, Knuble Wash (holding) 17:21, Laich Wash (delay of game) 17:43, Enstrom Wpg (holding) 19:50

THIRD PERIOD

4. Washington, Perreault 13, 0:27 (pp)
5. Winnipeg, Byfuglien 11 (Kane, Burmistrov) 9:21

Penalty — Chimera Wash (hooking) 2:43, Brouwer Wash, Wheeler Wpg (roughing) 7:41, Hainsey Wpg (high-sticking) 17:38

Shots on goal by

Washington	5	6	11	—	11
Winnipeg	7	14	7	—	28

Goal — Washington: Vokoun (L,25-17-2); Winnipeg: Pavelec (W,27-23-7)

Power plays (goals-chances) — Washington: 1-3; Winnipeg: 0-5

Referees — Mike Legge, Kyle Rehman. Linesmen — Mark Wheler, Brian Murphy

Attendance — 15,004 (15,004)

CAROLINA 4 / WINNIPEG 3

THE cost for this result figured to be high.

Forward Chad LaRose's goal with 1:22 left in regulation gave the Hurricanes a 4-3 victory over the Jets, effectively casting a black cloud over the club's post-season hopes.

A win would have vaulted Winnipeg into a tie with eighth-place Washington in the Eastern Conference. Instead, with 10 games left to go, the Jets made a difficult task that much tougher.

"To me, the bottom line with this game, if we don't make the playoffs, we don't deserve to make the playoffs," Jets coach Claude Noel said. "There's a price to pay to win games and there's a price to pay to get in the playoffs. And it's not a sometimes thing."

Ondrej Pavelec faced 35 shots; 19 of those came in the third period. With the score 3-2 Jets in the final frame, the emotional netminder felt he was hung out to dry.

"We didn't play the right way," Pavelec said. "Do you want to win the game or score the goals?

"It's 3-2, 10 minutes left. Play smart, play intense and wait. We wanted to score the goals. Every game we want to score six, seven goals. It doesn't work like that. At 3-2, that's enough to win the game. We just didn't play the right way."

BIG PICTURE

The loss hurt. No question. One felt the air being let out of the playoff balloon. And with the schedule headed to Pittsburgh, Washington and Nashville, a miracle was in order to keep a post-season pulse beating.

LITTLE PICTURE

Nik Antropov scored for Winnipeg, as did Antti Miettinen, who picked a great time to score his first two goals of the season.

72

GAME

HOME

Sunday, March 18, 2012

JETS vs. CAROLINA HURRICANES

SUMMARY

FIRST PERIOD

1. Carolina, Jokinen 11 7:41 (sh)
2. Winnipeg, Antropov 13 (Stapleton, Stuart) 11:41

Penalties — Jokinen Car (slashing) 4:08, Joslin Car (cross-checking) 7:30, Allen Car (boarding) 8:05, Wheeler Wpg (hooking) 12:12, Burmistrov Wpg (boarding) 13:07, Kane Wpg (tripping) 17:49

SECOND PERIOD

3. Carolina, Staal 20 (Brent, Tlusty) 5:46 (pp)
4. Winnipeg, Miettinen 1 (Kane, Enstrom) 10:29 (pp)
5. Winnipeg, Miettinen 2 (Machacek) 18:54

Penalties — Stuart Wpg (interference) 5:21, Dwyer Car (high-sticking, fighting), Machacek Wpg (roughing, fighting) 6:09, Tlusty Car (hooking) 8:29, Bogosian Wpg (charging, game misconduct, served by Wellwood)) 10:41, Ruutu Car (interference) 14:25

THIRD PERIOD

6. Carolina, Staal 21 (Jokinen) 10:24
7. Carolina, LaRose 17 (Staal, Jokinen) 18:38

Penalties — None

Shots on goal by

Carolina	7	9	19	—	55
Winnipeg	12	7	14	—	26

Goal — Carolina: Ward (L,26-21-12); Winnipeg: Pavelec (W,27-24-7)
Power plays (goals-chances) — Carolina: 1-5; Winnipeg: 0-5
Referees — Dean Morton, Chris Rooney Linesmen — Mark Wheler, Derek Nansen
Attendance — 15,004 (15,004)

John Woods / Winnipeg Free Press

ONDREJ PAVELEC

73

GAME

AWAY

Tuesday, March 20, 2012
JETS vs. PITTSBURGH PENGUINS

PITTSBURGH 8 / WINNIPEG 4

THE Jets plunged into deep waters and sank right to the bottom.

In a game they needed to have — a common theme as the season wound down — Winnipeg dropped a deflating 8-4 decision to the high-powered Penguins at Consol Energy Center.

The Jets were no match against the depth of the home side:

- Evgeni Malkin had two goals and three assists. The centre put up three goals and eight assists in three games against the Jets this season.
- Sidney Crosby set up four goals in his first home game since early December.
- And winger James Neal had three goals in the first two periods.

"Obviously their depth is their strength," Jets captain Andrew Ladd said. "Right down the middle. It's tough to play against that. At the same time we knew that coming into the game, we knew it was going to be a challenge and that we needed to play our top game and we needed it out of everybody.

"It just seemed like they scored every chance they got."

Winnipeg goals came off the sticks of Bryan Little (he scored twice), Tim Stapleton and Jim Slater.

Goaltender Ondrej Pavelec allowed five goals on 24 shots and was pulled in favour of Chris Mason with seven minutes to play in the second period.

BIG PICTURE
The Jets' playoff dream faded as they remained in 10th in the Eastern Conference with a 34-31-8 record. They sat four points behind eighth-place Washington and two back of ninth-place Buffalo with just nine games left.

LITTLE PICTURE
Winnipeg's abysmal road record fell to 11-20-4 after suffering its third straight road defeat.

BRYAN LITTLE
Mike Deal / Winnipeg Free Press

SUMMARY

FIRST PERIOD
1. Pittsburgh, Kennedy 7 (Crosby, Cooke) 2:04
2. Winnipeg, Slater 10 (Glass, Machacek) 3:35
3. Winnipeg, Little 20 (Ladd, Enstrom) 12:51 (pp)
4. Pittsburgh, Neal 33 (Malkin, Crosby) 16:44 (pp)

Penalties — Byfuglien Wpg (high-sticking) 9:36, Malkin Pgh (double high-sticking) 11:32, Enstrom Wpg (holding) 15:04.

SECOND PERIOD
5. Pittsburgh, Neal 34 (Malkin) 1:15
6. Winnipeg, Little 21 (Ladd, Enstrom) 3:54
7. Pittsburgh, Kennedy 8 (Crosby, Cooke) 6:55
8. Pittsburgh, Malkin 42 (Crosby, Martin) 11:31
9. Winnipeg, Stapleton 9 (Maxwell, Machacek) 14:39
10. Pittsburgh, Neal 35 (Malkin, Orpik) 17:03

Penalties — None

THIRD PERIOD
11. Pittsburgh, Malkin 43 (Kunitz, Neal) 2:07
12. Pittsburgh, Dupuis 21 (Staal, Sullivan) 13:27

Penalties — Little Wpg (tripping) 18:55

Shots on goal by

Winnipeg	12	10	8	—	30
Pittsburgh	13	15	7	—	35

Goal (shots-saves) — Winnipeg: Pavelec (L,27-25-7)(24-19), Mason (12:50 second)(11-8); Pittsburgh: Thiessen (W,3-0-0)

Power plays (goals-chances) — Winnipeg: 1-2; Pittsburgh: 1-3

Referees — Chris Lee, Kelly Sutherland. Linesmen — Scott Cherrey, Scott Driscoll

Attendance — 18,589 (18,387)

74

GAME

AWAY

Friday, March 23, 2012

JETS vs. WASHINGTON CAPITALS

WINNIPEG 4 / WASHINGTON 3 (OT)

THE Jets still had a pulse, faint as it might be, following a come-from-behind 4-3 overtime win over the Capitals at Verizon Center.

Tim Stapleton provided the late heroics when he snapped a quick shot over the shoulder of goaltender Michael Neuvirth midway through the OT session. That capped off a furious comeback by the Jets, who stared down the barrel of a 3-0 deficit with 26 minutes left in regulation time and the possibility of the season ending right there.

"I saw us go into desperation mode," said Stapleton. "We were just pressing and pressing and stuck to the game plan by just throwing shots on net.

"We all want to make the playoffs and we're going to do everything we can to just try and get in. Obviously we need to get help from other teams, but all we can control right now is getting every point possible, and that's what we did tonight."

Stapleton's line was the difference. Together with wingers Spencer Machacek and Ben Maxwell — both call-ups from the AHL's St. John's IceCaps — the three accounted for three goals and six points in the game.

The Jets outshot the Capitals 19-2 in third period and overtime play.

Alex Ovechkin scored twice for the Capitals.

BIG PICTURE

The win moved the Jets (35-31-8) to within four points of the final playoff spot in the conference, shared by Washington and Buffalo. Winnipeg had a game in hand on both clubs.

LITTLE PICTURE

Prior to the dramatic finish in Washington, the Jets were 0-22-3 when trailing after two periods. The Caps were 22-0 when leading after 40 minutes.

SUMMARY

FIRST PERIOD

1. Washington, Chimera 18 (Halpern, Semin) 16:06

Penalties — Wheeler Wpg (hooking) 13:27

SECOND PERIOD

2. Washington, Ovechkin 34 (Laich, Knuble) 1:42
3. Washington, Ovechkin 35 (Perreault, Chimera) 5:47
4. Winnipeg, Maxwell 1 (Stapleton, Machacek) 7:01
5. Winnipeg, Little 22 (Enstrom, Wheeler) 8:12

Penalties — Slater Wpg, Laich Wash (fighting) 7:07, Wideman Wash (interference) 8:59, Hainsey Wpg (cross-checking) 13:05

THIRD PERIOD

6. Winnipeg, Machacek 1 (Maxwell) 16:15

Penalties — Laich Wash (tripping) 6:58

Overtime

7. Winnipeg, Stapleton 10 (Byfuglien) 2:37

Penalties — None

Shots on goal by

Winnipeg	8	15	17	2	—	42
Washington	7	14	2	0	—	23

Goal — Winnipeg: Pavelec (W,28-25-7); Washington: Neuvirth (L,11-12-5)

Power plays (goals-chances) — Winnipeg: 0-2; Washington: 0-2

Referees — Steve Kozari, Marc Joannette. Linesmen — Michel Cormier, Mark Shewchyk

Attendance — 18,506 (18,398)

Joe Bryksa / Winnipeg Free Press

BEN MAXWELL

75

GAME

AWAY

Saturday, March 24, 2012

JETS vs. NASHVILLE PREDATORS

NASHVILLE 3 / WINNIPEG 1

THE peaks and valleys of a playoff chase landed the Jets at the bottom of the hill again, thanks to a discouraging 3-1 loss to the Predators at Bridgestone Arena.

Winnipeg (35-32-8) had lost three of its last four and sat six points back of eighth-place Buffalo, with a game in hand but just seven left in the regular season.

"We gotta win, that's all you can do," said centre Tim Stapleton. "I don't know what kind of record we've got to go (in the final seven games), but I'm pretty sure it's probably close to undefeated."

Stapleton scored the lone goal for the Jets.

Officially, the stat sheet showed the Jets fired 25 shots at Predators netminder Pekka Rinne but Winnipeg went long stretches without any decent opportunities.

"We got shots, but very few quality shots, very few scoring chances," said Jets coach Claude Noel.

"They did a good job of really keeping us to the outside. It was a tough night to get on the inside of anything, and when we got pucks to the inside, we didn't have enough traffic or people at the net.

"They defended very well. There was very little space out there."

The Jets, who won in overtime in Washington the night before, fell to 1-11 in the second game of back-to-backs contests.

BIG PICTURE

Seven games left, six points back of a playoff spot. Goaltender Ondrej Pavelec summed up the dire straits best: "It's pretty clear that we need the help from other teams. It's not in our destiny right now. It seems like everybody else is winning right now."

Little picture

The one-score output was the 22nd time this season the Jets had been held to a goal or less.

TOBIAS ENSTROM

Trevor Hagan / Winnipeg Free Press

SUMMARY

● **FIRST PERIOD**
No Scoring
Penalty — Enstrom Wpg (slashing) 5:11, Erat Nash (hooking) 12:52

● **SECOND PERIOD**
1. Nashville, Halischuk 13 (Radulov, Klein) 2:56
2. Nashville, Bourque 5 (Spaling, A.Kostitsyn) 10:01
Penalty — Jones Wpg (tripping) 12:29, Byfuglien Wpg (roughing) 18:38

● **THIRD PERIOD**
3. Winnipeg, Stapleton 11 (Machacek, Maxwell) 12:53
4. Nashville, Weber 15 (Fisher) 19:50 (en-pp)
Penalties — Byfuglien Wpg (hooking) 19:30

● **Shots on goal by**

Winnipeg	7	9	9	—	25
Nashville	10	5	13	—	28

● **Goal** — Winnipeg: Pavelec (L,28-26-7); Nashville: Rinne (W,40-16-8)
● **Power plays (goals-chances)** — Winnipeg: 0-1; Nashville: 1-4
● **Referees** — Eric Furlatt, Kyle Rehman. Linesmen — Jonny Murray, Steve Miller
● **Attendance** — 17,113 (17,113)

OTTAWA 6 / WINNIPEG 4

THE Jets put up another determined fight at the MTS Centre, coming back three times, but eventually they dropped a 6-4 loss to the Senators.

"We chased the game," said Jets coach Claude Noel, in analytical mode, not anger mode, after his team fell to 35-33-8. "We were forever chasing the game."

Winnipeg fell behind three times throughout the course of the night but squared things up each time. The fourth occasion when they lapsed, when Sens captain Daniel Alfredsson was the beneficiary of a Zach Bogosian turnover with 2:33 left in the third, the Jets couldn't answer back.

"Guys are trying their best out there to make plays, create offence, get the puck out of the zone," Jets winger Evander Kane said about his team's costly turnovers. "It happens to everybody.

"We battled all night. We had 48 shots, threw everything at the net. We had a lot of key chances, probably could have got eight or nine goals if we could have got those bounces. I thought we played pretty darn well and we lose."

Winnipeg also lost ground in the Eastern Conference playoff race. They trailed Washington and Buffalo, who shared eighth place with 84 points, by a full six and had just six games left.

BIG PICTURE

Inconsistency killed the Jets — again. Kane's 29th of the season tied the game with 2:57 remaining but the Sens answered just 24 seconds later when Alfredsson converted a Jets turnover.

LITTLE PICTURE

The Jets outshot the visitors 48-35 and had chances galore to score, but Senators goaltender Craig Anderson was up to the task.

SUMMARY

FIRST PERIOD
1. Ottawa, Neil 12 (Spezza, Karlsson) 19:34
Penalties — Burmistrov Wpg (boarding) 1:48, Gonchar Ott (tripping) 14:57

SECOND PERIOD
2. Ottawa, Daugavins 5 (Condra, Smith) 1:53
3. Winnipeg, Miettinen 3 (Bogosian, Wellwood) 3:02
4. Winnipeg, Wellwood 16 (Kane, Hainsey) 6:54
5. Ottawa, Turris 10 (Spezza, Gonchar) 17:26
6. Winnipeg, Miettinen 4 (Slater, Glass) 17:46
Penalties — Kuba Ott (tripping) 2:38, Spezza Ott (tripping) 12:05, Enstrom Wpg (interference) 13:09, Spezza Ott (tripping) 14:56

THIRD PERIOD
7. Ottawa, Alfredsson 25 (Karlsson) 2:54
8. Winnipeg, Kane 29 (Wellwood) 17:03
9. Ottawa, Alfredsson 26 (Kuba, Turris) 17:27
10. Ottawa, Michalek 34 19:26 (en)
Penalties — None

Shots on goal by

Ottawa	10	11	14	—	35
Winnipeg	13	17	18	—	48

Goal (shot-saves) — Ottawa: Anderson (W,31-20-6). Winnipeg: Pavelec (L,28-27-7)
Power plays (goals-chances) — Ottawa: 0-2; Winnipeg: 0-4
Referees — Dennis LaRue, Dan O'Rourke. Linesmen — Brad Kovachik, Thor Nelson
Attendance — 15,004 (15,004)

John Woods / Winnipeg Free Press
KYLE WELLWOOD

77

GAME

HOME

Wednesday, March 28, 2012
JETS vs. NEW YORK RANGERS

N.Y. RANGERS 4 / WINNIPEG 2

THE end-of-the-season nosedive for the Jets continued as the home side blew a two-goal lead and lost 4-2 to the Rangers at the MTS Centre.

Winnipeg lost three straight at home and had dropped five of the last six games.

"It's frustrating. Any time you lose, it sucks," said defenceman Zach Bogosian. "We're competitive people in here, no matter what... even if we're in first place or last place.

"It's our job to come out and play hard and win hockey games and we didn't do it."

Though still mathematically alive for a playoff position, the Jets were up against it. They fell to 35-34-8 and remained eight points behind the Buffalo Sabres, who held down the eighth and final spot in the Eastern Conference.

Players couldn't put their finger on why the club stumbled.

"There's a bunch of teams that are in the same situation we are, battling for their lives, and they're doing all right," centre Bryan Little said. "I don't think it's fatigue. If anything, we should have a lot of energy to get up for these games."

BIG PICTURE

Winnipeg had a 5-on-3 power play for 1:43 in the first period but failed to score. To this point, the Jets were just 2-for-12 in that situation, 16.6 per cent. That was below their overall power-play efficiency, which was 18.2 per cent.

LITTLE PICTURE

The powerhouse Rangers defeated the Jets four out of four times, the only conference rival the Jets failed to beat all season.

BRYAN LITTLE

Phil Hossack / Winnipeg Free Press

SUMMARY

FIRST PERIOD

No Scoring

Penalties — Bickel NYR (holding) 10:24, McDonagh NYR (tripping) 10:41, Stralman NYR (delay of game) 14:20

SECOND PERIOD

1. Winnipeg, Machacek 2 (Maxwell, Stuart) 3:58
2. Winnipeg, Little 23 (Wheeler, Ladd) 4:54
3. N.Y. Rangers, Del Zotto 8 (Callahan) 7:44 (sh)
4. N.Y. Rangers, Callahan 28 (Gaborik, Del Zotto) 18:23 (pp)

Penalty — Boyle NYR (boarding) 0:27, Dubinsky NYR (slashing) 6:35, Kane Wpg (slashing) 8:19, Burmistrov Wpg (holding) 18:00, Ladd Wpg (double high-sticking) 18:53

THIRD PERIOD

5. N.Y. Rangers, Boyle 9 (Fedotenko, McDonagh) 3:07
6. N.Y. Rangers, Stepan 17 (Gaborik, Richards) 10:06 (pp)

Penalties — Bickel NYR, Glass Wpg (fighting) 5:56, Burmistrov Wpg (holding) 8:46

Shots on goal by

N.Y. Rangers	4	15	9	— 28
Winnipeg	11	8	5	— 24

- **Goal** — N.Y. Rangers: Lundqvist (W,37-16-5); Winnipeg: Pavelec (L,28-28-7)
- **Power plays (goals-chances)** — N.Y. Rangers: 2-5; Winnipeg: 0-5.
- **Referees** — Gord Dwyer, Brad Watson. Linesmen — Ryan Galloway, Brad Kovachik
- **Attendance** — 15,004 (15,004)

WINNIPEG 4 / CAROLINA 3 (OT)

78

GAME

AWAY

Friday, March 30, 2012
JETS vs. CAROLINA HURRICANES

THERE wasn't much left to play for — the Jets were all but mathematically eliminated from the post-season, but some veterans were determined to not let the year simply fade away.

Players' meetings helped clear the air about what the approach would be moving forward.

"We're trying to change the culture and, excuse my French, make this a place where you come to work and bust your ass every day, no matter the situation," captain Andrew Ladd said after the Jets beat the Hurricanes 4-3 in overtime. "It has to be a thing that everybody does every day and if you don't, you don't play.

"We talked about showing the character we have in this room and that we owed it to our fans to finish the season on a good note. The first period was pretty disappointing and we came into the room after and talked about it. We needed to get it going and we did."

Ladd backed up his words: He scored the game-winner 16 seconds into OT.

The win gave the Jets a 36-34-8 record for 80 points, six back of Buffalo and Washington for the eighth and final Eastern Conference playoff invite. All teams had four games remaining on the schedule.

BIG PICTURE

Tanner Glass broke his foot blocking a shot in the second period but only missed a few shifts before coming back to help grind out a victory. He was out for the rest of the season.

LITTLE PICTURE

Nik Antropov, Jim Slater and Kyle Wellwood scored the other goals for Winnipeg. Defenceman Zach Bogosian had arguably his best game of the season; he picked up three assists and played a team-high 23:03 minutes.

SUMMARY

FIRST PERIOD

1. Winnipeg, Antropov 14 (Wellwood, Kane) 2:23
2. Carolina, Joslin 2 (Skinner) 11:22
3. Carolina, E.Staal 24, 16:46 (sh)

Penalties — Bogosian Wpg, Stewart Car (fighting) 10:53, Gleason Car (double unsportsmanlike conduct) 15:49

SECOND PERIOD

4. Carolina, Bra.Sutter 16 (Dwyer, Bowman) 3:49
5. Winnipeg, Slater 11 (Machacek, Bogosian) 10:25

Penalties — Little Wpg (roughing) 5:50, Antropov Wpg (slashing) 12:25, Harrison Car (tripping) 16:59

THIRD PERIOD

6. Winnipeg, Wellwood 17 (Miettinen, Bogosian) 15:13 (pp)

Penalties — None

OVERTIME

7. Winnipeg, Ladd 25 (Bogosian) 0:16

Penalties — None

Shots on goal by

Winnipeg	7	9	18	1	— 32
Carolina	12	12	9	0	— 45

Goal —Winnipeg: Mason (W,8-6-1); Carolina: Ward (L,28-23-13)
Power plays (goals-chances) — Winnipeg: 1-4; Carolina: 0-4
Referees — Rob Martell, Dan O'Rourke. Linesmen — Scott Driscoll, Pierre Racicot
Attendance — 18,860 (18,860)

Mike Deal / Winnipeg Free Press

NIK ANTROPOV

79 GAME

AWAY

Saturday, March 31, 2012
JETS vs. TAMPA BAY LIGHTNING

TAMPA BAY 3 / WINNIPEG 2 (OT)

STEVEN Stamkos scored 45 seconds into overtime to give the Lightning a 3-2 win over the Jets and with that, Winnipeg was officially eliminated from the playoff hunt.

Post-season play was the goal for this club at the start of the season. The Jets fell short of that standard and were left to reflect on what happened after the game.

"Coming into this year, the goal and expectation was to get into the playoffs, and to not get there is disappointing," captain Andrew Ladd said. "It's our job to get better and to learn from this and make sure this doesn't happen next year. In our minds, this is a failure. I feel we had the group in here to get into the playoffs."

Others shared that sentiment.

"I have a lot of feeling about this, and I'm not happy about it," said defenceman Mark Stuart. "The future of this team is bright. The pieces are in place, with obviously being better on the road a big part of that."

"Not making the playoffs is disappointing. We're out. Our goal was to make the playoffs and we didn't," goalie Ondrej Pavelec added. "It's tough, for sure, because that's why you play hockey, to make the playoffs. There's nothing we can do right now.

"We couldn't win the important games."

BIG PICTURE

The Jets were eliminated from the playoff picture and sat at 36-34-9 through 79 games. Winnipeg had 81 points, one better than they finished with last season when known as the Atlanta Thrashers.

LITTLE PICTURE

The dismal road record would feature prominently on many Jets obituaries after the season. With two visitor dates left to play, the club was 13-21-5 away from Winnipeg.

RON HAINSEY

Phil Hossack / Winnipeg Free Press

SUMMARY

FIRST PERIOD
1. Tampa Bay, Malone 19 15:37
Penalties — Clitsome Wpg (hooking) 6:35, Wyman TB (holding) 12:22, Wallace TB (roughing) 16:35, Enstrom Wpg (hooking) 16:50

SECOND PERIOD
2. Winnipeg, Miettinen 5 (Kane, Stuart) 6:20
3. Winnipeg, Wellwood 18 (Byfuglien, Stapleton) 9:28
Penalties — Kane Wpg (elbowing) 2:07, Hainsey Wpg (cross-checking) 12:27

Third Period
4. Tampa Bay, Malone 20 (Purcell, Hedman) 7:25 (pp)
Penalties — Hainsey Wpg, Malone TB (fighting) 0:44, Byfuglien Wpg (hooking) 2:47, Slater Wpg (high-sticking) 4:36, Little Wpg (hooking) 6:19, Wyman TB (high-sticking) 8:05, Ladd Wpg (roughing, fighting, misconduct, served by Stapleton), Wheeler Wpg, Brewer TB (slashing), Hedman TB (fighting, misconduct) 8:29

OVERTIME
5. Tampa Bay, Stamkos 56 (Lee) 0:45
Penalties — None

Shots on goal by

Winnipeg	12	9	7	0	—	28
Tampa Bay	7	10	21	1	—	39

Goal — Winnipeg: Pavelec (L,28-28-8); Tampa Bay: Caron (W,1-0-0).
Power plays (goals-chances) — Winnipeg: 0-3; Tampa Bay: 1-7.
Referees — Chris Rooney, Ian Walsh. Linesmen — Jonny Murray, Derek Amell
Attendance — 19,204 (19,204)

WINNIPEG 5 / FLORIDA 4 (OT)

80

GAME

AWAY

Tuesday, April 3, 2012

JETS vs. FLORIDA PANTHERS

ONDREJ Pavelec made 34 saves and helped the Jets play the role of spoiler as they erased an early deficit and beat the Panthers 5-4 in overtime.

The goaltender, who often wore his emotions on his sleeve after games, told reporters the players were playing for one reason: the people back in Winnipeg.

"We can't quit on our fans," Pavelec said. "They've been so good to us this year and we know they are watching on TV at home. We want to be good for them on Thursday in Long Island, too. And that last game on Saturday at home in Winnipeg is going to be so special.

"They have been such a big part of this season. We're disappointed that we're not going to the playoffs and we know they are, too. So we can't let them down in these final games. We have to do it for them."

Claude Noel talked about his team's leadership all season. Playing with fire in meaningless games is another example of his team's character, the Jets coach noted.

"It does please me. To me, there are a couple of signs and signals, and it's because you are led in the room. Guys have pride and they are well-led," Noel said.

Jets captain Andrew Ladd scored the OT winner.

BIG PICTURE

Ladd scored two goals and had a game-high seven shots. The captain was the Jets' best player down the stretch — even after the club was eliminated. Early-season doubts about his leadership were answered as things wore on and he never ducked a question from the media.

LITTLE PICTURE

Evander Kane's second-period goal gave him 30 on the year, 11 more than his previous career high. He would be Winnipeg's only 30-goal man this season.

SUMMARY

FIRST PERIOD

1. Florida, Sturm 3 (Kulikov) 12:03
2. Florida, Versteeg 23 (Fleischmann, Campbell) 14:00 (pp)

Penalties — Clitsome Wpg (hooking) 9:39, Thorburn Wpg (holding) 13:15

SECOND PERIOD

3. Florida, Fleischmann 27 (Versteeg) 0:25
4. Winnipeg, Kane 30 (Machacek, Bogosian) 13:15
5. Winnipeg, Bogosian 4, 17:21

Penalties — Garrison Fla (hooking) 13:40

THIRD PERIOD

6. Winnipeg, Ladd 26 (Byfuglien, Little) 0:53
7. Winnipeg, Little 24 (Wheeler, Byfuglien) 3:45 (pp)
8. Florida, Kopecky 10 (Sturm) 16:07

Penalties — Weaver Fla (delay of game) 2:00

OVERTIME

9. Winnipeg, Ladd 27 (Wheeler) 3:12

Penalties — None

Shots on goal by

Winnipeg	5	13	10	2	—	30
Florida	12	10	12	4	—	38

Goal — Winnipeg: Pavelec (W,29-28-8); Florida: Theodore (L,22-15-11)
Power plays (goals-chances) — Winnipeg: 1-2; Florida: 1-2
Referees — Stephen Walkom, Francois St. Laurent. Linesmen — Brian Murphy, Steve Barton
Attendance — 17,760 (17,040)

Trevor Hagan / Winnipeg Free Press

GRANT CLITSOME

N.Y. ISLANDERS 5 / WINNIPEG 4

SPEEDSTER Michael Grabner — a graduate of the Manitoba Moose program before he cracked the NHL — scored two goals in the third period to push the Islanders past the Jets 5-4 at Nassau Veterans Memorial Coliseum.

Grabner scored the game-winner with just 47 seconds to play. Defenceman Travis Hamonic — himself a Winnipeg product — took a shot from the point that deflected off the forward and past Jets goaltender Chris Mason.

Grabner also scored on a penalty shot earlier in the final frame.

For the second time in as many games, Winnipeg found itself in a hole early as the home side took a 2-0 lead eight minutes in and forced the Jets to play catch-up.

"I think it's very disrespectful the way we start games," head coach Claude Noel said. "The way we started again tonight and the way we got down I think is disrespectful to one another and what we want to accomplish as a team.

"The game is 60 minutes and whether you look at it as coming back, I think it's poor. It's poor. The game is 60 minutes and I don't like the way we play and the way we disrespect each other."

Kyle Okposo also scored twice for the Isles. The Jets' biggest gun was defenceman Dustin Byfuglien, who had a goal and two assists.

BIG PICTURE

Success, or lack thereof, against the Islanders was symptomatic of Winnipeg's inconsistency all season. The Jets only grabbed three of a possible eight points from New York, a club that spent most of the year behind Winnipeg in the standings.

LITTLE PICTURE

The Jets wrapped up the 2011-12 road schedule with a 14-22-5 record.

ZACH BOGOSIAN

Trevor Hagan / Winnipeg Free Press

SUMMARY

FIRST PERIOD

1. N.Y Islanders, Moulsen 36 (Tavares) 6:38
2. N.Y Islanders, Okposo 22 (Bailey, Nielsen) 8:06
3. Winnipeg, Enstrom 6 (Slater, Byfuglien) 9:42
4. Winnipeg, Ladd 28 (Little, Bogosian) 17:08

Penalties — None

SECOND PERIOD

5. N.Y Islanders, Okposo 23 (Tavares) 8:41

Penalties — Streit NYI (holding) 1:02, Wheeler Wpg (tripping, elbowing) 2:16, Kane Wpg (hooking) 6:08, MacDonald NYI (tripping) 13:42

THIRD PERIOD

6. Winnipeg, Bogosian 5 (Thorburn, Byfuglien) 7:03
7. N.Y Islanders, Grabner 18 (penalty shot) 11:45
8. Winnipeg, Byfuglien 12 (Enstrom) 12:21
9. N.Y Islanders, Grabner 19 (Hamonic, Nielsen) 19:13

Penalties — Jurcina NYI (holding) 15:50

Shots on goal by

Winnipeg	13	5	7	—	25
N.Y. Islanders	10	11	7	—	28

Goal — Winnipeg: Mason (L,8-7-1); N.Y. Islanders: Montoya (W,9-10-5)

Power plays (goals-chances) — Winnipeg: 0-3; N.Y Islanders: 0-3

Referees — Greg Kimmerly, Wes McCauley. Linesmen — Michel Cormier, Mark Shewchyk

Attendance — 13,048 (16,250)

TAMPA BAY 4 / WINNIPEG 3 (OT)

82 GAME

HOME

Saturday, April 7, 2012
JETS vs. TAMPA BAY LIGHTNING

THIS time, the last Jets game of the season wasn't the last game.

Teddy Purcell's goal at the 1:08 mark of overtime gave the Lightning a 4-3 win but it couldn't dampen the spirits in the 2011-12 season finale, as fans at the MTS Centre wrapped up a year-long celebration of NHL hockey's return to the city.

Everyone understood the Jets would be back again next season — and not moving to Arizona, as they did in 1996 — which is why the final ovation was more of a "see you later" than a "goodbye."

"I didn't want to get off the ice," said Jets centre Jim Slater, whose two goals included the game-tying marker with 53 seconds left in regulation. "Every fan stayed. I think it's more of us giving them applause than them to us. That's tough leaving the ice. I didn't want to go."

"That's something that was over the top," said Nik Antropov. "I expected this was going to be crazy, but that's overwhelming. Nothing but positive things about that."

The Jets gave lucky fans the jerseys off their backs after the game.

The subplot in all this involved Lightning sniper Steven Stamkos, who potted his league-best 60th of the season in the third. After some initial jeers, the Jets faithful gave him a nice ovation, too.

BIG PICTURE

The Jets finished the season with a 37-35-10 overall season mark, good for 84 points. They finished 11th in the Eastern Conference, eight points out of a playoff spot and six points from the bottom of the conference standings.

LITTLE PICTURE

Winnipeg's home record finished at 23-13-5. The MTS Centre was certainly kind to the club in the early stages (notably December) but the Jets' success fell off slightly as the playoff-push pressure started to materialize.

SUMMARY

FIRST PERIOD
1. Tampa Bay, Purcell 22 (Lecavalier) 17:49
Penalties — Stuart Wpg (tripping) 7:41, Clitsome Wpg (tripping) 13:40

SECOND PERIOD
2. Tampa Bay, Purcell 23 (Lecavalier, Brown) 1:12
3. Winnipeg, Antropov 15 (Miettinen, Kane) 8:53
Penalties — Brewer TB (hooking) 6:46

THIRD PERIOD
4. Tampa Bay, Stamkos 60 (St. Louis, Lee) 3:29
5. Winnipeg, Slater 12 (Clitsome, Enstrom) 4:59
6. Winnipeg, Slater 13 (Wheeler, Ladd) 19:07
Penalties — Malone TB (hooking) 13:13, Little Wpg (holding) 15:18

OVERTIME
4. Tampa Bay, Purcell 24 (Hedman) 1:08
Penalties — None

Shots on goal by

Tampa Bay	8	4	10	1	—	23
Winnipeg	3	15	12	1	—	31

Goal — Tampa Bay: Roloson (W,13-16-3); Winnipeg: Pavelec (L,29-29-8)
Power plays (goals-chances) — Tampa Bay: 0-3; Winnipeg: 0-2
Referees — Steve Kozari, Tim Peel. Linesmen — Mike Cvik, Brad Lazarowic
Attendance — 15,004 (15,004)

Mike Deal / Winnipeg Free Press

GRANT CLITSOME, JIM SLATER

Jonathan Hayward / The Canadian Press

THE TOP 5

BEST AND WORST OF 2011-2012 ›

5 MOMENTS TO REMEMBER

1 DRAFT DAY
June 24

A coach. A name. A draft pick. Beyond the actual announcement of the acquisition of the franchise, there was no more magical time than the Friday of draft week in Minneapolis/St. Paul. The team named its first head coach, Claude Noel, in the morning. Co-owner Mark Chipman went to the podium at Xcel Energy Center to speak the team's new/old name for the first official time. New GM Kevin Cheveldayoff winked at Mark Scheifele on his way to that same podium, then announced the young Kitchener, Ont., native's name as the new team's first first-round draft pick in the seven slot. It was a day unlike any other if you were a Jets fan.

ERIC FEHR MARK STUART

2 17 WING
Sept. 6

Real jerseys. Real jets. Real Jets in jerseys. A big day for the franchise and its look for years to come. A perfect, warm, sunny late-summer day and a perfectly choreographed event to unveil the team's uniforms and colour scheme. Classically understated and leaning to the traditional, the colours and the look were trending positive pretty much from the start.

General manager Kevin Cheveldayoff welcomes first-rou pick Mark Scheifel at the 2011 entry d in St. Paul, Minn.

Eric Miller/ Reuters

John Woods / The Canadian Press

‹ ANTROPOV ANDREW LADD

3 XCEL ENERGY CENTER JETS 4 WILD 3

Feb. 16

It was a game worthy of the "Games to Remember" list but this evening, at the downtown St. Paul arena, already the site of our No. 1 item on this list, seemed like it was a good place to be part of Jets Nation. Of all the road games this season, it was very likely the best spectacle and proved Jets fever travels well. The game itself was excellent, hotly contested. The building, which included about 6,000 Jets fans, was absolutely abuzz and the back-and-forth between the fans (as well as the teams) was something to behold, indicating this rivalry, when eventually the NHLPA approves, will be fascinating and worth waiting for six times a season.

4 " TRUE NORTH "

It is a moment prior to the start of each Jets game, at home and most of those on the road, that is actually better than the passé Whiteout. In the middle of the singing of the Canadian anthem, when fans get to the "True North strong and free" part, they bellow "True North." It is a salute and a point of pride and since its origin is fan-generated, all the more meaningful. It's obviously the name of the company that built an arena and then brought an NHL team back to Winnipeg, but it's got the perfect nationalistic overtones. Best of all, it's uniquely Winnipeg's.

5 " GARY, GARY "

There are so many other noteworthy moments, this list could have been a whole lot longer. Storytelling days by Jets coach Claude Noel are up there, the franchise celebrations downtown and at The Forks ought to be included, as well as the league-sponsored parties ahead of the season opener. But really, the overriding element in the entire season has been the fans, who are clever in a lot of places and do inventive stuff. The faithful at the MTS Centre acquitted themselves spectacularly this past season, making it the epicentre of something very special in sports. You've no doubt heard about "Sil-ver Me-dal," and "Cros-by's bet-ter," and "Prong-er." But when NHL commissioner Gary Bettman was here to help Winnipeg celebrate its season opener, the fans actually chanted his name in the arena's atrium. There aren't a lot of times or places you can ever have claimed to have heard that but it was just the right touch of enthusiasm and appreciation to again set Winnipeg fans apart. Adding to the legend.

GARY BETTMAN

Boris Minkevich / Winnipeg Free Press

Phil Hossack / Winnipeg Free Press

INDIVIDUAL NUMBERS:

Leading scorer:	Blake Wheeler — 17G, 46A, 63 pts.

› DID YOU KNOW? **The Jets/Thrashers franchise had not had a point-per-game leading scorer since Ilya Kovalchuk scored 91 points (43G, 48A) in 2009-09.**

Leading goal scorer:	Evander Kane — 30
Assist leader:	Wheeler — 46
Game-winning goals:	Andrew Ladd, Bryan Little — 6
Short-handed goals:	Alex Burmistrov, Jim Slater, Mark Stuart — 1 each

› DID YOU KNOW? **Only Tampa Bay and Detroit, with two, scored fewer short-handed goals than the Jets this season.**

Longest point streak this season	8 games; Kane (Feb. 16-March 12; 7G, 8A)
Longest goal streak by a Jet this season	4 games; Little, Feb. 16-March 1; Wheeler, March 1-9; Nik Antropov, March 14-30
Penalty minutes:	Mark Stuart — 96
Plus-minus:	Kane — +12

› DID YOU KNOW? **Recent call-up Spencer Machacek was a +9 in 12 games; third-best on the team.**

Hits:	Tanner Glass — 246 (tied for 10th in the NHL)
Blocked shots:	Mark Stuart — 178 (9th in the NHL)
Faceoffs won:	Bryan Little — 727 (11th in the NHL)
Saves:	Ondrej Pavelec — 2,011 (5th in the NHL)
Shooting percentage:	Kyle Wellwood, 19.4% (18 goals on 93 shots)

› DID YOU KNOW? **Wellwood was the NHL's top goal scorer among players with fewer than 100 shots on goal.**

— compiled by Ed Tait

Goalie Ondrej Pavelec ranked fifth in the NHL with 2,011 saves.

1 OCT. 9, 2011
Canadiens 5 / Jets 1

Will be one of those "Where were you when... " games in Winnipeg hockey history; 5,642 days passed between meaningful NHL games in the Manitoba capital. The buildup to the game was unprecedented. "It's such a unique situation that I don't know if it'll ever happen again," Jets captain Andrew Ladd said. More than 250 media credentials were issued for the opener. It seemed big at the time but it's entirely possible Montreal's participation will wind up being a mere footnote.

2 MARCH 16, 2012
Jets 3 / Capitals 2

There were some intense home results this season, including wins over Pittsburgh, Philadelphia, Phoenix, Minnesota, Boston (twice), Toronto (twice, much to the glee of Jets fans) and Buffalo, but this one took the cake in terms of arena decibels and commitment by the fans and their team ('Crosby's better!'). A high-water mark for noise and hope.

3 DEC. 17, 2011
Jets 5 / Anaheim 3

This game — the entire day, in fact — put all of the passion Winnipeg hockey fans possessed on display for the world. Second to the opener, this was the "event" of the season, with the return of Teemu Selanne of Jets 1.0, the in-game switches from cheers to boos back to cheers and of course, another win by the home team.

4 OCT. 17, 2011
Jets 2 / Penguins 1

Nothing like sending a message early. After flopping in their opener, the Jets corrected that issue in Game 2 at the MTS Centre, scoring eight seconds after the opening faceoff. Kyle Wellwood had that goal, and Tanner Glass added another before the first period was over for the team's first win of the season. On this night, the Jets and their fans started something good in downtown Winnipeg, making it a tough place for opponents.

5 OCT. 27, 2011
Jets 9 / Flyers 8

If ever a game had it all — or most of it, at least — this was it. Goals and comebacks and intrigue and a rare Jets road win. In particular, coaches and goalies were still twitching days after this one was over, but in the end, the Jets left town happy when Andrew Ladd scored with 1:06 left in the third period.

Mike Deal / Winnipeg Free Press

Teemu Selanne

1 DEC. 10, 2011
Red Wings 7 / Jets 1

Immediately after an encouraging win over Carolina at the MTS Centre, their fourth in a row, the Jets flew into Detroit. They might as well have stayed home. The beating illustrated just how much trouble the Jets had and would have: a) on the road, b) in back-to-back games and c) often against good teams. Those items make this the night to forget of the season.

2 FEB. 5, 2012
Montreal 3 / Jets 0

There are many games from which to choose during Winnipeg's puck-anywhere-but-in-the-net phase from January and early February. You've no doubt forgotten most of them already, but just to remind you of the pain — losses to New Jersey twice, the Rangers, earlier to the sad-sack Habs, San Jose, Carolina, Florida — preceded this weak afternoon in Montreal. Their offence was eventually rediscovered but this period of the season did not harbour a lot of happy memories.

3 NOV. 12, 2011
Columbus 2 / Jets 1

On the subject of losses to sad-sack teams, Winnipeg's one-off meeting against Columbus was a low-water mark in terms of record on the season, the loss sending the team four games under. 500. Having been booed off the ice by some fans two nights earlier in a sad home loss to Florida, the Jets had some game but not as much as the low-game, last-place Blue Jackets. This defeat, though, served as a rallying point in the weeks that ensued.

4 MARCH 20, 2012
Pittsburgh 8 / Jets 4

It's demoralizing to fans when their team is outmatched AND outplayed. The Jets tried to keep up with the Penguins in the first 30 minutes and almost did, but in the end had no answers to the weapons they faced. It actually happened twice, because an 8-5 result Feb. 11 was eerily similar. This one, though, was an ominous sign for the games to come that saw the Jets officially slide from the race.

John Woods / Winnipeg Free Press

The Flyers' Wayne Simmonds puts it past Jets goalie Ondrej Pavelec to force OT, which Philly won.

5 FEB. 21, 2011
Philadelphia 5 / Jets 4 (OT)

The Jets had their share of last-minute heartbreak during the season, a home loss to Washington, a late-season playoff-crusher to Carolina among them. But this defeat against the Flyers, Philly's only win over the Jets all season, really hurt momentum. The game seemed to be in hand for the Jets until the Flyers tied it with 10 seconds left, not on zone pressure but a mere rush, and then won it in overtime. It ruined a defining goaltending evening by Ondrej Pavelec and for the rest of the season, Winnipeg was unable to string more than two wins together at any one time.

1 MARCH 5, 2012
Blake Wheeler

As far as the definition goes, this one includes all the must-haves: style, pressure and relevance. Wheeler's game-winner on Buffalo goalie Ryan Miller came in the third period, on a breakaway and was a shot to the shelf, scoring an A in all categories. Oh, and it pretty much rattled the MTS Centre's four walls and roof to their max. We considered Chris Thorburn's quasi-toe-drag insurance marker just a few moments later because of the setting and style and drama of it, but Wheeler's mattered more because it was the deciding shot in a huge game.

2 FEB. 16, 2012
Evander Kane

Already with two goals during the game at Minnesota, Evander Kane's number came up during the shootout. With the game on the line, he hopped over the boards to witness a hat come sailing down from the seats before he started his attempt. No pressure there. Kane calmly skated in and buried the goal that decided the outcome. It was the closest a Jets player came to a hat trick all season.

3 MARCH 1, 2012
Bryan Little

Well, there's always room for a little humour, so we're abandoning our criteria to fit this amazing goal into the list. It didn't decide the 7-0 game against the Florida Panthers, but when was the last time you ever saw a five-on-one? Little converted the all-in rush — known now as the "Flying W" — by the Jets, clearly the exclamation mark on another important win at the MTS Centre.

Joe Bryksa / Winnipeg Free Press

Nik Antropov's historic marker on opening night.

4 OCT. 9, 2011
Nik Antropov

Same for this entry, since most of the drama and circumstance had left the building by the time Antropov pulled the trigger. But the first official goal of the Jets' new era is significant enough to remember, the setting for its scoring be damned. It took until early in the third period of Game 1, but Antropov's goal at 2:27 of the third on Montreal goalie Carey Price briefly made the game 2-1, though it quickly turned to 5-1 for the enemy. Mark Stuart and Alex Burmistrov were the official first helpers.

5 FEB. 9, 2012
Dustin Byfuglien

Known as the "magic puck" goal, Byfuglien's shot from the centre red-line skipped and hopped over the ice and behind Caps goalie Tomas Vokoun with 2:03 left in the third period, and combined with Evander Kane's goal 12 seconds earlier, tied the game and paved the way for a Winnipeg victory in a shootout. The Verizon Center was pretty good to the Jets in 2011-12, offering five out of six points and also included another stylish goal, Tim Stapleton's in overtime on March 23 that at the time kept Winnipeg's playoff hopes alive.

Jeff Parsons / St. John's IceCaps

Another city gets its team back

HERE'S some free advice from Winnipeg Jets assistant GM Craig Heisinger for anyone who might consider establishing two professional hockey teams in one off-season: "I wouldn't advise it."

But even prior to acquiring the Atlanta Thrashers, the Jets organization (previously the AHL's Manitoba Moose) was ahead of the curve when it came to landing a minor-league affiliation in St. John's, N.L.

In essence, it wasn't just the NHL that returned to Winnipeg. The American Hockey League returned to the Rock.

After all, the St. John's Maple Leafs left St. John's in 2005, after 14 seasons. The team, an affiliate of the Toronto Maple Leafs, relocated to Toronto in 2005-06, leaving Mile One Stadium without a tenant. On July 10, the AHL's board of governors approved the St. John's relocation. The team was named the IceCaps on July 29.

Just as in Winnipeg, though, the club sold the majority of its season tickets — 4,700 as of mid-July in an arena with a capacity of about 6,200 — before the new team even had a name. Throughout the 2011-12 season, IceCaps' average attendance was 6,297.

The Caps weren't just a success at the box office. Under the guidance of head coach Keith McCambridge (a former assistant coach of the Manitoba Moose), the IceCaps finished atop the Atlantic division standings (43-25-5-3) and advanced to the AHL semifinals before being swept 4-0 by the powerful Norfolk Admirals, who went on to capture the Calder Cup championship.

IceCaps' Patrice Cormier skates away from Charles Landry of the Norfolk Admirals during the 2011/2012 season.

Jeff Parsons / St. John's IceCaps

The IceCaps were led by leading scorer Spencer Machacek (18 G, 32 A) and all-star defenceman Paul Postma (13 G, 31 A), along with veterans Jason King and Jason Jaffray, two former members of the Manitoba Moose.

Several IceCaps players had brief stints with the Jets during the 2011-12 season. Forwards Machacek (13 games, 3 goals, 7 assists) and Ben Maxwell (1 goal, four assists) both finished the season in Winnipeg after getting late call-ups. Postma, an AHL all-star, was up for three games, while defenceman Arturs Kulda and forward Patrick Cormier dressed for nine games apiece.

However, it was former Manitoba Moose defenceman Mark Flood who had the most impact from the farm. After getting called up in November, Flood never went back to St. John's. The 27-year-old played 33 games with the Jets, notching seven points (3 goals, 4 assists), including his first career NHL goal against New Jersey's Martin Brodeur.

Heisinger said geography doesn't favour St. John's — "It's on a rock in the middle of the Atlantic Ocean, there's no coating that one." But the Jets were drawn by an ownership group that included former Newfoundland premier Danny Williams.

"Location isn't everything," Heisinger said. "The people that you're dealing with are everything. Airplanes can fix geography."

Besides, Winnipeg and St. John's have much in common. Both are considered relatively isolated by their respective leagues. Yet both have assets location can't buy: A devoted, hockey-mad fan base.

"It's the same response as Winnipeg, only smaller," Heisinger said of the welcome the IceCaps received. "They got their team back."

THE ST. JOHN'S **ICECAPS**

BACK ROW (L-R) — Spencer Machacek, Eric O'Dell, Mark Flood, Shawn Weller, Patrice Cormier, Ben Chiarot, Riley Holzapfel, Zach Redmond, Travis Ramsey,

Jeff Parsons / St. John's IceCaps

MIDDLE ROW (L-R) — Eqipment manager Ian Cox, Garth Murray, assistant equipment manager Shannon Coady, Brett Festerling, Paul Postma, Arturs Kulda, Carl Klingberg, Marco Rosa, Jason DeSantis, Jason Gregoire,Kevin Clark, John Albert, Shayne Wiebe, athletic therapist Alain Chabbert, video coach Ian Anderson.

FRONT ROW (L-R) — Peter Mannino, Eddie Pasquale, president and CEO Danny Williams, head coach Keith McCambridge, Captain Jason Jaffray, assistant coach Mark Morrison, chief operating Officer and AHL governor Glenn Stanford, Tom Maxwell, Jason King, David Aebischer.

Mike Deal / Winnipeg Free Press

Maj.-Gen. Alain Parent, Commander of 1 Canadian Air Division, receives a $100,000 cheque from Mark Chipman, chairman of the Winnipeg Jets True North Foundation, at a ceremony at 1 Canadian Air Division headquarters May 22, 2012.

A foundation for the future

IMAGINE a seven-year-old boy, from a family with modest or little means, who has neither the opportunity nor the money to play hockey.

Now imagine that boy a decade later, graduating from high school, with post-secondary options and a wicked slapshot from the point.

That's the vision of the the flagship program of the Winnipeg Jets True North Foundation, which during its first year of existence donated $1 million to 44 local charities.

In the 2012 season, about 150 Winnipeg-area schoolchildren took part in the True North Hockey Academy. In 2012-13, it will swell to include 425 kids, each provided with equipment, assistance, ice time and lunch once a week at local rinks.

The program will be open to Grade 2 to Grade 9 students initially, with the goal to keep the kids in the academy until high school graduation. There's a catch: Acceptance to the program is tied directly to school attendance. There's also a goal: that each student, upon graduation, would be provided career counselling and possible scholarships for post-secondary education.

"We want to help these children to know there's a larger community looking out for them," said foundation executive director Dwayne Green.

The academy falls under the foundation's three pillars of underserved youth: health and wellness (mental and physical), education, and character-building.

Most foundation revenue in 2011-12 came from 50/50 ticket sales, the Mike Keane Celebrity Hockey Classic, Jets licence-plate sales and the Flatlander's Beer Festival.

The foundation is also deeply involved with three military charities out of 17 Wing: the Military Families Fund, the Soldier On Fund and the Air Force Heritage Fund.

From the outset of the NHL's return, the Jets realized the team's ability to develop deep roots in the community wouldn't just be a possibility, but a necessity.

In fact, while the return of the NHL certainly meant increased ticket prices, it also meant the club's ability to raise funds for charities would be increased several-fold. For example, the Moose Yearling Foundation raised a much-needed and appreciated $2.3 million in 15 years. The Winnipeg Jets True North Foundation raised almost half that amount in Year 1, with plenty of room for growth.

"We understand the impact we have in the province," Green said. "And we want to give back in a meaningful way to allow our future leaders to excel."

"The program is enhanced due to the partnerships we have with various school divisions and our community corporate partners who donate staff hours to help run the academy."

Children having fun at the True North Hockey Academy, an inner-city hockey program funded by the foundation and held at the MTS Iceplex.

Ken Gigliotti / Winnipeg Free Press

Former pro hockey player Mike Keane and (below left) Lanny McDonald appear at the second annual Mike Keane Celebrity Hockey Classic in support of the foundation Nov. 10. 2011.

Wayne Glowacki / Winnipeg Free Press

Wayne Glowacki / Winnipeg Free Press

Wayne Glowacki / Winnipeg Free Press

Former NHL star Brad Park hits the MTS Iceplex in support of the foundation Nov. 10, 2011.

Individual scoring

POS	NO	PLAYER	GP	G	A	P	+/-	PIM	PP	SH	GW	S	S%	TOI/G
R	26	Blake Wheeler	80	17	47	64	3	55	6	0	3	208	8.2	19:04
L	9	Evander Kane	74	30	27	57	11	53	6	0	4	287	10.5	17:31
D	33	Dustin Byfuglien	66	12	41	53	-8	72	4	0	3	223	5.4	24:06
L	16	Andrew Ladd	82	28	22	50	-8	64	4	0	6	265	10.6	19:33
C	13	Kyle Wellwood	77	18	29	47	3	4	4	0	1	93	19.4	14:57
C	18	Bryan Little	74	24	22	46	-11	26	6	0	6	162	14.8	20:13
C	80	Nik Antropov	69	15	20	35	0	42	4	0	0	95	15.8	16:30
D	39	Tobias Enstrom	62	6	27	33	6	38	2	0	1	94	6.4	23:50
D	4	Zach Bogosian	65	5	25	30	-3	71	1	0	0	150	3.3	23:18
C	8	Alexander Burmistrov	76	13	15	28	4	42	1	1	0	123	10.6	16:39
C	14	Tim Stapleton	63	11	16	27	-2	10	4	0	3	74	14.9	10:08
C	19	Jim Slater	78	13	8	21	-9	42	0	1	1	118	11.0	14:45
D	24	Grant Clitsome	63	4	13	17	-9	32	1	0	1	87	4.6	17:00
L	15	Tanner Glass	78	5	11	16	-12	73	0	0	1	86	5.8	13:25
D	5	Mark Stuart	80	3	11	14	-4	98	0	1	1	60	5.0	17:12
R	20	Antti Miettinen	45	5	8	13	-5	0	1	0	0	58	8.6	11:42
R	22	Chris Thorburn	72	4	7	11	-6	83	0	0	0	69	5.8	10:10
D	6	Ron Hainsey	56	0	10	10	9	23	0	0	0	57	0.0	21:05
R	46	Spencer Machacek	13	2	7	9	8	7	0	0	0	12	16.7	7:30
D	36	Mark Flood	33	3	4	7	-1	10	1	0	1	30	10.0	15:20
C	49	Ben Maxwell	15	1	5	6	4	2	0	0	0	10	10.0	6:44
R	17	Eric Fehr	35	2	1	3	-6	12	0	0	1	54	3.7	9:41
D	12	Randy Jones	39	1	1	2	4	8	0	0	0	24	4.2	14:48
L	39	Brett MacLean	5	0	2	2	1	2	0	0	0	6	0.0	8:29
C	55	Mark Scheifele	7	1	0	1	0	0	1	0	0	5	20.0	10:56
L	41	Jason Jaffray	13	0	1	1	-1	7	0	0	0	10	0.0	6:30
D	44	Arturs Kulda	9	0	0	0	3	4	0	0	0	8	0.0	10:52
C	21	Aaron Gagnon	7	0	0	0	-1	0	0	0	0	6	0.0	9:26
D	53	Brett Festerling	5	0	0	0	-1	2	0	0	0	2	0.0	13:07
C	28	Patrice Cormier	9	0	0	0	1	0	0	0	0	8	0.0	6:21
L	23	Kenndal McArdle	9	0	0	0	-3	4	0	0	0	3	0.0	6:06
L	48	Carl Klingberg*	6	0	0	0	-1	4	0	0	0	7	0.0	5:29
D	38	Paul Postma	3	0	0	0	0	0	0	0	0	3	0.0	8:30
D	7	Derek Meech	2	0	0	0	1	4	0	0	0	2	0.0	11:26

Goaltending

NO	GOALIE	GPI	MINS	AVG	W	L	OT	SO	GA	SA	SV%	G	A	PIM
31	Ondrej Pavelec	68	3,932	2.91	29	28	9	4	191	2,036	.906	-	2	-
34	Peter Mannino	1	20	0.00	0	0	0	0	0	4	1.00	-	-	-
50	Chris Mason	20	995	2.59	8	7	1	2	43	422	.898	-	-	-

Winnipeg Jets roster (End of season)

Forwards

#	NAME	HEIGHT	WEIGHT	DATE OF BIRTH	BIRTH PLACE
80	NIK ANTROPOV	6' 6"	245	18 FEB 1980	UST-KAMENOGORSK, KAZ
8	ALEXANDER BURMISTROV	6' 1"	180	21 OCT 1991	KAZAN, RUS
28	PATRICE CORMIER	6' 2"	205	14 JUL 1990	MONCTON, NB, CAN
17	ERIC FEHR	6' 4"	212	7 SEP 1985	WINKLER, MB, CAN
15	TANNER GLASS	6' 1"	210	29 NOV 1983	REGINA, SK, CAN
9	EVANDER KANE	6' 2"	195	2 AUG 1991	VANCOUVER, BC, CAN
16	ANDREW LADD **"C"**	6' 3"	205	12 DEC 1985	MAPLE RIDGE, BC, CAN
18	BRYAN LITTLE	5' 11"	185	12 NOV 1987	EDMONTON, AB, CAN
46	SPENCER MACHACEK	6' 1"	195	14 OCT 1988	LETHBRIDGE, AB, CAN
20	ANTTI MIETTINEN	6' 0"	190	3 JUL 1980	HAMEENLINNA, FIN
19	JIM SLATER	6' 0"	200	9 DEC 1982	LAPEER, MI, USA
14	TIM STAPLETON	5' 9"	180	19 JUL 1982	FOREST PARK, IL, USA
22	CHRIS THORBURN **"A"**	6' 3"	230	3 JUN 1983	SAULT STE. MARIE, ON, CAN
13	KYLE WELLWOOD	5' 10"	181	16 MAY 1983	WINDSOR, ON, CAN
26	BLAKE WHEELER	6' 5"	205	31 AUG 1986	ROBBINSDALE, MN, USA

Defencemen

#	NAME	HEIGHT	WEIGHT	DATE OF BIRTH	BIRTH PLACE
44	ZACH BOGOSIAN	6' 3"	215	15 JUL 1990	MASSENA, NY, USA
33	DUSTIN BYFUGLIEN **"A"**	6' 5"	265	27 MAR 1985	MINNEAPOLIS, MN, USA
24	GRANT CLITSOME	5' 11"	215	14 APR 1985	GLOUCESTER, ON, CAN
39	TOBIAS ENSTROM **"A"**	5' 10"	180	5 NOV 1984	NORDINGRA, SWE
36	MARK FLOOD	6' 1"	190	29 SEP 1984	CHARLOTTETOWN, PE, CAN
6	RON HAINSEY	6' 3"	210	24 MAR 1981	BOLTON, CT, USA
12	RANDY JONES	6' 2"	210	23 JUL 1981	QUISPAMSIS, NB, CAN
5	MARK STUART **"A"**	6' 2"	213	27 APR 1984	ROCHESTER, MN, USA

Goalies

#	NAME	HEIGHT	WEIGHT	DATE OF BIRTH	BIRTH PLACE
50	CHRIS MASON	6' 0"	195	20 APR 1976	RED DEER, AB, CAN
31	ONDREJ PAVELEC	6' 3"	220	31 AUG 1987	KLADNO, CZE

Team home and road game-by-game results

HOME

No	Date	Opponent	Result		PTS	Goalie(s)	GW Goal	Record	PP	PK	SF	SA	GF	GA	Attend.
1	10/9	vs. MTL	1-5	Loss	0	Pavelec	[Plekanec]	0-1-0	0-7	3-4	31	22	1	5	15,004+
2	10/17	vs. PIT	2-1	Win	2	Pavelec	Glass	1-3-0	0-4	3-3	34	29	2	1	15,004+
3	10/22	vs. CAR	5-3	Win	5	Mason/Pavelec	Ladd	2-4-1	2-6	7-7	24	24	5	3	15,004+
4	10/24	vs. NYR	1-2	Loss	5	Mason	[Callahan]	2-5-1	0-1	3-5	28	17	1	2	15,004+
5	11/10	vs. FLA	2-5	Loss	13	Pavelec/Mannino	[Garrison]	5-8-3	1-3	3-5	27	20	2	5	15,004+
6	11/14	vs. TB	5-2	Win	15	Pavelec	Flood	6-9-3	1-2	6-6	39	32	5	2	15,004+
7	11/17	vs. WSH	4-1	Win	17	Pavelec	Kane	7-9-3	2-5	5-5	31	32	4	1	15,004+
8	11/19	vs. PHI	6-4	Win	19	Pavelec	Byfuglien	8-9-3	3-8	6-8	40	31	6	4	15,004+
9	11/29	vs. OTT	4-6	Loss	22	Pavelec	[Smith]	9-11-4	1-5	3-4	43	34	4	6	15,004+
10	12/1	vs. PHX	1-0	Win	24	Pavelec	Little	10-11-4	0-3	2-2	31	33	1	0	15,004+
11	12/3	vs. NJ	4-2	Win	26	Pavelec	Stuart	11-11-4	0-2	3-4	20	25	4	2	15,004+
12	12/6	vs. BOS	2-1	Win	28	Pavelec	Little	12-11-4	0-3	3-3	35	40	2	1	15,004+
13	12/9	vs. CAR	4-2	Win	30	Mason	Stapleton	13-11-4	2-4	2-3	37	25	4	2	15,004+
14	12/13	vs. MIN	2-1	Win	32	Pavelec	Little	14-12-4	0-4	3-4	27	35	2	1	15,004+
15	12/15	vs. WSH	0-1	Loss	32	Pavelec	[Ovechkin]	14-13-4	0-4	2-2	26	28	0	1	15,004+
16	12/17	vs. ANA	5-3	Win	34	Mason	Ladd	15-13-4	1-2	3-4	31	36	5	3	15,004+
17	12/20	vs. NYI	2-3	SOL	35	Pavelec	[Parenteau]	15-13-5	0-0	2-2	38	33	2	3	15,004+
18	12/22	vs. MTL	4-0	Win	37	Pavelec	Wheeler	16-13-5	1-2	5-5	34	27	4	0	15,004+
19	12/23	vs. PIT	1-4	Loss	37	Pavelec	[Neal]	16-14-5	0-3	3-4	19	39	1	4	15,004+
20	12/29	vs. LA	1-0	OTW	41	Mason	Kane	18-14-5	0-2	5-5	37	31	1	0	15,004+
21	12/31	vs. TOR	3-2	Win	43	Pavelec	Wheeler	19-14-5	2-6	2-3	35	24	3	2	15,004+
22	1/12	vs. SJ	0-2	Loss	45	Pavelec	[Couture]	20-18-5	0-2	2-2	24	37	0	2	15,004+
23	1/14	vs. NJ	1-2	Loss	45	Pavelec	[Elias]	20-19-5	0-2	2-2	23	25	1	2	15,004+
24	1/19	vs. BUF	4-1	Win	49	Pavelec	Enstrom	22-20-5	2-4	2-2	33	26	4	1	15,004+
25	1/21	vs. FLA	3-4	SOL	50	Pavelec	[Samuelsson]	22-20-6	1-5	3-3	44	23	3	4	15,004+
26	2/7	vs. TOR	2-1	Win	56	Pavelec	Little	25-24-6	0-2	2-2	29	18	2	1	15,004+
27	2/14	vs. NYI	1-3	Loss	58	Pavelec	[Parenteau]	26-26-6	0-3	0-1	38	25	1	3	15,004+
28	2/17	vs. BOS	4-2	Win	62	Pavelec	Little	28-26-6	0-2	2-2	25	33	4	2	15,004+
29	2/19	vs. COL	5-1	Win	64	Pavelec	Little	29-26-6	2-5	4-5	25	32	5	1	15,004+
30	2/21	vs. PHI	4-5	OTL	65	Pavelec	[Jagr]	29-26-7	3-3	2-3	26	55	4	5	15,004+
31	2/23	vs. TB	4-3	Win	67	Pavelec	Byfuglien	30-26-7	2-3	3-5	34	25	4	3	15,004+
32	2/25	vs. STL	2-3	OTL	68	Mason	[Perron]	30-26-8	0-2	1-1	41	16	2	3	15,004+
33	2/27	vs. EDM	3-5	Loss	68	Pavelec	[Hall]	30-27-8	2-3	1-3	32	25	3	5	15,004+
34	3/1	vs. FLA	7-0	Win	70	Pavelec	Kane	31-27-8	1-3	3-3	32	33	7	0	15,004+
35	3/5	vs. BUF	3-1	Win	72	Pavelec	Wheeler	32-27-8	0-2	2-2	31	24	3	1	15,004+
36	3/14	vs. DAL	5-2	Win	74	Pavelec	Fehr	33-29-8	1-3	0-0	28	30	5	2	15,004+
37	3/16	vs. WSH	3-2	Win	76	Pavelec	Byfuglien	34-29-8	0-5	2-3	28	22	3	2	15,004+
38	3/18	vs. CAR	3-4	Loss	76	Pavelec	[LaRose]	34-30-8	0-5	4-5	33	35	3	4	15,004+
39	3/26	vs. OTT	4-6	Loss	78	Pavelec	[Alfredsson]	35-33-8	1-4	2-2	48	35	4	6	15,004+
40	3/28	vs. NYR	2-4	Loss	78	Pavelec	[Boyle]	35-34-8	0-5	3-5	24	28	2	4	15,004+
41	4/7	vs. TB	3-4	OTL	84	Pavelec	[Purcell]	37-35-10	0-3	2-2	25	31	3	4	15,004+

ROAD

No	Date	Opponent	Result		PTS	Goalie(s)	GW Goal	Record	PP	PK	SF	SA	GF	GA	Attend.
1	10/13	@ CHI	3-4	Loss	0	Pavelec	[Bolland]	0-2-0	0-2	2-3	30	32	3	4	21,175+
2	10/15	@ PHX	1-4	Loss	0	Mason	[Ekman-Larsson]	0-3-0	0-4	4-5	19	34	1	4	17,132+
3	10/19	@ TOR	3-4	SOL	3	Pavelec	[Lupul]	1-3-1	2-4	2-4	29	23	3	4	19,514+
4	10/20	@ OTT	1-4	Loss	3	Pavelec	[Spezza]	1-4-1	0-4	3-4	36	30	1	4	17,919
5	10/27	@ PHI	9-8	Win	7	Pavelec/Mason	Ladd	3-5-1	2-5	4-5	25	48	9	8	19,588+
6	10/29	@ TB	1-0	Loss	7	Pavelec	[Lecavalier]	3-6-1	0-2	3-4	28	27	1	0	19,204+
7	10/31	@ FLA	4-3	SOW	9	Pavelec	Ladd	4-6-1	1-2	4-5	31	42	4	3	11,855
8	11/3	@ NYI	3-0	Win	11	Pavelec	Kane	5-6-1	0-0	3-3	26	34	3	0	10,157
9	11/5	@ NJ	2-3	OTL	12	Pavelec	[Henrique]	5-6-2	0-3	2-2	23	28	2	3	14,952
10	11/6	@ NYR	0-3	Loss	12	Pavelec	[Stepan]	5-7-2	0-4	5-6	23	27	0	3	18,200+
11	11/8	@ BUF	5-6	OTL	13	Pavelec	[Vanek]	5-7-3	1-5	8-12	31	45	5	6	18,690+
12	11/12	@ CBJ	1-2	Loss	13	Pavelec	[Johansen]	5-9-3	0-5	4-4	36	27	1	2	15,581
13	11/23	@ WSH	3-4	OTL	20	Pavelec	[Chimera]	8-9-4	0-2	3-3	25	37	3	4	18,506+
14	11/25	@ CAR	3-1	Win	22	Mason	Ladd	9-9-4	0-1	4-4	30	21	3	1	15,718
15	11/26	@ BOS	2-4	Loss	22	Pavelec	[Kelly]	9-10-4	0-4	5-6	42	36	2	4	17,565+
16	12/10	@ DET	1-7	Loss	30	Pavelec/Mason	[Zetterberg]	13-12-4	0-2	3-3	30	29	1	7	20,066+
17	12/27	@ COL	4-1	Win	39	Pavelec	Stapleton	17-14-5	1-1	1-1	26	33	4	1	18,007+
18	1/4	@ MTL	3-7	Loss	43	Pavelec/Mason	[Eller]	19-15-5	1-2	3-3	27	31	3	7	21,273+
19	1/5	@ TOR	0-4	Loss	43	Mason	[Kessel]	19-16-5	0-1	2-3	24	25	0	4	19,514+
20	1/7	@ BUF	2-1	OTW	45	Pavelec	Oduya	20-16-5	1-4	3-4	41	32	2	1	18,690+
21	1/10	@ BOS	3-5	Loss	45	Pavelec	[Seguin]	20-17-5	0-4	2-3	32	42	3	5	17,565+
22	1/16	@ OTT	2-0	Win	47	Mason	Slater	21-19-5	0-3	2-2	35	25	2	0	19,927+
23	1/17	@ NJ	1-5	Loss	47	Mason/Pavelec	[Sykora]	21-20-5	0-1	3-4	21	20	1	5	14,129
24	1/23	@ CAR	1-2	Loss	50	Mason	[Brent]	22-21-6	0-2	2-2	30	16	1	2	16,045
25	1/24	@ NYR	0-3	Loss	50	Pavelec	[Callahan]	22-22-6	0-2	4-4	22	31	0	3	18,200+
26	1/31	@ PHI	2-1	SOW	52	Pavelec	Little	23-22-6	0-3	0-1	24	28	2	1	19,874+
27	2/2	@ TB	2-1	OTW	54	Pavelec	Wellwood	24-22-6	0-2	2-2	24	31	2	1	16,923
28	2/3	@ FLA	1-2	Loss	54	Mason	[Bergenheim]	24-23-6	0-1	2-3	21	30	1	2	16,773
29	2/5	@ MTL	3-0	Loss	54	Pavelec	[Pacioretty]	24-24-6	0-5	3-4	23	23	0	3	21,273+
30	2/9	@ WSH	3-2	SOW	58	Pavelec	Little	26-24-6	2-3	3-5	27	33	3	2	18,506+
31	2/11	@ PIT	5-8	Loss	58	Pavelec	[Park]	26-25-6	0-1	1-3	32	39	5	8	18,602+
32	2/16	@ MIN	4-3	SOW	60	Mason	Kane	27-26-6	0-3	2-3	27	25	4	3	19,060+
33	3/8	@ VAN	2-3	Loss	72	Pavelec	[Pahlsson]	32-28-8	0-3	1-1	32	45	2	3	18,890+
34	3/9	@ CGY	3-5	Loss	72	Pavelec	[Tanguay]	32-29-8	0-2	0-3	45	27	3	5	19,289+
35	3/20	@ PIT	4-8	Loss	76	Pavelec/Mason	[Malkin]	34-31-8	1-2	2-3	30	35	4	8	18,589+
36	3/23	@ WSH	4-3	OTW	78	Pavelec	Stapleton	35-31-8	0-2	2-2	42	23	4	3	18,506+
37	3/24	@ NSH	1-3	Loss	78	Pavelec	[Bourque]	35-32-8	0-1	3-4	25	28	1	3	17,113+
38	3/30	@ CAR	4-3	OTW	80	Mason	Ladd	36-34-8	1-5	4-4	35	33	4	3	18,680+
49	3/31	@ TB	2-3	OTL	81	Pavelec	[Stamkos]	36-34-9	0-3	7-8	28	39	2	3	19,204+
40	4/3	@ FLA	5-4	OTW	83	Pavelec	Ladd	37-34-9	1-2	1-2	30	38	5	4	17,760+
41	4/5	@ NYI	4-5	Loss	83	Mason	[Grabner]	37-35-9	0-3	3-3	25	28	4	5	13,048

+ - indicates sellout

THIS is the second *Winnipeg Free Press* book on the Winnipeg Jets franchise and its return to the province in 2011.

Our first, *Back In The Bigs: How Winnipeg won, lost and regained its place in the NHL*, was also written by Randy Turner and co-published with Penguin Canada.

You can purchase a copy of the Canadian bestseller direct from the Winnipeg Free Press at 1355 Mountain Ave., 204-697-7000; or order online at www.winnipegfreepress.com, or www.penguin.ca

$1 from every *First Season* sold will go to the Winnipeg Jets True North Foundation, which supports dozens of local charities every year.

Winnipeg Free Press

WINNIPEG
JETS